The entangled city

Manchester University Press

The entangled city

city

Crime as urban fabric in São Paulo

Gabriel Feltran

Manchester University Press

The right of Gabriel Feltran to be identified as the author of this work has been
asserted by him in accordance with the Copyright, Designs and Patents Act 1988.

Published by Manchester University Press
Altrincham Street, Manchester M1 7JA
www.manchesteruniversitypress.co.uk

British Library Cataloguing-in-Publication Data
A catalogue record for this book is available from the British Library

ISBN 978 1 5261 3824 8 hardback

First published 2020

The publisher has no responsibility for the persistence or accuracy of URLs for
any external or third-party internet websites referred to in this book, and does
not guarantee that any content on such websites is, or will remain, accurate or
appropriate.

Typeset by Servis Filmsetting Ltd, Stockport, Cheshire
Printed in Great Britain by TJ International Ltd, Padstow

For Deb, Iaiá and Léo

We are not outlaws, 'cause the law we make by ourselves. (M.C. Orelha, 'Faixa de Gaza' (Gaza Strip), a 'forbidden Funk', Rio de Janeiro, 2009)

Contents

Foreword

Brodwyn Fischer

The most important deliberative bodies in São Paulo's contemporary body of crime have a funny name: *sintonias*. Like so much else involving the Primeiro Comando do Capital (PCC), the term is odd, unexpected, opaque. If we want to understand it, we need to move from the inside out.

Since its origins in a high-security prison in the early 1990s, the PCC has grown from a tight group of prisoners determined to curb carceral abuse and fratricidal violence to a transnational brotherhood responsible for the normative regulation of neighbourhoods and economies, from the organisation's native São Paulo to the peripheries of cities throughout Brazil and points of criminal economic activity across the globe. A good part of that rise, Gabriel Feltran argues, can be explained by the PCC's radically decentralised, anti-hierarchical and deliberative structure. No leader defines the PCC, and its ultimate aim is not to profit, but rather to create the conditions through which its 'brothers' in crime might do so – to foment 'peace, justice liberty, equality and union' among thieves. Those conditions are not commanded from high by a powerful mastermind, but created in practice through deliberation within cell-like groupings of 'brothers' who earn their status through action and should never be held above the collective notion of what is 'right' and tolerable in the world of crime. Each of those 'independent nuclei', functioning without full knowledge of one another or even of the PCC's operational map, is called a *sintonia*. When I recently had the chance to talk with Gabriel Feltran about his extraordinary research on the PCC, it occurred to me to ask: why? The word could be rendered in English as 'synchronicity' or 'harmony'. But Feltran honed in instead on the evocative power of concrete mechanics. *Sintonia*'s most powerful definition, he told me, is 'tuning'. It denotes that magical moment when one's clumsy fiddling with an old-fashioned radio dial or television antennae yields clear reception; the wavelengths are synchronised, the sound is plain. Those men in the Taubaté prison who founded the PCC in the 1990s – for the most part children of Brazil's poor peripheries in the economically disastrous 1980s – had probably messed with their share of rickety televisions and radios. They knew the intricate, tactile delicacy required for every successful tuning. And thus their deliberative bodies became *sintonias*, those intangible spaces where the clash of static becomes lucid sound.

In translating portions of Feltran's remarkable *Irmãos: Uma história do PCC* (2018), *Entangled City* illuminates the logic of the PCC's *sintonias*, allowing English-language readers to peer beyond the veil of bravado and drama that renders the rise of Brazil's criminal organisations as an exotic triumph of uncontrolled violence, straight out of *City of God*. But *Entangled City* is not a straight translation. It is, instead, a synthesis of Feltran's quarter century of intensive ethnographic research in São Paulo's vast peripheries, a crystallisation of forms of understanding that have emerged through the granular accumulation of everyday experiences: bus rides through dusty self-built neighbourhoods in which bodies, houses and commercial outposts gradually incorporate the trappings of global consumerism; everyday conversations in cramped homes where a crack addict and drug dealer is also a son taking a shower; decades of confessional tête-à-têtes with a single mother whose past of domestic abuse and family subsistence on fish-head gruel gradually becomes a present in which material stability and community integration coexist with wrenchingly violent loss. In juxtaposing these histories of granular everyday transformation with the parallel evolution of academic, political and media discussions of 'democracy', 'citizenship', 'urban violence', and 'crime', Feltran achieves a *sintonia* of his own, opening a space of clarity where strangers can apprehend the synchronicities and dissonances that order and disorder the urban world as it is experienced from the peripheries.

Gabriel Feltran began publishing his research about São Paulo in the early 2000s. In three major monographs, several edited volumes, and dozens of articles, book chapters and works of public scholarship, he has worked as both a translator and an intellectual, illuminating for outsiders dynamics that are so obvious as to seem banal to residents of São Paulo's periphery, but also shedding brilliant light on the significance of those dynamics within broader historical, urban, economic and cultural contexts. Feltran has written about peripheral social movements and regulatory regimes, about the music of crime and young people's encounters with the state and the law, about the structure of illegal economies and the dynamics of urban violence. These projects are layered, not linear, each building on intensive immersion in São Paulo's southeast periphery but focused on the threads of connection that link those peripheral cityscapes to economies, structures of governance, conceptual aesthetics and moral logics to greater São Paulo, greater Brazil, and alternate urban and civic orders stretching from Paraguay to Berlin. This book assembles fragments of all of those projects, but it is more fusion than collage, an extended meditation on the meaning that all of those disparate strands take on when they are entangled in our own historical moment, and apprehended from disparate and distant global contexts.

In that spirit, one conceptual and argumentative thread from *The Entangled City* stands in especially sharp relief. It emerges from the deceptively simple notion that 'specific stories' shape the worldviews of peripheral urbanites. In theoretical terms, Feltran's

commitment harkens back to multiple sociological and ethnographic traditions, and especially to those inspired by the theory
of action, as expressed in the notion that 'the social' is structured
'through everyday life ... and it is in pragmatic action ... that the
plausible is constituted (p. 31)'; 'the everyday plays a decisive role in
the objectification of the categories of difference (p. 41).' Feltran's
ethnographic method is built on the notion that the periphery's
multiple and shifting realities can only be understood through the
accrual of experience. The peripheral world he portrays is one in
which it makes no sense to think through important questions in
the absence of specific narratives – real people, real things, real
and infinitely varied interactions. It is more meaningful to say that
'Bianca has a new refrigerator' than it is to say that 'more money
is circulating' (p. 7); you convey far more by describing the deaths
of actual people – Fernando, Anísio – than you do by analysing
the causes and meaning of 'urban violence'. And the emphasis on
narrative is a moral logic as well as a discursive technique; one of
the reasons that the PCC's justice enjoys broad legitimacy is that it
is based on the interplay of moral principle and situational nuance,
told by the actors themselves and debated by 'brothers' with little
patience for abstraction or technicality. This is justice based on
'principles put to the test on a situational basis' (p. 221), not on
an opaque and impenetrable legal infrastructure that's actions
regularly belie its theoretical commitments.

Feltran's take on PCC justice is but one facet of a broader
set of arguments about the nature of urban order-making, and
in particular the ways in which contemporary cities are shaped
by overlapping, contradictory, competitive and interdependent normative regimes. There is nothing especially novel about
the notion that liberalism, citizenship and democracy coexist with their antitheses. In Brazil, these paradoxes inhabit the
core of national self-reflection, preoccupying thinkers as varied
as Joaquim Nabuco, Sérgio Buarque de Holanda and Roberto
Schwarz. The fact that Brazil's post-1988 democratic expansion

Foreword

has been paradoxically entwined with the rise of illicit economies, police violence and criminal governance has undergirded some of the most insightful analyses of contemporary urban Brazil, from Luiz Antônio Machado da Silva and Michel Misse to Teresa Caldeira and James Holston. Feltran pushes those insights a step further, with especially penetrating everyday logic. The issue in São Paulo is not only that there are competing notions of how to achieve a normative state that we might define as the rule of law or liberal democracy. It is, rather, that São Paulo's commitment to those principles – understood not through rhetoric or legal forms, but through the concrete workings of everyday life – is so aleatory and incomplete, especially on the peripheries, that progressive institutional inclusion and citizenship cannot operate as hegemonic ideals. The question in São Paulo's peripheries is not whether democratic governance can be best achieved by law-and-order crackdowns or through radical expansions of civil rights and formal equality; it is, rather, whether democracy and liberal governance are even relevant as ordering concepts. The PCC understands this, and has in response created – with violence, but also methodically and consistently – 'alternative and coexistent regimes of publicness' (p. 13). Like so many relational and informal orders that have historically co-governed cities in Brazil and around the globe, these operate not in opposition to laws and institutions, but in conjunction with them, becoming part of a repertoire of operative scripts that everyone calls upon on a situational basis. The PCC has grown not as a force of violent chaos, bent on disordering urban society, or as a militarised business hierarchy, bent on profit at all costs. It has emerged instead as an intricate pact capable of organising and protecting bodies, relationships, spaces and economies, that the liberal order has systematically failed to recognise or fully incorporate.

Feltran grapples frequently in these pages with the new meanings his insights have taken on in Brazil's current context of violent historical rupture. He reflects, as many have, on the ways in which elite imaginaries have shifted from paradigms of economic and civic integration to those of management, control and defence. He delves far more deeply, with sparser company, into the ways in which more than thirty years of democratisation and liberal economic reform have been experienced on the peripheries as 'a series of crises; formal employment, in Catholic religiosity, of the promise of social mobility for the working family, of social movements and their representativeness' (p. 69). By the new millennium, these crises were so endemic that they had become for young people 'a constitutive element of their being in the world'; their parents' ways of understanding progress, moral behavior, and societal pacts of protection and responsibility had fractured beyond recognition (p. 70). In their place, consumerism and 'old-fashioned religious morality' emerged as the only social logics capable of integrating peripheral and privileged spheres that no longer shared common understandings of the present or the future. Money connected illegal and legal economies and governing bodies, eye-for-an-eye morality and faith in divine jurisdiction linked 'citizens' and 'bandits' who no longer invested much faith in institutional jurisdiction. Seen in this context, Jair Bolsonaro's political rise doesn't seem like an aberration; it might be better understood as the lifting of a veil, the moment when 'the conflict that plagued the favelas … finally became a part of national politics … Police repression, religious fundamentalism, and radical liberalism, everything that was thought to be backwards in the era of building democracy, was now in the vanguard of a new national project (23).'

There is nothing remotely utopian about the urban periphery that Feltran describes. Since the early 2000s, Ivete – Feltran's most intimate informant, the person who helps him understand how normative regimes intersect to sustain family life – has seen two sons die violent deaths. A third is beaten to a pulp and sent to exile in the Northeast, one of her daughters is an addict, in and out of prison. The world of crime provided Ivete with day-to-day security when she arrived in the periphery, and gave both the material resources and the local legitimacy she and her straighter-arrow children needed to forge a more sustainable life. But the PCC also decreed her son's exile and forced his brother to participate in his brutal beating; the organisation facilitates the sale of the drugs that devastate her daughter, and cannot protect two of her sons from dying young, at least one from a police bullet. All of this during years when São Paulo's homicide rates were plummeting and the economy was booming, the golden age of both PCC and democratic governance.

At a broader level, there is no guarantee that the ethical strain that Feltran identifies within the tangle of PCC governance – its radical commitment to deliberative methods and to the principles of peace, justice, liberty, equality and unity – will be even as enduringly present as the ethical strains within liberalism and institutional democracy, especially as the organisation competes for dominance with other normative regimes and expands nationally and globally in a context of rising authoritarianism. Without that strain, criminal governance – like liberal governance – becomes simply the violent forging of an order suitable to those who hold the reins of power. As anyone who has ever manually tuned a radio knows, *sintonia* is ephemeral and sometimes impossible. *Entangled City* does not open our eyes to an urban order most people would choose if they had a better option. But it does allow us a brief moment of synchronicity, within which tangles become patterns and the peripheral worldview makes absolute sense. In allowing us to see the disjuncture of the liberal and democratic discourses emanating from the so-called centre, *Entangled City* lays the basis for a frank, honest conversation about the lived experience and moral underpinnings of contemporary urbanity.

Acknowledgements

I wish to thank Patrick Le Galès, Talja Blokland, Caroline Knowles and Angelo Martins Jr for their enthusiasm for this book. Marta Arretche, Eduardo Marques and Adrian Lavalle, as well as my colleagues at the Centro de Estudos da Metrópole, have been incredibly supportive over the last fifteen years. Evelina Dagnino and Daniel Cefaï trusted my fieldwork from the very beginning and helped me in every step of my research. I am also grateful to Valter Silvério, Jacob Lima, Rodrigo Constante and all my colleagues at the Sociology Department and the Sociology Graduate Programme of the Federal University of São Carlos. Our shared struggle for academic excellence and commitment to democracy in Brazil is still alive.

Luiz Antonio Machado da Silva, the late Maria Celia Paoli and Michel Misse were sources of inspiration for the research trajectory that I followed. I feel part of a collaborative network of urban ethnographers inspired by their way of doing social sciences in Brazil: Neiva Vieira, Heitor Frúgoli, Taniele Rui, Adriana Vianna, Mariana Cavalcanti, Patrícia Birman, Carly Machado, Vera Telles and Márcia Leite; and also Mariana Côrtes, Claudia Fonseca, Adriana Piscitelli, Natália Padovani, Jussara Freire, Alexandre Werneck, Marcella Araujo, Andrea Guerra and Robert Cabanes. The NaMargem – Núcleo de Estudos Urbanos, coordinated by Luana Motta, and the Núcleo de Etnografias

Acknowledgements

Urbanas of CEBRAP, coordinated by Ronaldo Almeida, are also important nodes of this network. Daniel Hirata and Willian Neves have been my closest intellectual partners during these years, and have always been references for my studies about cities, crime and PCC (Primeiro Comando da Capital) in Brazil, as also have been Karina Biondi, Reginaldo Nasser, Camila Dias, Leonardo Sá, Bruno Manso, Fernando Rodrigues, Marcelo Campos, Ben Lessing, Graham Willis, Fabio Candotti and Sacha Darke.

I developed part of the arguments presented here during periods spent as a visiting scholar at the University of Oxford, the Goldsmiths College, University of London, the Humbold University in Berlin, the Sciences Po in Paris and the CIESAS Golfo in Xalapa. Thanks to Andreza Santos, Caroline Knowles, Bill Schwarcz and Les Back, to Patrick Le Galès and Tommaso Vitale, as well as to Ernesto Isunza, and most especially to Talja Blokand her and team, for the invitations and close partnership. I wish also to thank Salvador Maldonado, Marie Morelle, Sebastien Jacquot, Jerome Tadie, Brodie Fischer, Gabriel Kessler, Sergio Costa, Natália Bermudez, Derek Pardue and Frida Gregersen for our discussions over these years. Mitch Duneier, Teresa Caldeira, Bibia Gregori, Paulo Arantes and John Gledhill urged me to go ahead when we met, and that was important to me. The Liebman family gave us a hospitable home in London and I have no words to thank Maggie, Sam and Tatiana for their continual generous support for this book. Matt Richmond worked with great enthusiasm and competence on the translation of most of the chapters.

The Comunidades do Parque Santa Madalena, Jardim Elba, Jardim Planalto, Pró-morar e Juta are part of my existential community and I am grateful for their hosting and friendship over the last decades. I thank Valdenia Paulino in the name of all those people who helped me so patiently during my fieldwork. I have been learning continually in Sapopemba, more than in any other place I have been. Our research team at the Centro de Estudos da Metrópole (CEM) project on illegal markets was very important

Acknowledgements

for this book: thanks to Deborah Fromm, Luana Motta, Janaína Maldonado, Isabela Vianna, André de Pieri, Gregório Diniz, Lucas Alves and Evandro Cruz. I wish I could thank properly Deb, Iaiá, Léo, Lulu, Paulo, Renata and my parents for their love and our beautiful moments together. I hope that our everyday life shows just how it is important to me.

I am profoundly grateful to FAPESP (Fundação de Amparo à Pesquisa do Estado de São Paulo – processo 2013/07616-7), the CNPq (Conselho Nacional de Desenvolvimento Científico e Tecnológico) and the Kosmos Fellowship Program (Humbold University) for their financial support for my research projects over the years. Tom Dark has been a splendid editor. Some material in this book has previously appeared in the following publications: O legítimo em disputa: as fronteiras do 'mundo do crime' nas periferias de São Paulo. *Dilemas Revista de Estudos de Conflito e Controle Social*, v. 1, n. 1, pp. 93–126, 2011; *Fronteiras de tensão: política e violência nas periferias de São Paulo*. São Paulo: Editora da Unesp/CEM, 2011; Governo que produz crime, crime que produz governo: o dispositivo de gestão do homicídio em São Paulo (1992–2012). *Revista Brasileira de Segurança Pública*, v. 6 n. 2, São Paulo ago/set 2012; The management of violence on the periphery of São Paulo: a normative apparatus repertoire in the PCC era. *Vibrant*, Florianópolis, v. 7, n. 2, 2010; (I)llicit Economies in Brazil: An Ethnographic Perspective. *Journal of Illicit Economies and Development*. v. 2, 2019; A categoria como intervalo: a diferença entre essência e desconstrução. *Cadernos Pagu*, Unicamp, Campinas. n. 50, 2017.

Abbreviations

CEDECA	Centro de Defesa dos Direitos de Crianças e Adolescentes 'Mônica Paião Trevisan' (Centre for the Defence of the Rights of Children and Adolescents)
CEM	Centro de Estudos da Metrópole (Centre for Metropolitan Studies)
FEBEM	Secure Centres for Young Offenders
MST	Landless Rural Workers' Movement
Nasce	Núcleo Assistencial Cantinho da Esperança (Corner of Hope Care Unit)
NGO	non-governmental organisation
PCC	Primeiro Comando da Capital (First Command of the Capital)
PT	Workers' Party
R$	Brazilian real
RDD	Differentiated Disciplinary Regime
UAI	Unidade de Atendimento Inicial, the unit for first-time offenders at FEBEM

3 September 2001, 9:40 a.m.

It's early and there's already loud music on the high street, and people talking loudly. The avenues of the periphery are noisy. Men on different sides of the street greet each other from a distance with shouts and jokes. Two passing young women try to ignore them, but become their focus. Crowded buses take maids, porters, security guards, cleaners to work. The noise of diesel engines is only surpassed by the pollution they produce. Old cars carry white builders, black electricians. Already long queues are waiting for the agencies to open so they can fill out forms in search of employment. Queues also form at the doors of banks and lottery stores, which serve many neighbourhoods. Street vendors set up their stalls, and many small shops raise their shutters. The day is beginning. I am in Mateo Bei avenue, in the East Zone of São Paulo, and it reminds me a lot of the main avenue of Carapicuíba, in the far west of the metropolis. Everything is similar. The graffiti decorating the shop fronts add some colour to an environment with so few trees, so grey with the cement and asbestos tiling, opaque orange with the Bahian bricks. Here and there, small bakeries and bars serve buttered toast, and an evangelical church between the 'Casas do Norte' sells products to migrants. (Field notes, handwritten)

24 May 2006, 6:40 p.m.

I'm on the bus back from Sapopemba, going to Ibirapuera. From the window, I see a sea of self-built homes. I feel like I've just been delivered a blow. Bianca filled me in on what was happening in her life; I met up with Clarice and Ivonete again. 'Fuck the police', graffitied on walls, in squares, in schools. 'Paulo Fiorilo', painted on the wall, is a councillor from the PT (Workers' Party). A woman with a child, an old man and a dog on a roof. A heavy home-security gate with a car on the inside. Another windy road, the bus is noisy, another PT star (party symbol) on the wall. Bianca cares for her three children and five younger brothers and sisters, she is 23 years old. We circle the Jardim Elbe favela. She was sexually abused by her stepfather aged 13 to 15. Her mother blamed her. A man selling brooms. Jehovah, a store selling religious goods. Casa de Carnes Serena, a butcher. Cleaning products in Coca-Cola bottles and a pool bar, interspersed with gated homes. Another mother holding her daughter's hand. Ivonete's son is called Vitor, he's 12 years old and has already had to repeat two years of school: 'There are times when there is only class once a week.' It's just favela, favela and more favela now, on the left side of the bus. Then a supermarket, which is a reference point in Parque Santa Madalena, the Nagumo. A business centre. Vitor does not go out with his uncles who are 'from the crime'; 'only with workers'. A beetle car, completely dismantled. More arcades and pool tables. Four teenagers on the corner, a small bar. Houses with small entrances and up to three floors. Clarice studied psychology at PUC (the Pontifical Catholic University), she passionately recounted a case she was dealing with at work. An 18-year-old boy, addicted to crack, who was sentenced to death, but had not yet died. Another woman with a child on her lap. Another bus stop and a notice advertising repairs for ovens, pans. Another staircase. Lots of favela now, well consolidated, and two more boys on bikes on the corner. A worker arriving home, a payphone in the grocery store, a health centre. (Field notes, dictated to voice recorder)

13 January 2019, 5:20 p.m.

We just had lunch at Ivonete's house in Santa Madalena Park. Matt, Ana Paula and Valeria accompanied me. We ate sitting on the bed where Ivete, her mother, sleeps in front of a huge, flat-screen television. There is much affection between us and we exchange news; we had not seen each other for months. Ivete's grandchildren surround us, messing with cell phones. I told her that my children are studying in France this year, and I miss them.

The entangled city

Ivete agreed it was hard to be away from the little ones, and then fell silent. I wanted to apologise, but I kept quiet. Ivete lost two children, murdered; she misses them painfully. Now she's worried about her grandchildren. Vitor is now 25, he was shot in the back running from the police in 2017, and went to jail for nine months. He is out now, is still involved in crime; he's has had a daughter, Ivete's first great-granddaughter. He bought a new apartment, he's got money. Ivete seemed drowsy; I asked her what medication she's been taking. There were seven pills a day. We talked about psychiatric care, about the Church, about her other children and grandchildren, about the refurbishment of her house, and then it was time to go. We continued walking from the favela to the station of the newly opened *monotrilho* (a suspended trainline, similar to London's Dockland Light Railway). The favela has been integrated into the metro network for the first time, and the journey to the city centre is now forty minutes quicker. We spoke about how the landscape had changed with the arrival of the train. The avenue, once full of informal businesses selling used and stolen cars and car parts, now has the air of a metropolitan avenue, with a bicycle lane painted red along the central strip between the gigantic concrete pillars of the *monotrilho*. I take photos of the landscape with my cell phone. Land and rental prices will rise here. On the way to the station, the sole of Ana Paula's shoe broke. She, who had lived so many years on the streets, threw the shoe away and kept walking barefoot, with no apparent problem. Upon entering the modern station, she felt embarrassed but kept going. Once you are on the suspended train, the landscape is once again a sea of self-constructed homes. I remembered 1997, when I noticed for the first time that the peripheries of São Paulo stretch out as far as the eye can see. The landscape had changed, cell phones and televisions had arrived, the *monotrilho*; the PCC, born in the *quebrada* (slang for poor neighbourhood), is now transnational. I'm feeling I understand it far better than before. But still not much. (Field notes, dictated to cell phone)

Introduction

The research for this book began in 1997, when Brazil's elites still hoped to achieve the integration of the country into a modern global order, and of the urban poor into a prosperous nation. Both integration projects placed their hopes in the city of São Paulo. The largest metropolis in South America, it was at the centre of the national economy and the drive for modernisation; it had the country's largest industrial sector and received millions of rural migrants from the 1950s to the 1980s. Within the space of thirty years, the population of the metropolitan region grew from 2.6 to 12.5 million. This demographic explosion manifested in the rapid expansion of poor, self-built peripheries. Favelas, clandestine subdivisions, grilagem,[1] working-class neighbourhoods. The peripheries became the primary spaces occupied by white workers, blacks and Northeasterners (Durham, 1973; Cabanes, 2003). Besides migration, the chief underpinnings for the occupation of these territories, until the 1980s, were factory work, the family and Catholic religiosity (Kowarick, 1979; Sader, 1988; Holston, 2007; Feltran, 2011; Machado da Silva, 2016).

These pillars of peripheral life have shifted radically since urbanisation. Rural-to-urban migration was slowed by the economic crisis of the 1980s, and followed by economic restructuring (Lima, 2016); there was a dramatic transition in popular religious practices (Almeida, 2018) with the aggressive expansion of the

1

Table 1 Population growth in the municipality and metropolitan region of São Paulo (absolute numbers)

	1950	1960	1970	1980	1991	2000	2010	2018
São Paulo	2,151,313	3,667,899	5,924,615	8,493,226	9,646,185	10,434,252	11,253,503	12,176,866
Metropolitan region	2,653,860	4,739,406	8,139,730	12,588,725	15,444,941	17,878,703	19,683,975	21,571,281

Source: IBGE census and bulletins – compiled by Prefeitura Municipal de São Paulo 1950–2010.

Pentecostal churches from the 1980s onwards (Almeida, 2004, 2019b; Birman, 2012; Birman and Machado, 2012). The large extended family, characteristic of the rural world, also contracted rapidly in the city: average fecundity plummeted from 7.1 to 1.4 children per woman over just forty years (Oliveira, Vieira and Marcondes, 2015). Since then, two generations have been born and grown up in an urban world radically different from that in which their parents and grandparents lived. However, it is none-theless still marked by what they lived through. The inhabitants of the peripheries today are no longer migrants, nor do they expect to be protected workers; their family arrangements, life trajectories and forms of insertion into the productive economy are far less stable than those of the previous generation. Schooling, access to key services and urban infrastructure, although still precarious, have all grown considerably. However, it is the expansion of the 'world of crime' – a social universe and form of everyday authority established around illegal markets like drug trafficking, the trade in stolen vehicles and other types of crime, especially robbery – that has most radically transformed the social dynamics of the peripheries.

In this book I tell the story of the emergence and expansion of the 'world of crime' – or simply 'crime' – in São Paulo and its con-sequences for urban life. This expansion is connected, on the one hand, to structural changes to everyday life in urban peripheries (Ferguson, 1999; Robinson, 2006) and, on the other hand, to the expansion of the Primeiro Comando da Capital (First Command of the Capital, PCC). By 2019 this faction, founded in 1993 in a single prison in São Paulo, had grown to become the main crimi-nal organisation in Brazil, if not in Latin America, and a key issue in the national political debate. My focus on the 'world of crime' and the PCC is not an arbitrary choice, given that there has been a surprising lack of academic attention to the subject over two decades (as well as major misunderstandings of the issue in public debates). The focus on violence and the PCC was also, effectively, imposed on me as an ethnographer who was close to people who were being murdered on a massive scale around the turn of the century, as well as to others from the middle and elite classes who had no idea what was happening and, in any case, cared little. This ethnographic study is the result of an experiment conducted at this frontier, of searching for the parameters of São Paulo's contemporary urban order. I argue here, at the outset, in favour of understanding São Paulo's urban conflict through the formal notion of normative regimes – in contrast to the view, dominant in the academic literature, which still presents 'urban violence' as the opposite of the 'modern order' or 'democracy'. Historically – and the metropolis of São Paulo is exemplary in this regard – these notions have been intrinsically related (Tilly, 1985).

Expectations of modernity[2]

When this ethnographic study began in 1997, international investors were only beginning to view our markets, recently opened up following the end of the dictatorship, as 'emerging'. The economy had recovered from the hyperinflation of the 1980s, thanks to the 1994 Real Plan, which led to Fernando Henrique Cardoso's election to the presidency that same year. However, the economic restructuring still underway was generating growing unemployment, reaching 16% in the São Paulo Metropolitan Region.[3] The government claimed that the country was modernising in every area and that education had become universalised for the first time. The opposition denounced the massive privatisations, which they argued had benefited banks and foreign capital. Jurists took pride in the 1988 Federal Constitution, a 'first world' normative framework, as they moved into gated communities. In the universities, democracy and neoliberalism, globalisation and popular participation were all being vigorously debated. Newly created non-governmental organisations (NGOs), focusing on peripheries, talked about citizenship and corporate social responsibility. Social

4

democracy, liberalism, left, right. Everyone was sure that Brazil was the country of the future; the debate was about which path should be taken to get there.

But the favelas were not part of this 'everyone'. The conversations happening there were quite different. 'Do you know that boy they killed in the football field last Saturday? He was the son of Dona Aurora, the brother of Jefferson, that boy who studied with Renan, remember?' The main topic of conversation in the favelas in 1997 was violence. 'He told me that Jefferson's brother was involved. Lord almighty!' By the early 1990s, cocaine trafficked from Colombia via the Amazon on an industrial scale had reached the peripheries of São Paulo. Marijuana came from the Northeast of the country, later from Paraguay. Cocaine paste came from Bolivia, and, with it, a few years later, crack. Multiple routes. In all cases, spectacular profits were to be made from retail, and favelados (residents of favelas) came to occupy the front line of this distribution chain, dealing directly with the consumer. 'Money is one thing; a lot of money is something else,' said Tim Maia, a musician celebrated in the peripheries. For the first time in Brazilian history, black and poor people were able to earn a lot of money.

The conflict to manage the accumulation of so much money was horrific. 'Poor people killing poor people, black people killing black people', as I used to hear. Weapons arrived to equip this conflict, illegally bought from the police, trafficked from Paraguay, diverted from the armed forces. The homicide rates of black youths exploded (Santos Silva, 2014). Between 1960 and 1995 they rose from 9.6 to 186.7 per 100,000 inhabitants, an increase of 1,800% (Manso, 2012, p. 28). Passing the bodies of young people murdered in the street, whether by the police or by traffickers, seemed to have become routine everywhere I went. It was the personal impact of this that led me to study violence.

In the 'hood' ('quebrada'), no one spoke about neoliberalism or democracy, but about concrete issues of everyday life, especially the violence that pervaded it. In the favelas, people tend not to speak in generic but, rather, in narrative terms. You need to tell a specific story, not a general story. 'Who was the cop?', not how the police act in general. 'Each case is a case,' people often say. Still, the 'quebrada' has its concepts, its tools of analysis. The 1990s, which are commonly regarded in the press as the period of the consolidation of democracy in Brazil, are remembered in the favelas as the 'time of wars'.

The soundtrack of the peripheries of São Paulo in 1997 was that of Racionais MCs, a quartet of young black men, 'represented' in every car, every set of earphones, every bar. A soundtrack punctuated by samples of urban sounds: police sirens, dogs barking, cars screeching, alarm clocks, gun shots. 'Sobrevivendo no Inferno' – Surviving Hell, not democracy – was the name of their latest album. A cross and Psalm 23 of the Old Testament appeared on the cover: 'Restore my soul and guide me on the path to justice.' The most played song in the favelas was 'A Fórmula Mágica da Paz' (The Magic Formula of Peace), which a black boy showed me, among the tapes kept in his father's car, in answer to my question: 'Do you think the favelas are better now than before?' In 1997 the song already spoke of the PCC offering hope of order and peace in the ghettos. As an outsider – despite being born in São Paulo – I did not understand what the boy was trying to say. It took many more years before I understood.

The 'Lula era'

The 2000s arrived, and with them the 'Lula era' in Brazilian politics. The minimum wage saw a real increase of 30% over the course of the decade, and popular forms of credit were made available. Global consumption reached the peripheries – the result of a bottom-up economic growth strategy. By 2010, unemployment in the São Paulo Metropolitan Region had fallen to 8%.[4] Big global brands of cell phones and televisions, as well as myriad Chinese and counterfeit products, became part of everyday life. There was talk of a new 'C Class', or even a 'new middle class', that had escaped from poverty (Richmond, 2019a and 2019b). This brief outbreak of prosperity brought new people to São Paulo, now from outside the country. On the metro it became more common to hear Bolivian Spanish, English with a Nigerian accent and Portuguese from Angola. These workers did not enter the formal market, instead joining the base of the Brazilian labour pyramid, dominated by informal and illegal activities.

Nothing seemed to deter Brazil, nor the poor, in their project of integration into the modern world via the market. The broad presidential coalition during the Lula and Dilma Rouseff governments lasted more than a decade and seemed to have created a consensus. Both the old landowners of the rural Northeast and the Landless Rural Workers' Movement (MST) supported the government. So did the large real estate developers and homeless movements; the agribusiness lobby and environmentalists; financial capital and the solidarity economy. This new-found political consensus clearly had economic foundations. There were massive resources for the richest political groups, and far fewer for the poorer ones, but in the latter case this was still much more than ever before.

Even so, the rampant profits of the banks and brokerage firms combined, somewhat counter-intuitively, with low unemployment and the expansion of core public services in the peripheries: electricity, water, housing, healthcare, social assistance (Arretche, 2015). By the end of the last decade, the urban peripheries were firmly on the economists' maps. Similarly, Brazil had become an attractive location for international investors, becoming more deeply integrated into global markets. In this favourable context, and thanks also to his own personal charisma, Lula finished his second term in 2010 with almost 80% of popular approval.

In the favelas, a lot of money circulated. Bianca had a new refrigerator and was expecting to soon move into a new apartment through the Minha Casa, Minha Vida (My House, My Life) federal social housing programme. She bought a new cell phone in instalments, and even thought about getting a motorbike. She went to the hairdresser more often. But, with more money in the economy, illegal markets also expanded. More money in people's pockets, more drug use, more guns, more stolen goods. Demand heats up the economy, bottom-up growth. With a more globalised economy, consumer markets also became transnational. Thieves and drug dealers talked about Dior, Lacoste, farms on the border with Paraguay, a yacht on the São Paulo coast. The world opened up for entrepreneurs, less so for workers.

By this time, the PCC, first created in 1993, had already been around for almost twenty years. Having emerged in the São Paulo prison system during its expansion, the faction ultimately ended the wars in the peripheries. The PCC slogan, 'peace between us, war on the system', echoed through the *'quebrada'*. The chapters of this book tell that story. 'Brothers' of the faction were already active in almost all the favelas of the state of São Paulo, which has more than 44 million inhabitants. In each neighbourhood, the Command negotiated with existing groups, securing a monopoly on the legitimate use of force in exchange for providing justice and protection. The regulation of retail drug pricing completed the arrangement. It worked.

One of the main effects of the PCC's hegemony in São Paulo was a radical reduction in homicides in the favela: the 'magic formula of peace' that had been sung for years. Official statistics have shown that homicides in the state of São Paulo fell precipitously over the decade 2000–10: a fall of more than 70% across the state (Manso, 2012; Waiselfisz, 2015). In peripheral districts, murders in 2010 had fallen to one-tenth of those registered in 2000 (PRO-AIM, 2012). How did this happen? In the universities, in government, in the press, the debate was intense (Feltran, 2012). But not in the favelas, where everything was already clear. In the public debate, the process was poorly understood, and remains so today, despite the solid recent body of literature produced on the faction (Biondi, 2016; Feltran, 2018; Hirata, 2018; Manso and Dias, 2018). By the time we'd started to understand what was going on, the PCC itself was already in another phase. It was no longer restricted to São Paulo, having expanded to practically every state of the federation.

In 2013 the largest popular demonstrations in Brazilian history took 'the population' to the streets. Middle classes banging pots, elites wearing yellow and green, trade unionists dressed in red, students and organised social movements all vied for space in the streets. The feeling of not being represented in politics was the only thing the protesters, of right and left, had in common. The peripheries, with the exception of the traditional workers' movements, were conspicuously absent from the protests. They had a different understanding of the world, one less connected to politics and more to markets.

In 2015 Racionais MCs no longer spoke of death, but of containers of cocaine sent to Belgium from the port of Santos; of R$400,000 in gross sales earned by a single cocaine trafficker, in a single deal. Growth opportunities in illegal international trade, in the financial market, between the legal and illegal spheres, were open to entrepreneurs. For those who had the inclination, competence and courage, money would follow. Money was at the heart of attempts to mediate the social and urban conflict in the peripheries.

Outlining the argument

The argument presented here, that urban order in São Paulo is maintained by normative, plural and coexisting regimes of action, is built upon direct dialogue, in a long tradition of Brazilian authors working on urban conflict and violence (Machado da Silva, 1993, 1999, 2004, 2011, 2016; Misse, 2006a, 2018; Feltran, 2010a, 2012; Hirata, 2018; Grillo, 2013; Cabanes, 2014; Machado,

2017). For these authors, crucial to thinking about urban conflict is the hypothesis that it occurs between subjects who do not share the same plausible parameters of action and, by extension, do not occupy different positions as subjects in a common urban order. Different analytical traditions discuss the same empirical issues in political terms. Concepts such as sovereignty, state authority, security and hybrid orders or governscapes are mobilised to account for empirical challenges to modern states,[5] but also for our interpretations in contexts of extreme violence (Mbembe, 2003; Das, 2006a; Stepputat, 2013, 2015, 2018; Willis, 2015; Arias and Barnes, 2017; Lessing, 2017; Darke, 2018).

Jacques Rancière, in his classic work *La mésentente* (1995), pursues a related conceptual argument. For the philosopher, the key conflict that helps us to understand contemporary politics does not occur when one says white and another says black. Following this tradition, we realise that the black versus white dispute is only a secondary, sequential and managerial dimension – what Rancière calls the 'police' – of the original, essential conflict that occurs when one says white and another says also white, but they do not understand one another. Because between these subjects there is a radical mutual incomprehension about the criteria (Rancière, 1995), the many plausible meanings (Wittgenstein, 2009; Cavell, 2006) and the pragmatic effects of whiteness as they are understood by each actant (Boltanski and Thevenot, 1991; Thevenot, 2006; Werneck, 2012).

Let us take an example. Three subjects in São Paulo, or in Paris, desire security and offer normative arguments about the form and content of the kind of security they seek. For the first, security means living his/her life far from the threat of crime in São Paulo, or from the threat of terror in Paris. For the second, security means the ability to arm oneself against the threat of crime, or the existence of active state repression of terrorist threats. So far, the disagreement is at the level of content and there are sequential, secondary themes such as access to arms, life in gated condominiums or repressive state action that can be discussed in common. How to achieve 'security' would mean different, or even opposite, content for the two subjects' arguments, but they share the fundamental belief that crime and terror cause insecurity. Such differences between subjects divide, for instance, left and right along the democratic political spectrum. In São Paulo, the former might defend disarmament, the latter the right of upstanding citizens to own guns. In Paris, the former would advocate active anti-terrorism security measures, but without linking terrorism to any specific culture, while the latter advocates active state surveillance and anti-immigrant laws, as she/he connects immigration to terrorism. In this way, whether under democracy or authoritarianism, things may unfold on such a rational and administrative plane. One says white, another says black, but both recognise the other as a plausible even if a horrible interlocutor, and recognise that white and black are categories of the same nature.

The fundamental problem arises when a third subject, radically different from the first two, enters into the conversation. This subject believes that in São Paulo it is the 'world of crime' that offers them security, or in Paris that terrorism itself represents the very struggle for security, justice and liberation. This third subject does not share the fundamental belief that crime and terror produce insecurity. This subject finds himself/herself on the side of the PCC or of the 'terrorist'. Her/his normative assumptions change the very nature of the conflict about the meaning of 'security'.

For residents of cities like São Paulo or Rio de Janeiro who experience the relationship between the police and criminal factions empirically, citizenship, democracy and the rule of law are not plausible frames of explanation. By contrast, anyone who studies social policies would have no problem seeing them as such. The conflict in these territories is situated and specific, rather than generic. The homogeneous profile of homicide victims in Brazil is indisputable in this regard: young, unskilled operators of transnational illegal economies, living in favelas, of whom 94.6% are men, 72% are black, 71% are shot by gunfire, 53% are between fifteen and twenty-nine years old (IPEA/FBSP, 2018). For a long time, generic or normative notions have failed to offer an effective conceptual framework for Brazil's plural and disjunctive social conflict. They cannot encompass the mosaic of regimes of practice and plural urban orders, coexisting in time and space, that are needed to explain norms, deviations and actions in each specific situation.

The fundamental problem with much of the literature on the urban conflicts in São Paulo does not have to do with their formulations, which in themselves are productive for debate (Caldeira, 2000; Holston, 2007). The problem is that they treat the normative framework of one of the conflicting sides as a naturalised set of assumptions; that is to say, that of the state, which, explicitly or implicitly, presupposes democracy, citizenship and the public sphere as universals to be reached. This construction renders invisible the alternatives to this normative framework that, empirically, have emerged in the urban peripheries of São Paulo and other cities in recent decades as an implausible discourse or moral economy (Cabanes, 2014). This implausibility 'sabotages our reasoning', as Mano Brown has sung and Teresa Caldeira has understood (Caldeira, 2006). As an ethnographer, and years after these seminal works were published, I can more easily identify the role of the aforementioned third subject that, pragmatically, even if unintentionally, disruptively modifies the plausible limits of the world and who is able to join it. To understand those 'violent subjects' who were not supposed to exist or be part of the world, and their implausible actions, we must look far beyond frameworks centred on categories such as state policies, democracy and citizenship.

This third subject introduces an epistemological fracture into the problematic of the urban order and the modern state, because the first two do not consider the third's claim to be plausible, and therefore there can be no negotiation between them. Therefore, no universalism. The practical consequences of this fracture are hugely significant. It invalidates the entire conversation of the so-called public sphere, because it destroys the common ground that the three had occupied or should occupy (Arendt, 1951, 1959, 1977). All could be good if they were forever distant, but the empirical relations between the three subjects continue to exist, despite the lack of mutual comprehension, in cosmopolitan cities or in a global world. However high the walls of gated condominiums, they still share the same city, state, country or world.

The third subject does not continue the ordered debate between constituted actors occupying the same normative space. It forces a rupture of the entire debate assumptions and, in this way, opens the possibility for a double movement. On the one hand, there are increasingly fierce clashes between actors who misunderstand one another. On the other hand, the first two subjects will discuss their differences between them, while the third subject will cease to engage with them and will engage only with its peers. As time passes and conversation is restricted only to those who share the same basis of understanding, the distinct and internally coherent regime of thought tends to become autonomous.

The rupture produced by such dissensus causes not only a radical departure of all the subjects from the public scene, but also their arrival at another place. They will probably misunderstand that the PCC is not the absence of the state but the positive representation of 'crime', understood as a world or a powerful instance for regulating a community. This 'exit' from scene of which Hirschman (1970) speaks, and which Hannah Arendt (1959, 1977) recognises as the destruction of the modern public sphere, is pragmatically productive, and not a question of counter-publics who tend to move towards a synthesis of presuppositions (Fraser, 1992; Habermas, 1992). This rupture instead produces alternative and coexistent regimes of publicness, without the possibility of synthesis, because there can be no plausible communication between them (Machado da Silva, 1993).

With the common ground between the three subjects fractured, with two on one side and one on the other, we not only witness the withdrawal of one subject from the public sphere, which nonetheless continues without her. In cases of fierce conflict we also witness the emergence of other normative regimes, which coexist with the first, as people still share common physical spaces in the city without there being any rational, deliberative communication between them. What remains as the main relation between them is violence. When a possible negotiated exit from the urban conflict can no longer be resolved administratively, the city of São Paulo, like other Brazilian and Latin American cities (Arias and Goldstein, 2010; Arias, 2017), enters into a spiral of accumulating urban conflict in the form violence, understood as the use of force or threat that produces a similar effect (Misse, 2006b, 2018; Stepputat, 2013, 2015, 2018).

The representatives of the paulista middle and upper classes are then left in a 'democratic space', the actually existing government or public sphere, discussing among themselves what to do with, or rather, to the criminals. Whoever thinks criminals do not do the same is fooling themselves. The claims of the government – we are working for everyone's security – and that of the third element – crime is a means to social mobility – cannot be heard side by side. Crime threatens the country's security, period, says the government. 'Crime' is the only route to security in the favelas, period, says the PCC. It is precisely at this limit of the acceptable, the plausible, that Michael Taussig's terror – pure violence – becomes the fundamental relationship between the parts, separated by an unbridgeable divide.

More than 63,000 people were killed in Brazil in 2017. The vast majority of them were young black men from favelas, low-wage workers in huge, transnational markets based in large cities, such as drug trafficking and car theft. Prisons keep filling up, armoured cars multiply and armed robberies nonetheless continue and grow. Not only in São Paulo, but, with different levels of intensity, such contemporary dynamics emerged between Nazis and Jews, Israel and Palestine, Tutsis and Hutus, Al-Qaeda and the United States (US), and there are many other examples. Assumptions are no longer negotiated, and this produces a fracture between distinct and self-contained sets of irreconcilable regimes of action and understanding about what constitutes the common good; about what the world is and how it should be.

These self-contained terrains, understood as formal structures of thought and action filled situationally with different content (Simmel, 2009), are what I have called normative regimes (Feltran, 2010b, 2013a). Empirical action and social forms are something else and come later. Normative regimes function as a plausible set of orientations for the empirical action of subjects. This makes such action convenient, which is to say, formally expected by peers (Thevenot, 1990). Action that is convenient for peers will be incomprehensible, because it is implausible, on the other side of the fracture. On that side, it is not even believed that such subjects exist, let alone that they might be able to speak meaningfully (Cavell, 2006). This essential political fracture has been in place in São Paulo ever since the promise of integration of the migrant into the modern city was – with rare exceptions – frustrated. It became deeper, therefore, as urban wage labour declined and hopes of social integration, and of the comprehensive provision of public services that would enable this, retreated ever further into the horizon (Misse, 2006a; Machado da Silva, 2016). Over time, the limits of the plausible, on each side of the fracture, concretised. A thief is a thief. A worker is a worker. Crime is crime, the law is the law.

This fracture poses problems for analysts, though not as serious as for those who are positioned close to the edges of the divide. Describing precisely (how the city is) requires moving across different categorical boundaries, which is a far from easy task. But thinking about the normative problem (of how the city should be) means addressing profound mutual incomprehension and the risk of violence. In São Paulo, for journalists, lawyers, doctors, the middle classes and even many working people from the peripheries, security means maintaining a safe distance from thieves, *bandidos* and the PCC, in gated condominiums. These days, violent forms of interaction are very plausible where the need for such distance is not taken seriously. Meanwhile, in the favelas, for at least three decades it is precisely thieves and *bandidos* who have seemed to offer security. 'Thief' is thus an offensive word within the state regime of action, but a celebration of intelligence and insight within the criminal regime. Thief thus has essential, closed, defined content in each of these terrains. However, formally, or analytically, the word thief becomes a polysemic notion, endowed with various meanings, capable of being filled with different content.

These theoretical and practical dilemmas are hardly new: Georg Simmel was already grappling with them in 1900. Neither are they problems unique to São Paulo. For decades modern cities saw republicanism and multiculturalism as successful alternatives to these fierce conflicts. Today these are clearly understood as insufficient solutions, even though we may not be able to find anything better.

The countries to whom the modern global order was promised, all from the 'Global South', and the subjects that have never even been part of their 'nation states' (indigenous, black and favela-dwelling residents of São Paulo are just one example), face the same theoretical-political problem: that of understanding what order allows them to exist, in a scenario of profound misunderstanding about who they are on different sides of the structural fracture. The ethnographer has a role to play in this drama, as she should be committed to avoiding ethnocentrism – that is, to avoid allowing the structural fracture to function as an epistemological one.

This book tells specific stories about the urban conflict in São Paulo, a conflict that is often lethal. Through these stories it traces the recent history of the not always peaceful coexistence between

the normative regimes of the state and crime; a coexistence mediated by religion and by money, which enable state and criminal
actors to regulate the urban order in São Paulo also in liberal
and Christian terms, not just in democratic or violent ones. My
main goal is to offer an ethnographic account of transformations
in São Paulo's peripheries and the emergence of the 'world of
crime' through the frequently violent tensions between what the
fractured urban order is and, especially, what it should be.

This book dives into a long-standing theoretical tradition in
sociology, especially the sociology of action, that has long emphasised the intrinsic relationship between order and violence (Weber,
1967; Goffman, 2003, 2005; Cefaï and Gardella, 2012). In doing so
it engages directly with other contemporary urban ethnographers
(Bourgois, 1995; Bourgois and Schonberg, 2009; Blokland, 2003,
2008, 2017; Das, 2006b; Cefaï, 2010; Hobbs, 2011, 2013; Duneier,
Kasinitz and Murphy, 2014; Goffman, 2014; Rodgers and Baird,
2015;), all recognised as broadly working within or inspired by
the ethnographic tradition of the Chicago School since Anderson
(1923) and Whyte (2005 [1943]).

Unlike the Thevenot's *regimes d'engagement*, Goffman's *frames* and
Bourdieu's *fields*, and updating Machado da Silva's (1993) proposed 'coexistence of orders', the formal notion of a normative
regime implies a specific relation to violence. A normative regime
is guaranteed not solely, but ultimately, by the capacity of its actors
to resort to force to internally order social relations, thereby giving
plausibility to individual and collective action in pursuit of values
and projects, as well as interests. Max Weber (1967) and Norbert
Elias (1978) have long demonstrated how social relations of civility
and citizenship, often regarded as the opposite of violence, are
guaranteed both by the legitimacy of governments, representing
deeply rooted customs and values, and, as a last resort, by the
state's capacity for coercion.

Charles Tilly (1985) has demonstrated how war-making and
state-making are directly related to the notion of 'organised crime'

as it is today understood. It takes material resources to sustain any kind of state or urban order, and the violence of pillage, but also of security, is fundamental to obtaining these resources. The formula that underpins the state regime with regard to violence is clear: without legitimacy there is no government and without police there is no order, but without armed forces there is no state. Bureaucracy may appear as a modern mode of governing without the need for explicit violence, but it persists only when recourse to the potential violence of the police, the prison system and the armed forces lie behind it. Still, it is not enough.[6]

'The crime', which functions like a government that coexists more than competes with the state in the favelas of São Paulo or Rio de Janeiro, regulates illegal markets, advocates community values, depends on being viewed as legitimate by a significant portion of those it governs. But it would not exist without arms. The greater the consensus and government hegemony, the less the need for violent coercion. In Rio de Janeiro there are different factions and militias openly armed and at war with each other; legitimacy among favela residents has been eroded by years of war, and explicit violence is used to maintain order (Grillo, 2013; Lyra, 2013; Arias, 2017). In São Paulo, especially during the 2000s, the strong legitimacy of the PCC in the *'quebradas'* made recourse to violence unnecessary. Dealers at drug sale points stopped carrying arms fifteen years ago (Feltran, 2011; Willis, 2015; Hirata, 2018). Police officers can enter any favela in São Paulo without the need to shoot.

In the ethnographic situations that I have encountered over two decades, when someone in the drug trade decides that he will no longer pay the police to leave him in peace, violent conflict erupts. The conflict between the criminal and state regimes in the favelas of São Paulo, unlike in those of Rio, is largely mediated by money rather than violence. In Rio de Janeiro, although there are payments, violence is more explicit. This book develops the argument about the role of money in mediating the urban conflict in Brazilian cities.

But another fundamental way in which this conflict is now mediated involves the evangelical world, especially in its more Old Testament variety. Ethnographic work clearly demonstrates the pervasiveness of such forms of Christian religiosity, whose central moral code is that of 'an eye for an eye, a tooth for tooth' (Côrtes, 2007; Marques, 2015). Thieves and police, workers, rulers and ruled have flocked to evangelical churches, which have expanded precipitously since the late 1980s and show no signs of stopping. Pentecostal expansion took place first in the favelas, then across the urban peripheries and finally among the middle classes and within the political system (Almeida, 2017; Côrtes, 2018).[7] In Pentecostal churches in the peripheries of any major Brazilian, African, Latin American or European city one can hear the testimonies of ex-thieves, ex-prostitutes, ex-killers and ex-drug traffickers now converted to Jesus (Côrtes, 2007; Teixeira, 2011).

At the same time, the same religious tendencies have expanded among the military and civilian police in Brazil and are now also heavily represented in the legislative and executive branches of government at municipal, state and federal levels. In 2018 this group was one of the influences, if not the decisive force, in the election of the first president of the Republic who was both a former serviceman and an evangelical, Jair Bolsonaro.

Money and God: from Lula to Bolsonaro

The 2010s did not deliver what the previous decade had promised, even if unemployment had fallen to 6% in Brazil by 2013 and remained low in the metropolis of São Paulo. Full employment had made the workforce more expensive. The middle classes and the productive sector were resentful, while bank profits hit record highs. The crisis was also moral: after so much change the younger generations were no longer living like the older ones. Government corruption scandals during the pre-electoral period began to weaken the consensus around lulismo and the ruling coalition.

The party that had been Dilma Rouseff's main partner became an opponent in the Congress. The press promoted the anti-corruption investigation Operation Lava Jato, inspired by Italy's Mani Pulite, and judge Sérgio Moro became a national hero.

In just a few years the mesdames of Jardins, an elite neighbourhood in São Paulo, who had once been able to employ three full-time uniformed servants in their homes, now had only one or two. The middle-class families of Pinheiros, who had had a live-in maid cooking, cleaning and clothing their children until the 2000s, now only had a maid coming three times a week. The lower middle-class families of Osasco had stopped paying for a cleaner to come once a week and gone back to washing their own clothes. Sapopemba's cleaners, who had washed their own clothes and those of others, were beginning to think about buying their own cars. That left a lot of people unhappy, and there was reaction.

While whites and blacks were simply naturalised as different in Brazil, it was not difficult to identify the social position of each. It was plain to see, and perceived as existential. Some blacks in the favelas and peripheries had begun to make a lot of money since the 1990s, but they became thieves and drug dealers, populating prisons and homicide statistics, until they realised that it was better to act quietly and not show off their wealth, as the PCC advises. But the natural difference between blacks and whites was truly shaken only around 2013, when it was realised that the entry of the poor into the world of consumption could mean a genuine flattening of inequalities between the middle and peripheral classes.

The cleaner felt that life was getting better, and her son was thinking about going to college. Meanwhile, the mistress who employed her felt that her life was getting worse and that she was paying for that change. After all, she was still the mistress. When the possibility of equality is felt, even distantly, those who stand to lose by it feel compelled to react, to reinforce the existing, unequal order (Arendt, 1997 [1958]). The 'June Days' of 2013, in which the middle and elite classes took to the streets to demonstrate against the government in the main cities of Brazil, were the first clear sign of this reaction. A similar outburst, in terms of both form and content, would appear in Paris a few years later in the form of the gilets jaunes movement. A spark which spread on the internet mobilised millions of people without a clear agenda but who were clearly dissatisfied with what was happening in their daily lives: they did not feel represented in institutional politics. However, the programme always arrives, after the mobilisation. And it was an agenda that was reactionary in its content, but even more so in the homogenising form in which it manifested. 'Against corruption', 'for more decency and security', in Brazil. Against corruption, immigration, generically expressed, elsewhere.

Corruption, violence and unemployment are then represented as novelties, and a general impulse asserts itself, demanding the restoration of an alleged previous order, of earlier values that had been lost with recent changes. In the Brazilian case, and even more so in São Paulo, it was easy to identify the causes of the problems in 2013. They were the corrupt politicians, and the thieves of the peripheries. Both were crooks. The impulse for order finds its most refined mechanism in criminalisation. Unlike in other contexts, but very similar to what happens in non-modern nations, the criminal in Brazil is not seen as belonging to the same community of human citizens. He is a radically immoral being who must be eliminated for the sake of the community. Mary Douglas's (1976) interpretation of purity and danger, written long ago and in a markedly different context, offers extremely relevant insights into what happened next in Brazil's political scene. Different 'pure' elements became 'impure' through mixing.

From 2014, with the narrow re-election of Dilma Rouseff, public life became polarised. The actors embodying social change, previously viewed as harmless to the general public when they remained separate, became impure once they mixed. The poor criminals came from the same place as the black cleaners, who had always been treated with suspicion, and were now buying cars; in the universities students from the peripheries mixed with people of the left, who supported human rights for criminals, and with LGBT groups who were already walking hand in hand without shame. 'I don't mind, but kissing like that is disrespectful, there are children looking ...'. The same 'decline in values' that undermined the family produced corruption. Everything came to be connected in a unity of meanings, now understood as coherent and impure. In conversations with family and old friends, it was as though rats had crept out of the sewer. Order had to be restored, quickly and radically, no matter what the cost. The Workers' Party, especially after the impeachment of President Dilma Rouseff in 2016, came to embody the pole of impurity against which elites rallied. Jair Bolsonaro, a Christian and former army captain, mobilising a radical anti-corruption discourse, represented the order that they wanted to see restored. In 2018 he became president.

In São Paulo, Minas Gerais and Rio de Janeiro, just three of Brazil's twenty-seven states, but concentrating 40% of its population, the governors elected in 2018 were all outsiders who had risen rapidly in the polls in the final days, at the point when they adopted the same discourse as Bolsonaro. Not only Bolsonaro, but also these governors, who play a crucial role in determining direction of Brazil's security agenda, were elected with impressive vote totals. Voting maps are clear in terms of distribution by social class, skin colour and religion: Bolsonaro won by far among the elites and middle classes, but also among the evangelical poor and some precarious workers. He lost by far in the Northeast, narrowly among Catholics and the poorest (Almeida, 2019a).

Paradoxically, the election of Bolsonaro put an end to the mismatch between the national public sphere and the peripheries. The conflict that was plaguing the favelas in 1997, when my research began, finally became part of national politics. A centripetal force seemed to flow from the peripheries to the centre over the course of two decades, to form a new political logic. Police repression, religious fundamentalism and radical liberalism, everything that was thought to be backwards in the era of building democracy, was now in the vanguard of a new national project: a project that was no longer modern, but Christian; no longer democratic, but military; no longer distributive, but ultraliberal.

Churches appear as a solution, offering *bandidos* who are under threat, unemployed or repentant a way out of crime. At the same time they provide police officers with divine justification for action that is 'righteous', even if it is completely against the law. Churches also facilitate the political legitimation of religious discourse within state institutions. On the one hand, the expanding, popular evangelical world reinforces the narratives of Christian popular autonomy vis-à-vis the secular state – also present in the struggle of the 'world of crime' against the 'system', commonly expressed in the peripheral slang of 'us for ourselves'. On the other hand, this same evangelical world instrumentalises the notion of 'religious freedom' to subvert democratic institutions, promoting the project of a 'Christian nation' (Fromm, 2016; Côrtes, 2018) at the centre of state political power. It is not surprising, in this mediating grammar between the two main regimes of the contemporary urban order, that on the one hand thieves and traffickers, and on other police and politicians, from low to high rank, convert to Pentecostalism (Machado, 2016, 2017).

Conceptually, I do not consider the Brazilian evangelical world as a normative regime, because its subjects cannot (yet) autonomously control legitimate violence in cases of strong conflict. Their intention to do so, however, is clear. Evangelical penetration of both the police and 'crime', in addition to their control of significant financial resources and means of communication, can effectively establish a system of mediation between the irreconcilable state and criminal regimes. The regulation of state and criminal violence, both framed in Pentecostal terms, is put forward as a synthesis, not yet accomplished but already plausible, between the fractured epistemological frameworks of the state and criminal regimes. If this project were to be consolidated in practice and become dominant, religious fundamentalism would replace secularism and religious authoritarianism would replace the institutional 'democracy' of the green and yellow homeland, transforming it into a Christian homeland. Violence between state and criminal regimes would fall. Markets do not seem to fear this possibility. Contemporary liberalism is just as able to coexist with fundamentalist and authoritarian regimes as with Western-style democracy.

Meanwhile, the brothers of the PCC, who had safeguarded daily order in the favelas, who used to live on the corner, are today in Mato Grosso, in Fortaleza, in Foz do Iguaçu and many other places. The faction operates at the borders, the ports, the airports. Big business. The PCC started to attract the attention of the US Drug Enforcement Administration, the CIA and the anti-terrorism groups of the Federal Police. Evangelical pastors have gained influence in the new administrations. A lot of money involved, in both cases. The story of this book begins in 1997 and runs up to 2019, in São Paulo. But the transition that it points to in the urban history of the peripheries of São Paulo, in the metropolis and in the country, has not yet ended. Different promises about what Brazil should be in the world, and how the poor should be integrated into the nation, have not yet been settled. The metropolis of São Paulo, the heart of the military and evangelical parts of the new project, but also the country's main financial market, remains central to all of them.

Method: from impact to interpretation

Marcela was pregnant, lying on the couch half naked, almost unconscious, and had defecated in the living room. When I came in with her sister, she said that what she needed was affection, repeating the phrase three times. Her crack addiction had reached a serious stage, her body could no longer handle it, but she seemed reflective, as she always seemed, ever since our first conversation. Soon after, Marcela was arrested again, and her son was born in prison. Her fourth son, like two of the others, has been raised by Ivete. She was to be released by March 2019 if she did not commit any disciplinary offences.

Naldinho showed me his right arm, which had been deformed by a high-voltage electric shock that he received when trying to steal a huge transformer from the top of a post. He said he had been high. His arm was atrophied and curved backwards, arched in the opposite direction of the normal elbow flexion. The skin was covered in severe burn scars, keloids, the hand practically removed by the shock, disproportionately small and similarly deformed on its back. The image of this bent arm with its mummified look, and the way Naldinho told me what happened, laughing, stayed with me for days.

Israel showed me the scars from the four shots he received in the head when a policeman caught him and threw him to the ground after a robbery. Four bullet marks, two on each side of the head. The hair no longer grew there, leaving scars that were always on display. He grabbed me by the shirt, at the neck, showing me how the officer had pointed his gun, at point-blank range, directly at his face. At the time of the shots Israel had bled and passed out, but he had a 'deliverance', he tells me. The term is Pentecostal; it means that God saved his life.

Bianca was sexually molested by her stepfather at the age of thirteen and was kicked out of the house by her mother, who blamed her. She took care of her little brothers, and a few years later of her own children, all together. One night her mother, drunk, set fire to the house with everyone inside. Fortunately, they managed to escape through a window. Bianca tells me that when she was receiving psychological treatment she had heard that it was not a sin not to love her mother. It was a moment of liberation for her; the most important moment she remembered in her life.

Ana Paula lived for fourteen years in institutions for orphans, then spent eight years in the street, around the Praça da Sé, in the centre of São Paulo. She was raped dozens of times by thieves and police officers, and regrets having beaten her son when he was a child. She has always welcomed me in the favela, she's a very fun person, and over the years she has become not only my friend but a friend of my whole family. A photo of her holding her granddaughter in her lap, very carefully, appeared one day on the screen of my cell phone, and thrilled me. Another photo of her in an air vent in the Praça da Sé metro, now aged forty-three, also struck me.

Maria lost two teenage children, murdered at the turn of the 2000s. A third was imprisoned for many years. In 2017, police killed one of two nephews who lived with her, who had been accused of stealing a cell phone. I went to visit her. She was very sad, and kept her composure as best she could. We made lunch together, we ate, we talked. While we were eating, the brother of the murdered boy arrived from the street and entered the house. Locked in the bedroom, he wept uncontrollably, and sometimes cried out and bellowed in pain, revulsion, despair. I had never seen such suffering. Maria told me that's what it is like when something like that happens.

João, now an old friend, tells me that there was a guy who worked in the hair salon we were passing in Jardim Planalto who had killed two people a few years ago. He recounted the story of the homicide in detail. Very cruel, I thought to myself. Coincidentally, a block further on the guy was standing on the corner, and João stopped to greet him. They quickly updated one another on their news and we said goodbye. As he said goodbye, the guy held me by both shoulders, looked me straight in the eye and said: 'Go with God, my brother. May God light all your paths.' For the rest of the day, I felt shivers run through my body as I remembered this scene. Even today I cannot describe what I felt, but it was something close to fear.

During these years of fieldwork, scenes of this intensity were repeated. Hundreds of times. Over many years, the physical and emotional impact, mediated by the work of keeping a research diary and discussions with many interlocutors, has been filtered into interpretations (Das, 2006b; Feltran, 2007). Translation still seems to me to be a relevant category for thinking about what ethnographers do. As is probably clear, the favelas seemed to me to be chaotic and immersed in violence. This ethnography involved verifying the existence of other orders unknown to me. They operated on an everyday basis and were bounded by this violence, producing a double movement that I did not notice at the beginning: that of making both the urban order, pragmatically, and also our categories for understanding it. What looked like chaos, remade through these two movements, gained greater intelligibility.

Urban peripheries have been the object of intense academic study in Brazil. The public agenda has followed behind. Since the late 1980s contemporary debates about these territories and populations have been marked by a preoccupation with urban violence, which has also become the focus of our studies. Every day, favelas are discussed in newspapers, television programmes and cinemas. Homicides, drug trafficking, robberies, police occupations and wars, and armed adolescents are thematised in direct association with peripheries and favelas, which are depicted as territories in conflagration.

Based on such representations, middle-class guys cross the street when they see a black boy in a baseball cap and shorts approaching, and surveillance systems in gated condominiums become ever more sophisticated. At another scale, both reformist and populist discourses develop, both social assistance programmes and the prison population expand. In any of these projects, however, it doesn't make much difference if we're talking about São Paulo, Rio de Janeiro, Salvador, Belo Horizonte or any other large city in Latin America. The characters of the peripheries are understood as internally homogeneous, everywhere and always representing the same problem: violence.

On the one hand, the literature has suggested a focus on walls

(Caldeira, 2000) and, on the other, on the connection between the social and political worlds (Zaluar, 2004; Telles and Cabanes, 2006). In São Paulo, it really is not difficult to notice either the walls and gates, or these connections. The entertainment industry, cell phones, the third sector, domestic and industrial jobs, television, construction, electoral and religious markets, drug trafficking, informal markets, the recycling industry, arms trafficking, among many other circuits, have clearly become embedded in the urban peripheries. However, none of these circuits and markets is restricted to these territories. On the contrary, they extend far beyond the peripheries, in some cases to the centre of political and economic power.

It was necessary, therefore, to qualify, in empirical and analytical terms, the mediations between the peripheries and those spaces that, looking from the outside, view them as peripheries. My proposal was to conduct an ethnography of the fracture, and the boundaries, that today regulate the relationship between the peripheries of São Paulo and the public world.[8] The category of 'boundary' is mobilised to preserve the sense of division and demarcation, while being also, above all, a mechanism that regulates the flows crossing it, simultaneously connecting what it divides. Boundaries are established precisely to regulate the channels of contact between social groups which are separated but necessarily related. Where there is a boundary, there is separation and communication – of a kind that is both unequal and controlled. If there is a boundary, it is precisely to control communication between the parties. Where there is a boundary there is also conflict, even if it is latent. If the boundary can be disputed, it is common, especially in very hierarchical societies, that latency gives way to violence. Analysing these boundaries therefore requires discussion of the relations between normative regimes and violence (Willis, 2015; Arias, 2017; Feltran, 2019; Richmond, 2019b).

These two categories, which appear in the title of this book, were arrived at via very different paths. Violence, understood here simply as the use of force, or the threat of using it that produces a similar effect, imposed itself upon the analysis over the course of the field research. It explicitly marked the trajectories of individuals, families and forms of collective action encountered in the field. Regulatory regimes came much later. This was not by mere chance, of course: norms and violence are themes that have been discussed together not only in the urban peripheries, but in different ways throughout modern history and social thought. From Weber and Clausewitz to Hannah Arendt and Foucault, the relationship between norms and the use of force is central to the analysis of modernity; nothing less than debates over the notion of power itself articulates them. Even ethnology has placed non-state regimes and violence as fundamental dimensions of the emergence of community (Clastres, 2003, 2004). Analyses such as those of Mandani (2001) on East Africa, and works such as Kessler (2004, 2007) and Auyero (2000, 2003) on contemporary Argentina demonstrate the urgency of comprehensive approaches to understanding violence.

In specific studies on urban peripheries and the popular sectors in São Paulo, however, norms and violence have remained largely disconnected. After the 1970s, in the wake of the critique of structuralist economism, most analysts of politics turned their attention to the peripheries and the 'politicisation of everyday life'. Popular movements had emerged and were reopening debates about where power lay, including within the state. These new 'political subjects' brought with them the promise of expanding citizenship (Sader, 1988; Doimo, 1995; Feltran, 2005). But then the scenario reversed. The social movements of the peripheries became institutionalised alongside the growth of the PT, as expected; three decades of institutional democracy have passed and, since 1985, it is raw violence, both police and criminal, that has drawn the attention of analysts to the urban peripheries (Caldeira, 2000; Telles and Cabanes, 2006; Holston, 2007; Telles and Hirata, 2007; Willis, 2015; Biondi, 2016).

The course of empirical work

Not all the significant experience that has shaped this book took place in the favelas studied. And not even in Sapopemba. This ethnography was produced in transit between the different favelas I visited in São Paulo and wherever my home was, both because I would dictate my reflections into a tape recorder while I was driving, on planes or in metro stations, and because, symbolically, my transit between the favelas and other urban spaces provoked so many reflections. At the same time as I was studying different neighbourhoods in the peripheries of São Paulo, and even within Sapopemba, the research was also informed by my daily, unsystematic experiences in the five other cities that I lived in during this period: São Carlos, Paris, Xalapa, Berlin and London. I was not familiar, but a stranger to four of them (Martins Junior, 2014; Hall and Schwarz, 2017). On the one hand, I realise clearly that I can say far more about Sapopemba or São Paulo, which I studied methodically, than about those places where I only lived, such as São Carlos or Paris, where I did not produce systematic notes or immerse myself in the relevant literature. On the other hand, through the contrasts they offered, each of these ordinary cities (Robinson, 2006) helped me to formulate the questions and themes I present here. This book is about the peripheries of São Paulo, based on the district of Sapopemba. But it would not have been written in the same way if I had not left that place. In each of these cities, I experienced 'the field' of differentiation in different ways.

Sapopemba, one of the ninety-six districts of the municipality of São Paulo, is a very heterogeneous territory, with a population of slightly under 300,000 in 2019. The landscape has also changed dramatically over the last few decades: the desolation of large, dusty, vacant lands at the frontier of the growing city in the 1970s gave way to a consolidated form of urbanisation, initiated by self-built subdivisions and later by housing projects, public facilities and favelas. The distribution of urban infrastructure, commerce and services follows a similarly heterogeneous logic. The transition from the political regime of this period also contributed to a significant change in local forms of associativism, as the emphasis on trade unions, social movements and leftist parties was gradually replaced by a myriad of professionalised local associations that establish agreements with different spheres of government, as well as NGOs, foundations and businesses.

In Sapopemba, but also in every other city I lived in, I had the opportunity not only to discuss my work in the peripheries of São Paulo with students, researchers, teachers and favela residents but also to experience the everyday life of these spaces. It is through routine that what is deemed plausible is established, placing limits on what is expected and can be tolerated. It is therefore observable in every context. For authors dedicated to the theory of action, it is through everyday life that the social is structured (Das, 2006a; Bayat, 2013; Machado, 2016; Blokland, 2017; Simone, 2018), and it is in pragmatic action, which is always framed, that the plausible is constituted. The last chapter of this book is devoted to this theoretical debate. Dislocations between different urban settings, which interfere directly with personal routines and everyday action, were – without my knowledge at the time – the trigger for the analyses that are presented in this book.

The fieldwork itself, over these more than twenty years, has passed through different phases, some of them overlapping with one another. Between 1997 and 2003 I frequented the Residencial 1º de Maio, a former housing cooperative in Carapicuíba, a municipality in the west of the São Paulo metropolitan region. Also at that time, I first went to the favela of Vila Prudente, in the city's East Zone, and, later, Sapopemba, which would later become the main focus of my empirical work. Fieldnotes, but especially dozens of transcribed interviews, hearing the life stories of the generation that had built these neighbourhoods and of some members of the younger generation, as well as activists, religious leaders and public sector professionals, constituted my initial material from the field.

Between 1999 and 2001 I had the opportunity to visit dozens of favelas, social movement branches and community centres across the São Paulo metropolitan region, working full time in the area of children's policy. Circulating through the peripheries almost every day, but without stopping for long in any one place, I noticed that the situation that had impressed itself on me in Carapicuiba, of young people being murdered with alarming frequency, was similar all over the metropolis. It was the period in which São Paulo's homicide rates peaked. I became interested in the statistics, but especially in the stories being told to me of the circumstances surrounding the murders. They seemed to throw into relief the radical nature of the urban conflict I was now observing, but which was simply ignored by the middle and elite classes. But the stories of these deaths also crossed analytical lines that, at that time, seemed to me to be separate: urban segregation, armed violence, security, justice, religion, work, illegal markets. There was much for me to try to understand.

Between 2005 and 2009 I had my first intense period of fieldwork in the district of Sapopemba, in the East Zone of São Paulo, when the experiences that gave rise to the initial chapters of this book mainly occurred. We will encounter the neighbourhoods and the characters that inhabit them later. Apart from the one-year interval during which I lived in northeastern Paris, these were years in which I would spend at least one week per month walking around Sapopemba. At some points, I had longer periods of fieldwork, at others they were more spaced out. The years 2005, 2007 and 2009 were especially intense. Field notes and in-depth interviews – almost always focused on life stories – were my main research material. Diverse documents and analytical timelines were used to complete a more general picture of these changes. Over time, they began to form into stories that were not only of individuals but also of families and neighbourhood institutions, as well as of transformations of the peripheries as a whole and of the PCC. Analytically, this period was primarily focused on understanding the multidimensionality of transformations in the peripheries, and how these transformations interacted with the expansion of the 'world of crime', which had already become a legitimate power for many favela residents.

Between 2009 and 2017 my fieldwork gained new dimensions and became much more collective. I followed the same group of interlocutors, families and institutions that I already knew well, with periodic visits to the neighbourhoods of Parque Santa Madalena and Jardim Elbe in Sapopemba. But I started to supervise a series of students at different levels (especially Liniker Batista, Matthew Richmond, Gregório Zambon, Valéria Oliveira, Moisés Kopper and Janaína Maldonado), who also carried out ethnographic research, focused on different themes, in Sapopemba. I was able to share my fieldwork, my contacts and my experiences with each of them. This has brought a wealth of information and reflections that were unavailable to me as an individual researcher.

My proximity to these researchers kept me even more closely connected to these neighbourhoods, and even when I was not there news constantly flowed to me. This was also the period in which I visited numerous other favelas, in São Paulo and many other cities, at the invitation of students, activists and fellow researchers. Periods as a visiting professor in Mexico, Germany and the United Kingdom have added to these unsystematic, comparative experiences. New, systematic research efforts also got underway. Two new collective research projects have helped me to develop the arguments presented here. Between 2010 and 2018 I supervised more than forty students at NaMargem, a research centre that I coordinate, between *Universidade Federal de São Carlos* and CEM. The vast majority of these students have developed individual research on different forms of urban marginality. This group has allowed me to gain empirical knowledge not only of many other 'quebradas' in many cities, but also of homeless people and crack users, prisons and youth offender units, clinics and therapeutic communities, contexts of prostitution, urban art collectives and a lot of peripheral music.

In addition, between 2015 and 2019 I have conducted systematic field research with a team of eight other researchers, at different stages of formation, that I coordinate at CEM. We investigate the theme of illicit economies by following the destinations of cars stolen in São Paulo. To summarise, we have conducted fieldwork in scrapyards, auctioneers, insurers, we have been to the border regions between Brazil, Bolivia and Paraguay, and through this research I have also learned a lot more about transformations in peripheries, and in Brazilian politics. Above all, for the first time, we have been able to gain insight into the dimensions of the illegal economies and the regulatory capacities of governments, market actors and criminal factions in São Paulo today.

Organisation of chapters

This book's narrative starts from some very small interactions extracted from ordinary life with the intention to give an account of how meaningful those are. Then, I describe individual and family stories lived in the city of São Paulo's favelas in the boundaries of 'crime' which led to broadening the interpretation of the city's parameters, as well as of its institutions' practices related to managing urban order and violence. As the will see, violence permeates the whole ethnographic experience described throughout this book.

What I experienced during fieldwork is that different life stories and moral thoughts were impacted upon by what is 'the crime' and the PCC represented in those settings. The so-called organised crime emerged from people's everyday experiences, produced by the inescapable way they experience life, and not the other way around. Other central categories to understand urban order, such as the state, the territory, the productive restructuring, race and gender, emerged in the same way. Throughout the book, fragments of everyday life have combined to compose a *bricolage* of São Paulo's regimes of urban order and violence, as well as its mediations.

The first chapter puts together empirical and theoretical thoughts to present the book's analytical framework. Here I analyse three micro-scenes of interaction, arguing that everyday life plays a critical role in the objectification of *differentiation*. Paying special attention to the third situation, which involves the representation of peripheries and the 'world of crime' in São Paulo, I debate how difference operates when the marginals appear to be getting closer to the established middle classes. Native categories and analytical concepts are both understood here as intervals of plausible meanings, a formal structure where contents are always *mutually situated and constructed* within the normative ideal boundaries established by routine use. The ethnographic reflection upon these three empirical situations gives rise to a broader interpretation of how the recent authoritarian wave in Brazil is based on the categorical construction of ideals. The authoritarians rely on how gender and state, as well as of *race, religion, family, class, sexuality* and *crime* are entangled to serve their national project. I do not discuss all of these categories in detail during this chapter, as my aim is to debate how the contemporary social life-flows intertwine the production of those ideals simultaneously. In other words, I reflect upon how the *aesthetic* of their emergence in the quotidian impacts the construction of the general public spheres.

Chapter 2 leads us to Pedro's trajectory, which goes back and forth to the boundaries that circumscribe São Paulo's 'world of crime'. The young man describes violent persecutions, shootings and what he ought to do in many different situations, experiencing both sides of these boundaries. 'Crime' appears as a set of normative codes and social practices established primarily at the local level, around markets such as illegal drug trafficking, robbery and theft, yet equally established through family relations,

35

gendered status and through courage and respect. Based on São Paulo's peripheries' transformations and Pedro's narrative, I argue an interpretation of the expansion of 'crime' boundaries in recent decades, as well as the patterns of coexistence between crime and other normative legitimacies in the outskirts of the city.

The third chapter focuses on a family story. Ivete's family life guides us through a world where migration from Salvador meets hunger and struggle for protection and social mobility in São Paulo. After following her family for the last fourteen years, I show how disjunctive patterns of understanding 'crime' and 'work' differ within the family as time has passed. Second and third generations split the family into two different social ascension projects: one where children work legally, and other where the 'world of crime' is seen as a possibility. Capoeira (an Afro-Brazilian martial art), hairdressing and private security meet drug trafficking, robbery and incarceration at home. Money and violent deaths appear after some years of clash and assemblage between brothers and sisters. The chapter is entitled 'Coexistence'.

My ethnography then moves to a broader scenario. São Paulo's urban violence has several unique features. During the 1990s, while Ivete struggled with her eight kids in a 'time of wars', São Paulo became the first Brazilian state to implement mass incarceration policies. By consequence, it was also the first state to witness the strengthening of a single hegemonic criminal faction, the Primeiro Comando da Capital, or PCC. In a recent work I have argued that PCC's organisational framework is a brotherhood formally similar to that of Freemasonry; organised since the 2000s across the entire Brazilian territory, for the last twenty-five years it has been acting in a coordinated way both inside and outside the prison system (Feltran, 2018). This criminal group is deeply related, as we shall see, to the most striking aspect of São Paulo's urban order, which is the dramatic fall in the homicide rate that occurred between 2000 and 2010, amounting to around 70%.

In chapter 4 an ethnography of the PCC justice system will

describe the modus operandi of the 'crime courts' employed by criminals in the outskirts of São Paulo. I argue that the spread of this way of doing justice by the commons, completely 'institution-alised' in the studied territories, became possible only after 'the crime' ascended to the position of a legitimate normative regime among a minor but relevant part of the residents of the city out-skirts. Mapping these 'courts' on three different levels, including a 'debate' via cell phone conference in seven of São Paulo's prisons, I argue that these mechanisms are central factors in explaining the drop in homicide rates in São Paulo. Recognised publicly by the state's government and its military police, these courts themselves became important sources of legitimacy for PCC's expansion in Brazil.

Chapter 5 argues that violence, and especially lethal violence, is strictly managed on the periphery of São Paulo. I argue against the idea of banalisation of violence in favelas, as my thesis is that there is a strict control of the use of force in favelas and neighbourhoods of the peripheries of São Paulo. To support my thesis, I present three ethnographic situations of the 'PCC era' in which members of the 'crime world' interact in a particular way with police officers and lawyers. The diverse normative repertoire of PCC's practices is analysed vis-à-vis the state's violence management tools as I verified that they coexist in the peripheral zones of São Paulo in 2010. Thus, four dimensions are specifically analysed in this chap-ter, namely: (i) state justice; (ii) the court-room justice of 'crime'; (iii) the selective justice of the police; and (iv) divine justice. My ethnography shows how this repertoire divides different projects of regulation of violence in the city, which gave birth to the different normative regimes analysed in this book.

Chapter 6 shows how the management of homicides in the state of São Paulo since the 1990s was already carried out by at least two coexistent regimes of justice and security policies. As these regimes can be understood only in their constitutive relation, I recover the general lines of two decades of their development, from which have emerged the fundamental elements of São Paulo's contemporary urban order. I argue that state policies have offered the best conditions for the current hegemony of PCC policies in the regulation of both homicides and illegal markets, both inside prisons and in favelas. Many ethnographic situations exemplify the argument of São Paulo as an entangled city, where urban conflict could be much better understood if it were theoretically reframed.

Lastly, in the conclusion I argue that in the 2010s the Brazilian urban peripheries have two dichotomous public façades: on the one hand, they are the cause of 'urban violence' that calls for more repression; and, on the other hand, they are the focus of the 'nation development' project which would turn poor people into middle-class individuals – where I again refer back to the ideas of the expectations of modernity. The idea of urban violence, as commonly known, has displaced the core of the contemporary social question from 'the worker' to the 'marginal people'. As a side-effect, tensions between 'crime' and 'state' regimes have increased and the two have found a common basis for their relationship in monetised markets. Money seems to mediate the relationship between forms of life which, from other perspectives – legal or moral – would be in radically different from one another. Consumption emerges as a common way of life and mercantile expansion, above all connecting legal and illegal markets and fostering urban violence that otherwise would have been under control, had those territories seen economic development. Religion, and especially Pentecostalism, emerges as a plausible source of mediation between the regimes.

1

Boundaries of difference: on essence *and* deconstruction

An eighty-six-year-old white woman watched television footage of São Paulo's traditional New Year's Eve road race dedicated to Saint Silvester and reflected on her past – another habit traditional at the year's close – and on her stage in life. For Vitória, it was family gatherings like the one held that day that proved her efforts had been worth it. Widowed for a few years now, Vitória had just told me how much her life had improved over the years. The daughter of poor Italian immigrants who had arrived in Brazil a century ago, she had grown up as one of many children in the strictly Catholic environment of her foster mother's rural home. Now, here she was in the living-room of her sizeable house, with her days of hunger behind her. She congratulated herself on the 'standard of living' the family enjoyed. 'Life is good,' she repeated to me.[1] While we spoke, images of the Kenyan athlete Robert Cheruyot lingered on the television screen for a few minutes, a strong black figure with a shaved head, his long strides carrying him into the lead.

Vitória's four daughters were also present that day. Two of them were doctors, married to a doctor and an entrepreneur, while the other two had studied engineering and dentistry and married men in the same professions, one of Japanese heritage. With two children each, their generation was one of urban nuclear families. Surrounded by all of the close members of her family, including sons and daughters-in-law and family friends, Vitória exclaimed:

> Thank God life is good! Thank God there are no negroes in my family, nobody married a negro, nobody's kids are negro ... Life is good for all of us ... thank God for that! (Personal notes, São Carlos, 31 December 2007)

Her family's reaction came as something of a surprise to Vitória, two of her granddaughters exclaiming: '*Granny, what a terrible thing to say!*'. Another two turned to me, one of them apologising on behalf of her grandmother, embarrassed by her overt racism. Disapproving looks were exchanged across the sofa and then gave way to pronouncements of '*leave it ...*', '*it's her age speaking*' and '*how embarrassing*'.

Anyone who knows Vitória knows that the aesthetics of 'white', 'Japanese' or 'black' were not all the same to her, each carrying very different evaluative meanings in terms of marriage, family, national identity, work and religion. However, the boundary demarcating those for whom 'life is good' included white and Japanese people, and left black people in the shade. Categories are not words, concepts or expressions that are learnt by listening to explanations, regardless of whether they are 'native' or not.[2] Categories are intervals of meaning delineated by the boundaries of what is plausible in each lived context. It is in everyday life that the relations between experiences and language produce the *use* and thus the categorical meaning, serving as practical normative parameters, activating an *order* for action and its matrices of valuation in the world as we experience it.[3] In this experience of living, and therefore the sequence of interactions, whether routine or disruptive as in the case at hand,[4] that meaning is produced in the light of a *continuum* of possibilities within the category boundaries.

This chapter introduces the book's theoretical framework while reflecting in depth on three situations of interaction. Detailed description and analysis break with the immediate and sensory everyday order of understanding that offers an almost instant location and value for each subject or interaction. This immediate order produces essences, which give birth to fixed meanings and labels which, for the good and bad, guide us through life. In the living room, it was about racism. But having the time to reflect on an interaction is very different from experiencing it. I argue here that the *everyday* plays a decisive role in the *objectification* of the categories of difference, including conflictive ones, consequently conceived of as analytical categories (Brah, 2006; Piscitelli, 2008).[5] Such a reflection paves the way for a wider interpretation of the categorical assumptions of the recent authoritarian reaction in Brazil, based on the mutual construction (within the sphere of the categorical assumptions) of everyday ideas of 'gender' and 'state', as well as those of 'race', 'religion', 'family', 'class', 'sexuality', 'crime', 'nation' and 'violence'. Obviously, this chapter can not be expected to provide a discussion of each of the categories, but aims to consider the *regimes* of their simultaneous production in contemporary urban life, and therefore how the *aesthetic* of their emergence in everyday life relates to the urban conflict.

Misunderstandings

As we have seen, Vitória's words did not have the expected effect on those around her. There were no congratulations for her family's achievement of a better standard of living, nor for her grandmother's struggles on behalf of the women of the household. Vitória fell silent, the Kenyan athlete went on to win the race and the family gathering continued to ritualise the bonds present. Nothing was said about race, gender, family or religion. Nor about politics, for that matter. I will have to do so instead, seeking to identify the meaning that the categories formulated in such a disruptive situation and, going a bit further, the regime that structured Vitória's speech.

Vitória's words would readily be identified as racist, both in form and in content.[6] The category of 'negro' (*preto* in Portuguese), which has recently been reclaimed by a significant section of the hip-hop movement for purposes of self-identification in São Paulo, is strongly naturalised as a marker of inferiority in the racial puzzle in which Vitória was socialised, also denoting filth, ignorance and poverty. With her words, this ancient, specific racial diagram emerged, proving itself to be alive. The contemporary dominant racial puzzle is different, leading to the misunderstanding in its clash with the racial framework of her granddaughters. The categories that Vitória employed have no defence against any of the critical elements brought about by the Black Movement which has gained ground in Brazilian urban peripheries since the 1960s, emerging in political debate after the dictatorship. Vitória's socialisation in race relations dates back to the early decades of the twentieth century and, remaining as she did within the white social pole, there was no need to revisit it.

If racism is explicit and voiced readily, such as in Vitória's case, we do not, however, learn much about the *form* by which gender, family and religiosity is simultaneously constructed. Lateral social markers of difference in Victoria's racial discourse are also found in precise content which is hardly noticeable at the moment of speaking. The expression 'thank God' is repeated and used to evaluate Vitória's own course through life: sacrifices in life that lead to a final redemption in the Christian sense informed by God and his designs. To be on God's sacred side and far from the 'negroes' is a cause for contentment: 'Life is good.' Religiosity thus has evident racial content, and vice versa. God is not black.

The marks of gender and class are also less explicit; however, they emerge upon later analysis. Narrating the end of a journey, Vitória offers another three elements justifying her contentment, all of them reflecting her construction of gender in the light of a social mobility project based around family, but also on *class*. (i) *'there are no negroes in my family'*: the family was strengthened by its shunning of black people; the frame of reference possibly dates back to before the 1930s, when the national ideology of 'racial democracy' emerged for construction in the decades to come; (ii) her daughters' marriages: '*nobody married a negro*': for Vitória, as the mother of four daughters born in the 1950s and 1960s, when women were a minority in the Brazilian labour market, the possibilities for improving quality of life were derived from marriage. Education was undoubtedly a definitive route to finding a spouse, as universities were distant from the black social pole, which, according to Vitória's perspective, was fated to occupy the base of the social pyramid; (iii) children: '*nobody's kids are negroes*', reflects the fundamental hallmarks of the female role identified with marriage and reproduction and, as a consequence, the distance from black people as a family ideal. The situated ideal found in Vitória's representation of mobility therefore serves as a matrix of references for concrete experience as considered in this book. As in classical theory of action, categories of difference or labelling are both theoretically and empirically located, routinised by hegemonic practices of interpretation or otherwise subordinated. It is what Bourdieu calls a naturalisation effect of the 'mental structures' which define social positions:

> The great social oppositions objectified in physical space (as with the capital versus the provinces) tend to be reproduced in thought and in language as oppositions constitutive of a principle of vision and division, as categories of perception and evaluation or of mental structures. (Bourdieu et al., 1999, p. 125)

Stepping a bit further, we can see that their everyday construction as a coherent composite, by means of these pairs of opposed values in different teleological series (different formal courses of action, for Simmel, with content related to gender, class, race and mobility in Vitória's case), is therefore *aesthetically recognisable*. The recognisable, a relational product, is nevertheless understood as a self-reifying and self-embodying feature, in body shapes, but also in forms of social performance and orality. If Vitória's white daughter were to have a child with a black phenotype, this would constitute a defeat in the complex family-gender-class-race-religion project that emerges from the collective experience in which Vitória was socialised. Throughout the flux of everyday life, the construction of this 'intersectionality' is not evident at first glance, except in terms of its sensory dimension: the politics of the composition of the social markers of difference is reflected through a set of signs and boundaries coherent to anyone who shares their meanings, effectively serving as an *aesthetic of difference*.

> There is thus an 'aesthetic' at the base of politics that has nothing to do with the 'aestheticisation of politics' belonging to the 'age of the masses' of which Benjamin speaks. This aesthetic should not be understood as a perverse capturing of politics by an artistic will, by the viewing of people as a work of art. Extending the analogy reveals it may be conceived of in a Kantian sense – eventually touched on by Foucault – as the system of *a priori forms* determining what one feels. (Rancière, 2005, p. 16, emphasis added)[7]

This sense of a priori forms, opening up to make way for the interpositioning of the most diverse of contents – sexuality and madness, for example – that Jacques Rancière identifies in Michel Foucault's '*dispositif*' [apparatus] (1976), is in close dialogue with the formal sociology as suggested by Georg Simmel (2010a [1918], p1):

> Man's position in the world is defined by the fact he constantly finds himself between two boundaries in every dimension of his being and behaviour. This condition appears as the formal structure of our existence, filled as it always is with different contents in life's diverse provinces, activities and destinies. We feel that the content and the value of every hour lies somewhere between a higher and a lower value; every thought between a wiser and a foolish value; every possession between a more extended and a more limited value; and every deed between a greater and a lesser measure of meaning, adequacy and morality. We are constantly orienting ourselves, even when we do not employ abstract concepts, to an 'over us' and an 'under us', to a right or a left, to a more or less, a tighter or looser, a better or a worse. The boundary, above and below, is our means of finding direction in the infinite space of our worlds.

> Along with the fact that boundaries are both constant and perva-
> sive, we are boundaries ourselves. For insofar as every content in life
> – every feeling, experience, deed, or thought – possesses a specific
> intensity, a specific hue, a specific quantity and a specific position
> in some order of things, each content produces a continuum in two
> directions, toward its two poles; participating contentedly in each of
> these two continua, which both collide in it and are delimited by it.

Categorical regimes are difficult to study and particularly difficult to compare, because the meanings expressed invariably refer
to *situated* series of interactions that are therefore always distinct
from one another. The categorical systems used by each group are
also theirs for a variable period of time. Catholics ritualising their
beliefs on a weekly basis tend to remain Catholic for longer than
Catholics who never participate in such rituals. Categories can
also serve as causal elements or consequences of series of action:
'gender' in one example both constructs the marriages of Vitória's
daughters and is constructed by them. In light of this reflection, I
believe it is possible to affirm that categories always simultaneously
constitute:

1 a situated position in an interval of values naturalised by routine, a regime, therefore serving as a classification according to
   parameters of valuation supported by a situated *ideal* for a given
   group in a given space and time. Our lives see us *evaluating* and
   valuing all of the situations we find ourselves in, involving actions
   as diverse as other drivers' manoeuvres or our children's draw-
   ings, with the way things are said and Instagram posts being a
   basis for the ideal parameters in each situation ('you can't expect
   any better from a five-year-old …'), in each era (you wouldn't
   have imagined it possible to rate a Skype call as 'poor' thirty
   years ago) and in each aesthetic specific to our situated experiences (amateur photographs are evaluated differently to those
   taken by professionals). We both express and withhold these
   judgements based on categories or categorical silences. The

category of 'negro', for example, occupies a position in terms of an evaluative series of races and ethnicities in different contexts, and Vitória employed it in a significant scale of values learnt by socialisation, in order to *evaluate* her life story. The problem with categories – and categorical silences – is in this sense that of value judgements (Simmel, 1990 [1900], particularly part 1);

2 an interval itself among many others that could potentially be applied and an interval socially elected by a given group as suitable for evaluating a given situation, in its historical construction and according to the agency of its subjects; one which, between an infinite number of other passive intervals or scales, potentially offers pragmatic parameters for the action or daily performance, from the most intimate to the most public. Vitória chose race to place in the centre of the evaluation of her social mobility. Subjects are often used from completely distinct criteria (different categorical intervals, different series of meanings) in order to evaluate the same situation. In one example, homo-affective love may be read as the categorical scale of carnal love or of romantic love, or of Christian sin, or of citizens' rights, depending on the group and situation at hand. Categorisation therefore implies a choice on the scale of values, a choice which is made while simultaneously issuing its value judgement – which, however, constitutes a formal choice and not one of content. A choice of the interval of contents therefore belongs to the classification to be employed in accordingly each situation;

3 a practical definition of *appropriateness* to a situation, even if it runs against categorical values. You might detest the Brazilian Workers' Party – or gay people – with every fibre of your being, but avoid getting involved in debate on politics or homosexuality with your family. The interval to be taken as a reference for action is related to what is appropriate: the relevance of preserving the family is greater than that of politics, in this particular context. However, in maintaining silence on the Workers'

Party or on homosexuality, judgements are still produced, to be exposed at another moment.

The racism which Vitória expressed therefore leads us to wider dimensions of analysis. The social mobility project that she expressed with it and through it, expanding into an aesthetic in which race also refers to family, gender, class and religion, does not belong just to her. It is a categorical project objectified in a political national project in the first half of the twentieth century, while she was being shaped as a subject, that has become hegemonic since then. Readers of this text who do not identify with 'Brazilian whiteness' may also be able to identify this project in their own families, as I can identify it in mine. It is a national project, but also is disseminated by countless institutions, while simultaneously constructing them: from the Brazilian Catholic Church to Kardecism, from Freemasonry to the Rotary Club, from conversations on cinema and literature in elite circles to their children's French (or Chinese) classes, from business ethics to professionalism and from Cartesian logic to strategic planning. The project has had particular impetus in São Paulo, but also in the Southeastern and Southern regions of Brazil as a whole. Its influence has been particularly strong among white working-class Catholic families, and politically hegemonic where modern, Western rationality has been consolidated quite radically in Brazil, thanks to the national initiative of importing people-subjects such as Vitória, the children of Italian, Spanish and German immigrants. Such a national and international project for a white nation has violently and cordially fated its 'others' ('negroes', *bugres* and indigenous peoples) to a subordinate position. Now that their voices are much louder than in the past, such subordination is much less cordial.

Over half a century later, following much sacrifice and the construction of many boundaries of meaning, the 'family's' successful project should be celebrated by the victorious: 'life is good for all of us, thank God!' Victory has been secured, in terms both of the social order it fought against and of the state order it constructed. Racism is therefore much more than a *mere* attribute of Vitória's personality: it is a boundary erected as plausibility for social relations within this project-nation. Racism, along with social puzzles of gender, sexuality, family and religiousness, thus activated as *practices* with hegemonic bases extending beyond white people, is the practice of national order, state processes and, in Brazil's case, both state-idea as well as state-system, in the definition produced by Abrams (2006). In the Weberian sense, Vitória's situated *social action* contents, the *social relations* that give them boundaries of plausibility (the racism in the diagram mentioned) and their belonging to a *legitimate order* (that of the hegemonic class-race-nation-family-religion project at the time) are connected in the very course of the action, in the social performance, objectifying social difference markers. Meanings and parameters for the maintaining of the social order are constructed in this categorical use, only objectified in state institutions.

Vitória's granddaughters did not appreciate their grandmother's words, not because racism no longer exists but because they grew up in the 1980s and 1990s, under another puzzle of race relations. The racism of the past was no longer accepted, with more modern variations instead in play. The amalgamation had been positivised to the point of forming the core of the national project, a basis for 'racial democracy' that also formed my perspective of Brazil in my academic education. The Black Movement had already grown in its opposition to this project, institutionalising many of its victories; hip-hop had made strides, forming another puzzle of race relations in the country. However, distanced from the 'negroes', Vitória would not have known any of this. In her everyday life none of this existed: the world is the size of our relationships, the set of spaces between people, as Hannah Arendt affirmed. If I have no experience of aborigines, what they think simply does not appear between us, and does not exist to me. You could not say things like what Vitória said publicly, in such an environment, without social sanctions. The everyday had implemented other parameters – in other places it is still possible to affirm them – for the race relations in Vitória's family. However, these parameters were not perceived in the same everyday context to be connected to a project involving class, gender and family-religion, and the nation itself, which could go on being ritualised, continuing to serve as the basis for the (white) social order that the state must respect, incentivise and foster.

Assumptions

For although the boundary as such is necessary, every single specific boundary can be stepped over, every fixity can be displaced, every enclosure can be burst, and every such act, of course, finds or creates a new boundary. (Simmel, 2010a [1918], p. 2)

Junior is a very young, white, heterosexual man buying a baked snack in a juice bar, pragmatically pretending not to have noticed the male gender identity of the black trans server, who is just as young as he is. He chats with his friend about other subjects, asking the server if his snack is filled with meat or with cheese. What may be observed from the interaction with the server is practical, business-like and impersonal, stripped of any objective sense of gender. Junior pays for the snack and leaves. However, gender and sexuality are constructed in the scene, becoming explicit immediately afterwards (although they could have remained implicit[8]): as he moves away from the interaction, Junior asks his friend, smiling: '*would you screw a girl like her?*'[9]

Both of them amble down the road, laughing as they consider the possibility. I can't hear the rest of the conversation. Junior undoubtedly became aware of a *disagreement* with his gender and sexual norm and his categorical ideal, marked out by the binary of male-female. The server's *aesthetic* confuses his desire: the typically masculine haircut and tattoos, linked with a feminine tone of voice and hands, as well as the sizeable breasts underneath the shirt, combine to form a question. This question, and the gender destabilising, undoubtedly serves as a *political* moment, in the sense described by Jacques Rancière:

> Misunderstandings do not only involve words. Generally speaking, they also concern the situation of those speaking. (...) An extreme misunderstanding is one in which X cannot see the common object proposed by Y because X doesn't understand that the sounds issued by Y form words and agencies of words similar to X's. As we will see, such an extreme situation is essentially one of politics. (Rancière, 2005, p. 13).

There is no way of doing politics without destabilising the categories objectified. However, the author does warn that situations like these of categorical destabilisation do not come to a predictable end, and, furthermore, are no guarantee of political virtue. It is not about imagining that, once a priori destabilised (politicised), the boundaries of gender identity or of the category of 'woman' would pave the way for the emancipation of the man-woman binary. Such a moment would obviously open up the boundary of what is thinkable on gender, and this is politics. Neither Rancière nor Simmel sees evolution, teleology or redemption to be necessarily coupled with such an opening. It instead involves the insertion of a wedge, giving rise to a series of investigations (Dewey, 1927, 1938; Menezes, 2015) which for their part contain the (ultimately violent) conflicts involving the contents that would – ideally – fit in this formal interval, that of the category. The aesthetic destabilisation adds a normative question to the interaction which was previously implausible: what *should* gender *be like*? This is a normative question that appears as an 'emic' question to ethnography.

As Rancière maintains, this destabilisation produces a sequence of arguments concerning aesthetics (whether spoken or not) on their appropriateness. We are always therefore in a political interval: on the one hand, the *form* of this dispute indicates if we are closer to the democratic pole (a site of dialogism, argumentation, more open categorical intervals, more mobile boundaries, the non-definition of conceptual limits, the opening up of boundaries and hybridisms), or the authoritarian (ultimately totalitarian) pole, in which the world's meanings are relatively more fixed, assumed and dogmatically offered a priori. In the micro-scene touched upon here, it is not hard to notice the modern hegemonic position on this scale or in this topological network of positions and code-territories (Perlongher, 2008).

The destabilising of Junior's desire produces a reaction that has nothing to do with indeterminate assumptions. Junior does not question the boundaries of the category of 'woman'; he already *assumes* the elements essential to the order that he knows of: the server *is* a woman. And he also of course assumes that he and his male friend, as men, can define the position destined for her in the order of things, that order being the heteronormative order of desire, within the hegemonic social order. The notion of order – specifically in the Weberian sense, referring to the legitimacy and parameters for social relations and actions – is of such interest to me because it is in its very production that state reason emerges. Ordering processes in this text are also processes defining the game of forces, and even the potential use of violence, marking the state operation. Ordering is also state building.

Junior's question thus represents a call to the hegemonic order of gender and sexuality. It is within the context of sexuality that he and his friend learnt about gender: worthy of being a desirable woman, the server would form part of the sector of women whose femininity conforms to heterosexual desire; unworthy of such a position, the server is another figure downgraded in the order of classification of the sexes. 'She' will never be a peer among men, as long as these assumptions and boundaries of the category of 'woman' are upheld. And the indeterminate area should be tackled (Douglas, 1976). The question therefore serves a selective purpose: that of offering the chance for classifying the server in the order of naturalised, heteronormative and hegemonic desire, or downgrading 'her' from this order. It does not, however, question the order itself, which is objectified in the question and reinstates itself following a brief disturbance. The hetero ideal is updated (the normativity, the a priori 'what should be') not just for women but for all 'family women', according to the perspective of the masculine order which utters the question, and, furthermore, that of all men, who should desire only women.

As works in progress themselves, the two men discuss whether or not a man should 'screw' a 'girl like that', and therefore of that 'type'. In order to avoid future disturbances, a location must be created to frame girls for their existence to be *read*: as they multiply in everyday life, a strategy for dealing with them must be developed. The debate on the edges of the state is based on the problem of legibility (Das and Poole, 2004; Das, 2006a; Lancione, 2016). Junior's direct question constructs a *type* of gender and sexuality, while simultaneously seeking to frame this type within the wider heteronormative order. It produces criteria of legibility in a gendered social order which also harnesses this everyday mechanism to inform state processes (Vianna, 2005). Junior's question therefore reinforces the state claim for the legibility of the social, and the predictability in terms of future possible disturbances. It is therefore preventive. It is also undoubtedly a *reaction* to the categorical destabilising provoked by an emancipatory movement from decades ago which has since become more aesthetically radicalised – formed by the various LGBT and feminist movements – whose assumptions, particularly on gender equality or the implosion of gender, not only are not shared hegemonically but also do not represent a growing trend in Brazil nowadays. Furthermore, such assumptions are now read as an affront to the format of the social order. Walter Benjamin warned us of the risks of reading history as an evolution or a teleology. Nothing could be clearer in the country's present climate. In being surpassed and destabilised, boundaries are called upon to be rebuilt, just like in Simmel's epigraph above.

Categorical order and violence

Hello? / Dad? / Hi, love … */ There's someone here wants to speak to you and … /* Who wants to speak to me? */ Clayton wants to speak to you./* Who's Clayton, do I know him? */ He's a friend of mine. /* Now you've got me worried … what's happened? You can tell me… */ I bought a test at the pharmacy and went to Carla's gynaecologist, and I'm pregnant, and well, Clayton's the father. /* You're joking … */ I'm not, it's true… /* It's a … */ It's not, Dad … /* Does your mother know about this? */ No, nobody does … /* But what the hell? You're pregnant? */ It's not my fault! /* How is it not your fault? It's your life! And do I know your little friend? */ He's the office boy here, he works with us! /* Holy shit! The office boy?

The above dialogue introduces a 'prank' aired on the Rádio Jovem Pan programme *Pânico* at the beginning of 2007.[10] From the radio station's studios, the young woman calls her father, accompanied by an actor playing Clayton (a common name in Brazil's peripheries, but not among its elites).

Dad! Do you want to speak to him? / It's hardly a question of 'speaking', love … you're going to have to take responsibility for looking after the baby … listen, love … and as for that playboy? What are you going to do with this guy you just told me about? Are you going to get married? */ In … [*Clayton takes over:*] */ Hello? Nice to meet you, this is Clayton* [his way of speaking imitating a young man from the periphery makes the father sigh, both laughing and scorning him]. / Well, let's hear it, my friend! What do you have to tell me?

The sketch begins to gather pace. The father of the pregnant girl must interact with the guy who got her pregnant, and whom he knows to be an office boy (one of the least valued positions in a company). The male role of ordering a world going off track is thrown onto his lap. The relationship shifts to one between men. The scene unfurls, as may be noted, according to all of the stereotypical values (idealised yet still hegemonic) of what constitutes a 'family', under the same white, middle-class, urban nuclear model of father-mother-children. It therefore deals with the same frame of references that we have just glimpsed in the female perspective of Vitória's words. However, 'family' is now envisaged from a strictly masculine point of view, and, as is well known, this features the man as protector and as provider, especially in economic terms, according to the means available to him.

The comic aspect of the episode lies in Clayton's radical unsuitability for the model, which is gradually revealed to the girl's father. Running against the virtues expected by the model, and therefore breaking with the situation's desired normativity, the stereotype called upon by the actor provokes reactions which are highly instructive to our debate. Clayton's participation unfolds thus:

> *Well, at least I'm accepting responsibility for this shit right here* … / [father interrupts] This shit?! You're nothing more than a playboy, son … and here you are referring to it …, the baby … as shit? / *Of course not, sir* … / Look, here's how it is: I don't want you in my daughter's life! I don't want you … / *Calm down, bro* … / Bro? Bro, my ass! Watch your mouth! / *Okay bro, sorry, sir* … *let me just give my humble opinion* … / Your humble opinion? [teasing] … you fuck my daughter up, son, get her pregnant, and you come offering me your 'humble opinion?'. Tell me one thing, son, are you going to marry my daughter?

The father questions the categories employed by Clayton one by one, in sequence. Shit? Bro? Humble opinion? The sequence reveals the implausibility of the marriage in seconds. The 'family' is outside the plausible circumscription for *a guy like* Clayton. It also must be noted that the act of 'screwing' a woman – the sexual act – is again at the centre of the problem of the definition of gender, family and order. In encroaching on the father's territory – as if there is a woman, there is a male territory in which she circulates – and 'screwing' his daughter, Clayton challenges the father's authority, and thus the order in that *territory* (Perlongher, 2008). He is therefore encouraged to confront him, or, more appropriately, enact his subordination and accept the paternal imposition, even if ritually. What is transcribed above is merely the beginning of this male confrontation, of the dominant forces over the female in question, but mostly over the possibilities of taking responsibility for the maintenance of the hegemonic family order, which also means social and state order. As the girl is going to become a mother, a family will be born with that child, and, as we are told on a daily basis, 'family is the basis of everything'.

Further underlying the narrative is a debate on the daughter's dignity, violated by Clayton's virility.[11] Only marriage can restore this dignity, demonstrating that she is 'a woman worth marrying' and not just some 'slut'.[12] Clayton must therefore 'assume ownership' of the man's daughter, asking her father for permission to marry her, proving that he will be able to sustain her. Her agency is completely irrelevant, according to this male perspective. Clayton then responds as to whether or not he will marry her, spurring a ritual (comic for listeners and maddening for the girl's father):

I don't know … I don't know if I can. That's why I wanted to talk to you / You don't know if you can … well you were certainly able to something else very well! / *Listen, you can't talk to me like that!* / Like hell you don't think you can! How is it that you can get her pregnant and yet you can't look after her? [angrily] Can you look after a family? Can you pay rent? / *Calm down, bro!* / Can you look after a family? Can you look after my daughter? / You're crazy … / But one thing you can do is make a baby! You bum! / *Can you just calm down, bro?* / Calm down? My daughter gets pregnant from some office … [they start shouting over each other, until Clayton says: – *I have a job, bro!*] / How much do you make? /

The situation of confrontation gains more precise contours. With marriage implausible, the girl's father turns to insults and the clarifying of Clayton's subordination. At least each of their positions should be made explicit. The insults alternate with the connotation that makes the passive inferior (Misse, 2007), in the classic opposition between 'worker' and 'bum'. With the father representing the worker, and white male order, Clayton is on the other side of the boundary, outside order, even though he shares the male codes in the norm. The question about how much Clayton earns objectifies the observation.

I make 250 [the minimum monthly wage at the time was R$350.00]/ Are you fucking kidding me? 250 real? [he imitates Clayton's intonation and says 'real' in the singular on purpose, emulating what would be this way of speaking]. / *No, that's not all, on Saturdays I help a bro of mine out, he has a copy shop … I make another fifty there* / Listen to me while I'm talking to you, you need to go and get a life! Put my daughter on, let me speak to her, I don't want to speak to you anymore, you're trash!

The figures merely confirm what was already known. The girl's father doesn't want to continue with the conversation, there's no more to be said. The signs of urban poverty in São Paulo are harnessed by the actor to form the stereotype desired for the framework: Clayton is not only an *office boy*, but also helps out at a copy shop, speaking like a youth from the periphery of São Paulo in the 2000s. His 'work' is not enough for him to be a 'worker': he needs to 'get a life'. There is nothing left to say. 'I don't want to speak to you anymore, you're trash!' However, the insistence in the dialogue renders the focus on gender even more explicit, in the maintenance of respect for this order:

You're not a real man! A real man wouldn't do this to another man's daughter! / *I am a man and I'm a hard worker and I want you to listen to me, sir!* / What you have achieved in life, you bum? Now that you earn 250 reals a month, you bum! / *I don't make 250, man! I make 350!* / Do you know how much it costs to keep a family, you son of a bitch?! Get my daughter on the line, I don't want to talk to you anymore, you piece of shit! You're trash! You're a piece of shit! Get my daughter on! Trash! You can go to hell! Put my daughter on, I want to speak to her! / [he calls her] Love …

What did Vitória achieve in life? What has Clayton? The trajectory of social conquests forms the values objectified in the subjects. Vitória was able to 'rise up in life', building her family. The girl's father asks: 'what have you achieved in life?' He thus affirms that he hasn't achieved what he should have in order to be a 'man'.

Outside this boundary, he is a 'piece of shit', 'trash', a 'bum' and a 'son of a bitch'. 'Real men don't do this to other men's daughters', or, in other words, to other men. The order is between men, after all.

> [The daughter calls for calm:] *Calm down!* [Clayton pretends to start crying in the background. By this point, the dialogue is highly stereotyped, but the girl's father does not notice the staging, taken in by the seriousness of the situation.] *Dad?* / [hearing her voice, he changes his tone, assuming the lexicon used to speak to women in this key] Darling, for the love of God,… you can't get with a guy like that. .. / *Dad, he wants to speak to you!* / You can't just go around having sex like that, love … / *You can't speak to Clayton like that, Dad!* / Huh? / *If you can listen to me you can listen to him! You're more stressed out than we are!!* / Ah, and I'm not allowed to be stressed out? You call me up and announce you're pregnant, that the father is an office boy who makes 250 reals a month! / [Clayton comes back on the line] *Calm down love, stay here …* / Tell him to go to hell! Darling!

The categories shift when father and daughter speak. An order (categorical system) exists between men. Within family, and mainly when 'speaking to women', manners must be remembered. 'Getting with a man', 'having sex' and 'the love of God' are activated; but not Clayton's love. The plausibility of the father's agitated state is reinstated, given his family position. To all of those listening to the programme, his anger is fully justifiable. Speaking to his daughter and resuming his role as father, he calms down a little, which allows Clayton to resume speaking:

> *Calm down bro, let me just say my piece, sir …* / Fuck this 'bro' shit! You're an animal! Fuck you, bro! Who are you to talk to me like that? Bro?! Shit?! Fuck you! You're going to have to learn how to talk before you speak to me! / *Excuse me then, sir …* / What? / *All I need is an opportunity… I want a proper job, all you have to do is help us out in the beginning, okay?*

The actor thus skilfully constructs the public categorical framework for the debate on young men from Brazilian peripheries. On the one hand, the 'family' a priori states *holy shit, office boy, darling?*, and confirms each sign of the narrative that proceeds as though such young men are in fact 'bums'. It is explicit for them, objective! On the other hand, the 'defenders' of 'human rights' would relate the 'issue' concerning these young men to the 'lack of opportunities' and the 'social problem', as in the stereotypical Brazilian view of human rights as bum's rights. Clayton therefore appears not just as the ideal type of office boy as a young man from the periphery, but also as someone who embodies the public discourse that 'sustains such bums'. The father therefore uses irony and once again inserts gender and sexuality into the centre of the construction of order:

> Okay, why don't you just have my ass too? Will you screw me too? I'll give you a job, I'll give you everything you want … I'll give you 80% of what I earn each month, how about that? Help you out! What has my daughter got involved in? What did I do wrong? / *It's not help … it's just whatever you have, okay? Even if it's just R$50 in the beginning … I already have a kid, okay?* / Another one? / *Yeah …* / With a different mother? / *Yes … but calm down for God's sake, listen to me …*

The expression 'kid with another mother' refers to the boundary of the 'family' category again. Everything seems to make more sense. 'What did I do wrong?' is an unequivocal indicator that the subject is not individual but belonging to a family, in this order which is white, hard working, family oriented, male, heteronormative, public and hegemonic, and therefore state.

> [nervous laughter] You have a kid with another woman, do you? Let me tell you something, son … you need to disappear fast! You're asking me for money?! / *Whatever you can! Even if it's only R$50, R$100, it's only the beginning …* / Ah and you already want this money, do you? / *I need help at the moment, sir, do you understand?* / Ah you want it now? My daughter tells me she took the test just today and you're already crawling to me for money? / *For the love of God!* / You want money? Okay, let's calm down here … I'm a pretty calm guy too, my daughter will tell you, come round to my house and I'll give you money …

Boundaries of difference

This is the first moment in which the force of the verbal insults threatens to escalate into physical violence. Clayton is told to 'disappear', as the girl's father devises a scene of physical confrontation with him. I am particularly interested in this passage, which leads on to others with a similar meaning and the same script for interaction: with the order threatened, the conflict fails to be resolved within the discursive framework and insults are called upon in order to produce securely defined boundaries. With such a technique also failing, violence is naturally justified.

> *Listen, here's what I'm going to do: I've got somewhere to be, I'm going to the Corinthians match, and then … / Ah, don't tell me, Corinthians? / Yeah … / Great, man … then you must be a good guy! Now I'm in awe …*

Football is of not insignificant relevance among men, inserted into hegemonic masculinity across various social strata, countries and spheres of belonging, and the dominant representation of Corinthians supporters in Brazil is of those who live in the country's favelas, the most socially subordinated of all. The actor playing Clayton is radicalised at the moment of this revelation, in order to push the girl's father to his limit, employing the 'bro' (*mano* in Portuguese) used in São Paulo's favelas in an even more exaggerated fashion:

> *Listen, I'm no loser, you jerk! I don't want anything from you. I'll work it out. I'll go down the copy shop, I've got my mate there, Marcão, and Binoco, he works at the pizzeria, so I can do the deliveries for him too … /* Do you know how much rent costs? */ Well, where do you think I live, bro? In a house, right bro? /* Oh yeah, where do you live bro? [undoubtedly assuming he lives in a favela] */ I crash at my auntie's … I do the dishes for her … /* Ah, you crash there, do you? Go to hell! Stop fucking with me! Get my daughter back on the line, I have nothing to say to you. Get lost, you piece of shit! You can go to hell! You … you crash at your auntie's, you don't even have a home, and then you go and get another man's daughter pregnant? You irresponsible piece of trash, you're a cretin and an idiot! God will punish you! */ I've had enough! /* You have nowhere! You're not coming anywhere near my home, or near my daughter!

We know from Max Weber that state immanence lies in the monopoly's claiming of the use of force in a given territory. All legitimate orders ultimately constitute violence. This is no different in the order of white men, who have state violence in their favour (according to official data, the Military Police of São Paulo alone kills an average of two people – two Claytons – per day in São Paulo state).[13] God 'will punish you' is a trusted norm for those who violate this order. It is particularly radical to note that the girl's father threatens Clayton and, in doing so, projects danger onto him: 'you're not coming anywhere near my home, or my daughter!' Any similarity to the state repression of the peripheries inherent in the projection that they constitute violent threats to order would not have been a coincidence. Such cases, where everything is more than evident, constitute war. After the battle, the territory (of class-gender-race-religion) belongs to the victor: 'you're not coming anywhere near my home, or my daughter!' The only thing left for Clayton to do is to mock the order, selecting another. The world is full of possibilities:

> *Here's how it is: I'm not going to call you again, if you want to speak to me, I'll be at the Dogão do Betão, look me up there and we'll talk!* / And we both know what I would do there, don't we? Go to hell! Go fuck yourself! / *I'm going to get on with my life and you can get on with yours, you jerk!* / That's enough you piece of shit! You're scum! Disappear! Get out of here! Put my daughter back on! / *Well you know where to find me! You want a hot dog, I'll see you there!* / Fuck that, you idiot! You're trash, how could my daughter get involved with trash like you! / *I deserve a … / You're nothing but a piece of shit!* [the girl intervenes: *Dad?* – but her father keeps talking]: you're a loser! People like you would be better off dead! Darling, I'm sorry, but I didn't bring you up for this! [at this point, background applause becomes audible and the girl says: *Dad, it's a joke! Dad, I love you! You're on Pânico!* Her father hangs up. The girl says: *he'll never speak to me again …* laughter]

As seen in the previous situation, it is ultimately not just Clayton himself that has to 'go fuck himself', 'disappear' and 'go to hell'. What is also being questioned is his social type, whose morals are easily read – marking another emergence of the question of legibility – by the signs expressed in the way he speaks, his job and his salary, his stance against 'society', his uncontrolled virility, which invades the 'family's' carefully sheltered everyday life. It is therefore Clayton's aesthetic (which has nothing to do with visuals, which is evident in this case, but which undoubtedly informs a mental image – nobody imagines Clayton as a white man with blue eyes) informing his legibility to the 'family man': he knows who he is talking to. Police 'suspicion' and that possessed by private security services operate in a similar fashion in Brazil. Experience dictates that 'trash like you' is 'a waste of space'. As our national and state histories know very well (Oliveira, 2014; Gomide Freitas, 2014), the war waged by white men and its legitimate violence are and have always been based on an aesthetic concept (as a combination of very different elements, from very different categories) demarcating the enemy's social spaces.

Opening reflections

Vitória's racism is upfront, as is the misogyny in Junior's utterance and the elitism in the 'family man's' words. What is not as evident, however, is the edifice of gender and the heteronormativity that Vitória constructs while pronouncing her racism; or the state immanence inherent to Junior's question. Constructions of race, gender and sexuality (also state) are also not evident, inherent to the classist, hegemonic masculine and monetised discourse embodied by the 'family man'. Even less noticeable in an everyday context is the fact that his words suggest (in the ability to turn to the police forces) that legitimate violence should be available to tackle this kind of marginal social type, stereotyped in its race-class-performance as non-human because what Clayton represents is 'trash', 'shit', a 'son of a bitch' and an 'animal'. Such a type is even anti-human, because it destroys men's homes.[14] 'Real men don't do this to other men's daughters.' Even less evident is the claiming of the legitimate monopoly of contents and values able to fill the categorical interval of 'woman', or that of 'family', 'order' or 'state', in each of the everyday situations described.

Even if not notable, these evaluative contents are also objectified in each of these situations, thus impacting on the production of order and categorical structuring. If required, as in Clayton's case, subliminal calls to order are easily translated into an explicit harnessing of violence against those who threaten the categorical boundaries, as well as the enemies of gender, class, race, family and religion, and the law itself (Moutinho, 2004), experienced as a social norm. The production of outlaws or criminality is nowadays undoubtedly one of the most powerful contemporary drivers of radical distinction (Hirata, 2018; Feltran, 2014; Mattos, 2016), at the core of the warlike mechanism that impinges on the modern-day 'democratic' political forms and the 'racism of the Brazilian state' (Foucault, 1997; Rui and Feltran, 2015).

It may always be argued that other young, heterosexual men, other middle-class fathers and other white grandmothers would say different things when exposed to similar situations, and that the scenes described here were cherry picked, with no scientific representation for the 'opinions' related here. And this is undoubtedly true. What is much more important, however, is the fact that the *interval of categorical contents* demonstrated by the scenes, the *ideals for action* and the *formal boundaries* of the categories, noted by the performance of the protagonists, lend plausibility to many other scenes of every interaction in modern-day São Paulo or Brazil as a whole. The intervals of plausible contents revealed in each scene give cause to the hegemonic categories, in the Gramscian sense, that lie within assumptions in the 'constitutive nexus between culture and politics' (Dagnino, 1994) that allows us to consider how the national community is imagined (Anderson, 1991). We are therefore not only dealing with a way of thinking pertaining to the elites in São Paulo, but also about the very composition of the bases of public debate in contemporary Brazil.

Representatives of these contents have become relatively well situated in the worlds of economics and state administration after the 1980s; however, their presence is now more explicit in schools, universities, condominium committee meetings, in the courts and in the legal system, in churches and religious associations, in the police forces and their WhatsApp groups, in white families (and their WhatsApp groups), in hospitals and their corporative initiatives, in class associations and their Facebook pages, always marked by a religious, family-oriented and elite aesthetic. God, the white family and the heteronormative police order are returning to governments and the public scene, set to occupy hegemonic positions potentially for quite some time, because they have more than enough public legitimacy – that is, religious, hard-working and orderly – in everyday life. Via this hegemony, many poor black families also share similar things in their WhatsApp groups.

The tension at the boundaries of these premises remains, however. As Gramsci also pointed out, the hegemony is produced via doses of active consent and coercion, with the active construction of the consensus using all of the apparatuses available, and, when these fail, violence. If such a degree of violence is required to produce the contemporary state order of gender-class-race-sexuality-religion-family-nation (Brazil registered over 60,000 homicides in 2015), it is a sign of a lack of a categorical consensus. Violence must be called upon, and it resides at the limit of authoritarianism.[15] The formally democratic experience in Brazil since 1985 has sparked an authoritarian reaction, as has happened in the past.

I spent some years writing on the modes of the social and political subjectification of the 'worker' (Feltran, 2007), and the 'gangster/thief' (Feltran, 2010b, 2011, 2013a), as well as the 'consumer/entrepreneur' (Feltran, 2014) in São Paulo's peripheries. The argument underpinning these works is that all of these cases feature a brand of subjectification shaped in the framework of a fundamental conflict – political, violent and monetised – in the light of the boundaries of the plausibility of the order of the imagined community (the city, the public world, the nation). In the light of this idealised order and in the conceptual sphere, and despite various attempts to enter it, the peripheries I studied find themselves in disparate places such as those belonging to Clayton, the Kenyan athlete and the trans server, in places all considered to be outside the norm. From the perspective of this hegemonic community, they are explicitly referred to as opposites of the desired forms of family, work, class, gender, race and sexuality that are normal, correct and natural. This objectified and hegemonic normativity is manifested on a daily basis in the search for political legitimacy and state order.

Means for overcoming this boundary have been sought. The opportunity offered by the insertion of the 'worker' did not find community redemption; the Workers' Party, which was most explicit in its support for this project, abandoned it after a while, and the party's long-term crisis has intensified since the election Bolsonaro in 2018. The raising of the minimum monthly wage and the powerful monetisation of everyday life also failed to produce subjects suitable for a guaranteed stable space in the division of community plots. The 'new C class' did not flourish, defending itself as far as it could against the increase in unemployment and the cost of living. The ideas of criminal 'revolution' inherent to the viewpoint of the PCC criminal faction are now outgrowing it, with no expectation in its narrative of the construction of a national community. Perhaps this is why evangelical churches and the presence of police forces in politics – that explicitly represent the project for national order – are experiencing such as boom. The constitutive tension found in any boundary is still simultaneously present, producing countless everyday syntheses, in directions which are certainly not unequivocal. The radicalisation of identities and places of speech is undoubtedly a constitutive part of this tension.

Unlike my previous output, this chapter has not sought to situate the analytical point of view in the margins of the social and the state. I have inverted here what I attempted to do some years ago, taking, however, the same *relationship* of otherness as an object. If I sought in my previous output to translate my discoveries – the markedly political modes of thinking and acting in marginalised worlds – to the sectors which were not seen, not even by my own eyes before studying them, now the task has been mirrored. The perspective reconstructed here, as has been seen, is that of the family, racial, social, class, sexuality and gender group that I was brought up in. As is perhaps implicit in my way of considering these issues – because it is in the way these frameworks most directly operate – it is the white, Christian family project belonging to Vitória, Junior and the 'family man' studied in the state of São Paulo that constitutes my own social trajectory and shaping as a person. However, carrying these frameworks does not imply their infinite reproduction, precisely because there are many teleological series of social action operating in each situation and obeying distinct regimes of everyday objectification. Vitória's 'Brazilian white' may not be my 'Brazilian white', for example, with these in turn surely not being the same as German 'white' or 'white' in the United States. The multiplicity also does not necessarily lead to the possibility for absolute emancipation in the light of these frameworks; they are once again objectified in each rapid, everyday or routine interaction with people and subjects whom I don't know well. I will remain as white as Vitória.

Nobody white is ever just white when we have gained experience from weeks, months or years spent by their side. For our peers in particular, we are always more than what we appear at first glance. In the great majority of rapid interactions in the social world, however, and particularly when there is a significant otherness, a categorical boundary comes into play, often reducing us to our race, gender or class, or the aesthetic of their routinised, essentialised and objectified associations. It would be easier for a business man to forget the name of the woman who serves the tea and coffee, black and poor as she is (because in everyday

Brazilian life she is a routine type without a name), than the name of the company's chief executive officer. This woman looks at the white men in meetings and believes them to be as close socially as she is distanced from them, while they distinguish between themselves and ignore her presence. The woman, meanwhile, is probably more likely to know the names of her female co-workers than those of the men she serves. The boundary which is more radically significant is that separating them, aesthetically and politically (Feltran, 2007). Within the categorical boundaries, both individuals and a community may be recognised. Peering behind the boundary, we will make out categorised, conceptual, abstract social types. They are white, 'cool', 'playboys', 'successful' and 'rich'. 'They' are not like 'me'.

We are always inside and outside these categories in everyday life, whether we like it or not. This is why strategic essentialism works, and why it is not redemptive, in the struggle among movements of differences. This is why racial democracy works, and has limits, in the struggle between hegemonic groups. Both function in specific situations, are limited in other situated scenes, depending on the categorical boundaries in play and the performance of the actors facing them. As Butler stated, performativity (which is both aesthetic and political) plays a decisive role in the objectification of these boundaries. Sometimes, depending on how we behave, we situate ourselves on one side for a matter of years, with this experience potentially changing in a single day.

The everyday tendency towards categorical objectification by means of routine is thus eventually challenged by the time-consuming routines, by the contingency that ignores them. The daily exposure to misunderstandings and conflicts calls for an order, while simultaneously spurring research into other possible and plausible orders. Institutions, movements, families and people reproduce their cycles for generations, becoming different in each cycle. Favelas are and are not the new *senzalas*, depending on the sequence of actions deemed to be relevant for analysis. The perception of 'advances' and 'setbacks' on the political scene specifically concerns this shift within the legitimate order of categories, objectified by routine use, which also carries its worm. The recent authoritarian reaction in Brazil, effected by the radical objectification of the hegemonic categorical boundaries of difference and by the demand – violent, if necessary – that they remain in place, fixing them, is radical enough to request effective reaction. The essentialist radicalisation of sectors of minority groups in the public and conceptual scene – like that which opposes the PCC, on the one hand, and the police and evangelical Christians, on the other, for example – is the most noticeable and strongest effect, although there are many other effects to be understood. We know that it is in everyday life, however, that the practices of its groups often locate it within the same categorical limits. The public conflict that tends to become strengthened in Brazil therefore has unpredictable consequences. At least we know that understanding the world is not merely a question of gender or of sexuality rather than of race. The struggle between the classes is not the only thing driving history.

In a theoretical scenario in which the categorical 'emancipation' (of class, gender and race) has definitively lost its universal validity, the politics of categories seems to become polarised between the *aesthetic* limits of essentialisation and of deconstruction, both to the right and to the left. To bring a specific interpretation from Georg Simmel's latest works to this debate, I believe it is possible to turn to a situational analysis of categories that contemplates essence *and* deconstruction, but more particularly the *continuum* of the places between them, challenged by time, as positions that are a priori equally valid in the everyday, practical structuring of difference.

2

Legitimacy in dispute: the boundaries of the 'world of crime' in São Paulo

It is not possible to trace the boundaries of the 'world of crime' in relation to the broader social fabric without also examining the relations between this 'world' and social spheres considered legitimate, such as work, family, religion and so on. No boundary establishes a watertight division between two domains; rather, what any boundary seeks is to regulate the terms of the relationship, the flows (of people, goods, discourse, etc.) between them. A boundary, therefore, denotes a distribution, according to Jacques Rancière (1995, p. 7): 'distribution means two things: participation in a common set and, conversely, separation, distribution in instalments'. In order to study the expansion of the boundaries of 'crime' in São Paulo, it is therefore necessary to understand the broader social dynamics on which they are based, beyond their internal dimensions.

In the first part of the chapter I argue that the emergence of a 'world of crime' in the peripheries of São Paulo must be understood in the context of at least three decades of crisis and dislocation in the spheres of work, family and religion. These were been the main pillars structuring projects of social mobility among the migrants who occupied the peripheries from the 1960s onwards. In the second part I present in detail the story of Pedro, a young inhabitant of Sapopemba in the eastern periphery of the city. Recounted in 2005, Pedro's story directly addresses family, work and religion, as well as their boundaries with the local 'world of crime', which he crossed several times in both directions. Through his deft ability to describe his own experiences, Pedro demonstrates how boundaries operate in these areas and the social function they play. In the third part I offer some reflections synthesising the argument, which offer a preliminary interpretation of the struggle for legitimacy and the 'expansion of the world of crime' in the peripheries of São Paulo.

The contemporary social dynamics of the urban peripheries can be read through a series of crises. Crises of formal employment, of Catholic religiosity, of the promise of social mobility for the working family, of social movements and their representativeness. The term crisis, rather than collapse, is used because social relations and sociability continued to be primarily structured around the category of work, in spite of growing unemployment; Catholic popular morality remained dominant, despite the growth of neo-Pentecostal evangelical churches; popular collective actions continued, even though their representativeness had been thrown into doubt; and the prospect of family social mobility survived as an aspiration, revived by access to credit in popular chain stores like Casas Bahia, even if the dream of achieving it through Fordist employment was no longer viable.

In my respondents' testimonies it was also very common to hear all these crises linked, in negative terms, to the growth of violent crime in these territories. It was these crises that had brought the frontiers of the 'world of crime' closer to the realms of family and 'community' life. The theme of 'violence' and references to this 'world' thus emerged, in my own and other studies in the peripheries of São Paulo (Cabanes, 2014; Hirata, 2018), as closely linked to dislocations in those other spheres that structured popular life. An entire social world had been dislocated, and another was presenting itself as an alternative. And in the tension and coexistence between the two, the boundary marking what could be considered as socially legitimate was redefined.

When, beginning in 2005, I began to study the younger generation living in the peripheries more systematically – in particular
those adolescents who had been born in the period of the most
radical dislocation (the 1990s) – the interpretative hypothesis that
I had been working with seemed to hold up. For this younger
generation, the crises of work, family, religion and the project of
social mobility, which characterised the collective experience in
which they grew of age, were already constitutive of their being
in the world. The lifestyles of young residents of the peripheries of
São Paulo are already shaped by a representation of these crises
as inevitable and, therefore, of a reality that needs to be accepted
and dealt with. I began to realise that, with the passage from one
generation to another, a new layer of the social fabric was being
superimposed over that established by the previous generation
and came to coexist with it. Generational succession catalysed the
transformations that I was observing and allowed me to examine
their horizons. Since then, I have carefully studied the trajectories
of dozens of adolescents and young people living in the peripheries of São Paulo. Among these trajectories, I have given special
attention to those in which the 'world of crime' appeared as a
feasible 'option' considering the privations of the social context.
The following story is one such example.

Bounded life: Pedro

I was introduced to Pedro in May 2005, during my first days in
Sapopemba. We sat down, two researchers and Pedro,[1] at a round
plastic table in a room at the Núcleo Assistencial Cantinho da
Esperança (Corner of Hope Care Unit, Nasce), an organisation
where Pedro worked that attended to children and adolescents
with special needs. The idea was to conduct an exploratory interview. Pedro didn't know exactly what we wanted. We had just
asked him to tell his life story, about how it was that he ended
up in the neighbourhood and that job. We knew that a few years

earlier he had passed through the Centro de Defesa dos Direitos de Crianças e Adolescentes 'Mônica Paião Trevisan' (Centre for the Defence of the Rights of Children and Adolescents, CEDECA) – a non-governmental organisation in Sapopemba that supports adolescents from the area who have been required to undergo socio-educational measures ('Liberdade Assistida e Prestação de Serviços à Comunidade' / 'Assisted Freedom and Community Service') after having being convicted of a crime. We also knew that he had been through difficult family circumstances, from which he had managed to 'recover'. This first interview lasted two hours and was the only one I recorded with him. All the excerpts quoted are verbatim and I present them in the order in which they were made. I interrupt Pedro's account only to provide context and offer partial syntheses. Two more years of field research with Pedro, his family, his peers and organisations in the neighbourhood where he lived were needed to gain a fuller picture. I kept in touch with him until the end of 2007.

> On the day of her burial I turned thirteen. I saw myself in this scene: on my birthday, my mother dead, at home without nothing to do, without coffee, without any support, with nothing, only my godmother helping me. And my father had also just had surgery on his leg. He had an operation and almost lost his leg and could no longer work. And my godmother was like, seeing my mother in that state. She had just died, and my father stuck in bed, unable to walk, without anything, he barely had a thigh, only pure flesh. They did the operation, put a pin in the leg. (...) My sister went to live at my uncle's house, she stayed with my aunt. We stayed at home, my brother and I. I was thirteen, he was fourteen.
>
> My father had liked to drink since he was a kid; he started age nine and always drank, guzzled it down, even with his leg all messed up. (...) And my brother comes down, and says: 'I saw some kids in the middle of the street, with a gun, with a car, like. Sometimes with the police there, shooting.'
>
> I went to live with my godmother for a while because of these kids, 'cause I was very close to them. But it didn't help. I was at my godmother's house, she gave me everything; but at home we had

71

nothing. My father like that, my brother in the street, going around from place to place, and me with nothing. Just an odd job here and there. And I thought, 'These jobs I do... it's not working'. I saw the kids stealing, guns in their hands ... I'd never anything like it in my life before. One day a boy said to me, 'Ah, go and get a beer there for me'. I took the money and went and got the beer for him. I started being friends with them.

I got into a lot of fights with this crazy guy, who wasn't from the crime, but his brothers were. He was my age, and the others who were a bit older were the ones who were in the crime, who had already started to steal. (...) I saw that scene, the boys wanted to impress me: 'Look how much I've made! Look what my brother made, he did this and that. Look what I've got. My brother bought me a new bike; bought me some clothes.' 'At home we have everything we need, do you need help, Pedro?' I would say, 'I don't need any help, no.' So as not to take the money from them, you know? And I was trying to keep going with the odd jobs, things like that.

So far Pedro has recited, almost word for word, the standard account that a boy from the favela gives to people who resemble the teachers, social workers and psychologists he has met in his long journey through different institutions. Although he didn't know exactly what we wanted from him, he didn't ask for any clarification and just began telling his story, working his way through the different dramas that made it up. Even so, his narrative builds up a picture that primarily acts as a multi-layered *justification* for his involvement in crime – the mother who died, the poverty, his father's alcoholism, the brother who was gradually becoming involved, the sister who had left, the temptations in the neighbourhood, the odd jobs that did not pay enough, the attempts to avoid the 'world of crime', the objects of desire – designer clothes, the bicycle, etc. Pedro paints a largely realistic, at times hyper-realistic, picture of the context in which teenagers from the peripheries enter the crime. The recurring narrative is based on a bipolar opposition between *home* and *crime*, two worlds sealed off from one another. It can be summarised as: 'when the family disintegrates, crime embraces'. This formula is very well known, having become almost a cliché within social organisations in the peripheries of São Paulo. Like all clichés, however, these phrases must be read with attention to both their wisdom and their limitations.

It was bothering me a lot because there was nothing at home. I finished one day … a boy said to me, 'I have a toy gun'. It was plastic. The older kids, who wanted more, had loads of things: cars, beautiful things, money, children's toy, loads of things. I looked at all of that, it was a lot of money.

One day I was running and I accidentally hit him [*another boy*] in the face like … [*makes a gesture of turning around and bumping into someone else's face*]. Then the kid punched me in the face. I accidentally hit a guy who was armed. And he punched me in the face. I looked him in the face and walked up to him and he pulled out the gun. Then I went quiet, just looking him in the face. The kids talked, but I stayed mute. I left.

Then I became friends with this crazy guy who lived there by the house. And he said, 'Pedro, you know that I know how to drive a car?' And I said: 'What? No you don't!' Then the next day, he says: 'Come on, my uncle has a car key.' He even took the key from his uncle's car and his uncle beat him. We wanted to know more about messing around …

Well, we had a plastic gun, always playing cops and robbers. Then a kid asked me: 'Pedro, are you brave enough to steal a car?' I looked at his face, like, 'No, I don't have the nerve!' And he says: 'Come on, come on! You'll make money! My brother gave me almost fifty bucks right now.' And he showed me the money. Then, his brother arrived with an accordion. He had just robbed a car and now he had an accordion, and a load of other stuff. Then my brother said he was going to try to sell it to my uncle. And he told us to try and sell the accordion for him. I stayed at home playing with accordion. And the guy gave my brother fifty bucks, and my brother managed to sell it. He was delighted and started hanging out with those kids.

I saw my brother getting involved, the guys smoked marijuana, there was this 'neguinho' [pejorative expression meaning a little black guy] who was really out of control; my brother was there in the middle of it: 'Get us a beer!' (…) And my brother would go, and would earn a *real*, or more. So I saw my brother getting involved and I tried to stop him. I got an odd job handing out flyers and called my brother. But my brother messed around there. So I left for a while and he stayed. But eventually I came back and the kid says: 'When will you have the guts?' And I said: 'No, I don't think I have the nerve for that!' And he says: 'Let's try it one day.' And I said: 'Okay, one day we'll try.'

As the narrative progresses new elements appear that are similarly recurrent in such accounts. The first image is of the seductiveness of consumer goods and of the power of the firearm within adolescent hierarchies. 'Cars, beautiful things, money, children's toys, loads of things.' 'He pulled out the gun'; 'I went quiet'. In the second image, the friend 'borrows' his uncle's car. In the third, the accordion found in a stolen car enters a circuit of informal deals between friends and relatives, and the teenagers earn $50 by selling it. We can observe here, then, that relations between relatives and friends also feed into small networks that sustain and circulate stolen goods. From this perspective – and it is only the first – the house is no longer completely sealed off from the circuit of crime, is no longer its opposite. And there is one further image, 'I saw my brother getting involved', and the bridge between the home and crime becomes a little stronger. This means that, without even 'entering the crime', key elements of the criminal world are already clearly visible: 'kids smoking marijuana', 'the black guy who was really out of control', 'get us a beer!' The boundary is right there. Another *real* in the pocket, the story continues:

Then I started getting more angry. There was one day when I didn't eat anything. Nothing. My father hadn't eaten for four days, was drunk, dying, at home ... He would get to the bar and drink without stopping. (...) I began to feel hatred, to miss my mother, and I had hatred inside me, and I didn't know how to let it go. Then I got a gun and said: 'Let's do it then! Let's give it a try!'

I was halfway there and I saw a police car passing by, my heart was racing. And the boys [*who were with him*] said: 'it's fine, it's fine!' They had never stolen a car either. They said, 'It'll be our first and it'll be great!' Then I see a lady with a car full of shopping: 'You go first!' 'No, I'm not going.' We let the car pass. Then I saw this little old man. He was on a cell phone, counting money, and he got into the car, and I didn't have the nerve either! Then I passed it [*the gun*] to this kid: 'You go.' And he said: 'No, I'm not going!'

Then a rage came over me! I saw a car. The guy had just come in. Then I got the gun: 'This is a robbery, go, go, go, go'. Then the guy stared at my face and when he looked, I punched him right in the chin, whack!, with the gun. Then he gave me the key, his wife got out with his daughter and we got in, we got in the car and we drove off accelerating. And then there was a traffic light, with a truck going passed, the light [*inside the car*] was on, and we didn't even see it. And my friend hit it and turned off the light, and we almost hit the truck. But, the first time it went well. We got about R$ 150 each. I bought a load of things to take home.

And the guys asked, 'Where did you go?' And I said, 'It was like this, and that'. The guys kept looking at my face: 'You're cool! Do you really steal?' And I said: 'Ah, I don't steal, but I just did'.

At this point, Pedro breaks with the initial phase of the interview, during which we had regularly prompted him with small questions, beginning an uninterrupted phase of continuous narrative. If initially we had felt the need to ask him to describe some of the scenes in greater detail – the stories about his mother and his brother, the comings and goings of his odd jobs distributing flyers or washing cars – now we needed only to nod our heads to keep him talking. The more standard and familiar narrative then gave way to a detailed description of his criminal activities. Pedro was already elaborating his experiences like images. They felt like movie sequences, constructed from his memories of events that had occurred five years previously. He created metaphors to help us understand the codes in question, his relationship with them.

The boys saw a car full of shopping, a 'little old man counting money', but Pedro plucked up the courage, and felt sufficient 'anger' only with the third potential victim. Clumsily and without much planning, but without major problems, the first robbery was successful. Pedro was fourteen years old and using a plastic gun. He encountered the boundary for the first time. Coming back with the stolen objects, the 'older guys' from the favela showed them recognition. The boys were good. The first robbery, then, was almost a rite of passage into another world. Pedro felt he was between two different conditions: 'I don't steal, but I just did.'

Sitting in the traffic, new feelings arose within the group that gave them satisfaction: they recognised they had shown the courage, adrenaline and disposition necessary to carry out the act. At this point, Pedro's family still appears in the narrative, but the terms of their inclusion are changing. The home continued to provide some rhetorical protection from crime, but at the same time Pedro's brother is described as a bridge to people who are 'involved'; his father didn't like this, but there is a counterpoint: he was drunk and did not provide enough for the household to survive; his sister disapproved of the company he kept, but she was no longer around. The money he was bringing home was met with disapproving faces, but was nonetheless accepted. The uncle, aunt and godmother, who never seemed particularly close, are already disappearing from the testimony. School had already disappeared earlier in the story, shortly after Pedro had recounted his childhood memories. Previous jobs are no longer read simply as unprofitable, and start to take on associations of precariousness and humiliation. Now Pedro was envisioning the possibility of making real money. He had this 'option' (a term he used frequently). A new group (friendship, money, beer, cars) and new objects (clothes, bicycle, accordion, toy gun) become part of Pedro's life. His mother has been dead a year, a year and a half.

From trainee to professional thief

So I went on stealing with the boys. My father didn't like it; he drank, but he didn't like it. We hid the money. Then I started stealing and I started to get to know the older people. I made friends with these bigger guys and I went and put R$50 in their hands. And they said they were selling the gun for R$150. And I said, 'What is this weapon?' 'It's a weapon we have, if you want it ...'. I joined together with a colleague of mine: 'Let's buy it [together], it's easier.' So I bought it. And we started … this guy, who was older, who was getting good, reliable business, [said]: 'So I have a good earner for you. It's a lot! If you go there with two other kids, you'll get it because you're with me.' (…) A firm, there's was a lot of money. So I went; we picked it up from these older people, and it all worked out; we stole like hell.

The older boys were already more organised than Pedro and his friend. It was easy enough for them to buy a gun. 'Making friends' with these characters also meant access to a world of more profitable crimes, the 'earners' they could make, a kind of subcontracting of thefts and robberies. They had more means to organise an action to make good money, and they could hire teenagers and young people to run it. They paid for the service, they organised the tasks to be carried out: 'I have a good earner for you. It's a lot!' 'You'll get it because you're with me.' Subcontracted businesses work best when they have the necessary equipment and tools: 'Let's buy it [together], it's easier.' Time passed quickly. Pedro was 'becoming a thief':

Then I started assaulting the victims. There was a victim, a strong guy, he tried to hit me, I hit him and threw him to the ground. And he was like, 'No, no, no!' and I said 'I'm not here to kill you, I just want your money, that's all. I just don't want you to lean back, put your hand on your waist! I just want your money, I don't want anything else from you, your can keep your ID. I just want your money.' And he said, 'Okay, okay, okay!' Then I took his money and left. There was a victim who was armed, one time. We went for her car and she tried to escape, and I shot at the car. I took the gun and started to shoot, but I didn't hit it. My friend almost did. 'This is normal, this happens' [he said].

Then I started getting braver. And because of the hatred that I felt because of my mother's death, I began to get really bad. Then I made friends with these guys. One day we went on a robbery and one guy got shot in the hand. When I saw, I started shooting, but I didn't manage to hit anything. There was a victim who was armed, a 9 [mm] appeared. 'Are you armed?' 'No, I'm not, I'm not!' I had a deadlier weapon, I cocked it, and I pointed it in his mouth. 'Open your mouth!' 'No, I'm not going to open it!' I hit him with the gun and he opened his mouth: 'Don't move, if you move I'll blow your face off.' My friend saw, and he also had a gun. 'Are you a cop?' 'No.' My friend was going to kill him. I said, 'No, don't kill him. Let him live. I just want his money that's all.' We took the revolver too.

Another turning point. Now, Pedro no longer knows whether he chooses the narrative of the 'good thief', who steals without harming his victims, who only wants money and nothing more, or whether he presents himself as one of those who attack the victim, who act with violence, who show signs of actually being *bandidos*. The first image is more palatable to us, the second is more highly considered in the 'world of crime'. He knows the discourses and arguments of both, and can effectively choose between them. His indecision makes this part of the interview confusing, full of back-and-forths. The figure of the mother reappears, another recurring image: in accounts given by 'guys from the crime', the mother commonly appears as a saintly figure. Pedro's mother had died, making her even more so, at the same time as her absence generated more 'hatred' in him. At this point in the conversation, I had the feeling that he had doubts about how to proceed. We looked at him, waiting for him to continue. He decided he would: 'I started to get very bad.' 'Then I got braver.'

Pedro's narrative recovered its flow. The key markers then passed to the other side of the boundary between crime and family morality, and became virtually internal to the 'community' of crime. Pedro now spoke as though he were a 'professional' of this world; he made sure to demonstrate that he knew the craft. His actions no longer had the innocence that they had previously: he began to use technical terms – those used in police jargon – to describe his acts (what had been a 'little old man counting money' was now referred to as 'the victim', 'hitting' someone became 'assaulting' etc.); the dangers of these activities also began to appear – an armed victim, a poorly fired shot – and Pedro gained experience in dealing with such situations. He reflected on each crime, became better at executing them. He then became involved with more experienced, more skilled people. Pedro was passing the boundary into 'crime'.

> I made friends with some older guys, like twenty or thirty years old already. Some of them had already been in prison. And my hatred kept growing. I started to fight with other thieves. I started shooting thieves, that kind of trouble. There was a group that came ... I call just it naughtiness, because they were nothing, but thank God they all died. But it wasn't me who did it. They realised one day that I was unarmed outside the favela. They stole a motorcycle in the favela and my colleague said [to other people who were trying to find it]: 'It was so-and-so.' Then I went for a ride on his [his friend's] Monza. I was with him. These thieves caught up and said, 'Which one of you ratted on us? Which one of you?' So an argument started: 'It wasn't me, it wasn't me!' 'You're going to get it. You were together, all three of you are going to get it.' I said, 'I'm not going to get it, I didn't do anything to you.' Everyone was afraid of them because they were not afraid to kill. If you opened your mouth to them they killed you, without thinking ... Even playing football they'd already killed a guy. He kicked his leg ... He went and killed this guy who had kids. Nego [his friend?] was really afraid of them. And so one hit me, he punched the other guy; one hit me with his pistol in my chest, and the gun fell to the ground. When he dropped the gun I tried to bend down, he hit me in the face: 'Go down and see what I'll give you in your head!' Then, okay, I breathed deeply, I had a pain in my chest, my friend was crying. The other one didn't get hit. When he was leaving: 'Look, he's got some money!' He pointed at me. I had money in my pocket, a hundred *reais*. 'Give me the money!' 'No!' He started to hit me, picked up a piece of wood, and hit me over the head. I gave him the money and left.

Pedro was fifteen years old. But he was already a 'thief' and therefore could be treated according to the norms of the 'community of crime'. 'Community' here is used in the traditional sense, since among members peers are seen as 'equals', and also 'others' in relation to those 'outside crime'. Perhaps the first rule of this community is not to give others away. Pedro's friend did this, in response to another internal norm having been transgressed (not stealing in the favela), and trouble ensued. Pedro was with his friend at the time they caught up with him, and so he got embroiled in the conflict. The two weren't killed only because the codes were changing and the episode occurred precisely during the period of transition. With the entry of the PCC (the main criminal faction in São Paulo) in Sapopemba, organising all drug trafficking and interfering in the organisation of other criminal activity, getting permission to kill another 'thief' had become more complicated. You needed higher authorisation, you needed to assess what threats might lead to, you needed to know if other sanctions might not work. If all else fails, you would need to participate in a 'debate', the extrajudicial and summary judgments conducted by members of criminal organisations, especially the PCC. This mechanism, which emulates a court of law, with prosecution and defence witnesses, 'judges' and 'lawyers', has been widely used in the peripheries of São Paulo.[2]

Moreover, under the PCC's command, the rules of 'traffickers' and of 'thieves' also seem to have been unified. The subordination of different illegal markets under a single criminal command represents a process distinct from what has occurred in other Brazilian cities, including Rio de Janeiro. If in Rio the 'dangerous connections' between drug trafficking and other illegalities and crimes continue to shift over time (Misse, 2006a), in São Paulo these markets have tended towards an ever clearer integration and are currently subordinated under relatively centralised management. This unusual situation in São Paulo accelerates the circulation of what Misse (2006b, 2007) called 'political merchandise' inherent to 'protection markets'.

Thus, at difficult moments, Pedro, who never sold drugs, turns to the '*dono da boca*' (the boss of the local drug trade) to arm himself, and as he buys the weapons he receives instructions from the 'Command' (PCC) to 'ignore' the problem with the rival group:

From then on, I saved, bought a car, started to steal again. I got a gun and beat the two of them, I started to shoot at them. One in the arm and one in the leg. I said, 'Now it's on!' I bought like four guns, I became friends with these guys, the *dono da boca*, I started to get angry: 'You want to mess with me, then come!' After that they didn't come any closer to me; when I was in the favela, they would avoid me. Then they told me to stop, and I ignored it because otherwise I would end up dying because they were stronger than me. I was alone, because my friends …

In a job that I ended up going on, I almost died. I went to rob a guy, there were three policemen. I went to rob him, he was armed, but he didn't manage to be quicker than me. But I also didn't manage to kill him. I'm thankful to this day that I didn't kill him. But anyway. I pointed the guns at him: 'Go, go, go, this is a robbery, it's a robbery.' He stared at my face, an Alemão [literally German, in this context meaning a white guy], you know. I saw that there were two bigger guys, one short one, so I went. When he came up to me, I shot him in the chest on the side … It wasn't in his chest, it was in his hand, like that. I saw that it wasn't going to work because the other one was coming up on the other side. That's when I thought, I didn't even want to rob them anymore, I started moving away in fear. With them there, armed. When I looked around, I had no friends there. Luckily I had two guns. So I started to shoot at those guys and the policeman started shooting too: 'Okay, okay!' (…) I saw those bullets and ran into the middle of the woods. A friend of mine passed with a car. He was in a car and stopped, and gave a couple of shots; but didn't hit anyone. Then the policemen managed to get out of the house, I jumped on top of some, I fell, I almost broke my leg, I was all scratched up, scared. Then I saw a car, I hid. Then the cops went straight past. I left. I arrived in favela. The guys: 'You okay, you okay? I thought you were dead!' There was one, I shot him in the foot: 'Ah!' 'That's so you learn not to abandon people; you're all out of order.' Then I started to get more angry at these guys, and I started to cause trouble. I got into a lot of trouble because of this, and I tried to calm myself down.

And thank God, I managed to calm down. I tried to make friends with them again, because there was no other way, I was living there, there was no way I could leave, leave my family if I tried to do something crazy, because I was going to die. But I also wasn't afraid of dying anymore. My family didn't care about me anymore. It took a while to become friends [again], then I went robbing with them, we stole like five or seven cars in just one day.

Then, on the last one, we shot at the car. Then, the ROTA [Rondas Ostensivas Tobias de Aguiar from the Military Police] cornered us and began to shoot. So my colleague throws down his gun. [Police:] 'Sit down there!' They make us lie down on the floor, heads down. Then they start to beat us without pity, what a beating ... He pulled my friend's hair and hit him in the face. Then, my friends begin to shout, I just sat quietly. Then there was a guy who said, 'You're the only one who's quiet?' He was wearing an iron boot and gave me a kicking, that felt like it crushed my ribs: 'Ouch!' I had some [stolen] objects, and I was arrested. The guy came and I had to get some stuff that was in the house, otherwise they were going to beat us more. There wasn't even that much stuff, and I handed it all over. So the boys [local traffickers] saw what was happening and thought it was normal, okay. Because he [the police officer] said, 'Otherwise, your friend dies'. And me: 'All right, I'll get it!' My dad was wasted, you know? And, my godfather: 'That bastard.'

The criminal actions were narrated one by one, as if there were no interval between them, or as if the interval had little relevance. In short, the life that Pedro remembers – or believes to be more relevant – when narrating this period involves the succession of criminal actions in which he is involved. Pedro arrives at dawn accompanied by the police, on their way to the police station. His father was 'wasted'. The narrative long ago stopped mentioning family members, severed by the boundaries of 'crime'. These relationships were already exhausted. 'That bastard.' In fact, at this point it seems that the relationships internal to the 'world of crime' become the totality of his life. This is a world of extreme violence for young guys, who are at the front line in the battle against the police. Pedro's trajectory – and not only his, the phenomenon is widespread – becomes dominated by conflicts internal to the community of 'crime', leading him to further restrict his personal ties to those outside this world.

Legitimacy in dispute

The risk of death grows, gun battles become more frequent, armed violence starts to mediate not only criminal acts, but also daily sociability: penalties for breaking the codes, internal threats to the group, conflicts with other groups. Likely homicides appear, which we suspect from Pedro's insistence on saying that all the shots he fired were 'in the foot', 'in the arm', or when he corrects himself, after having said that he shot someone in the chest. Negotiated coexistence with police repression, always associated with illegal violence and corruption, becomes ever closer. The police clearly appear as agents shaping the experience of those immersed in the 'world of crime', rather than outside of it.

There is yet another recurrent feature in the accounts of individuals who, like Pedro, have reached this level of immersion: that radical moment when they claim to have nothing to lose. At this stage, the loss of ties to people, institutions and values considered socially legitimate translates into daily coexistence with the very real possibility of death. The fragility of bonds of social belonging, overwhelmed by the intensity of criminal life, effectively renders the individual non-existent in the legitimate world. This makes him feel that, ultimately, his death would only confirm this absence (Feltran, 2004). Numerous young men whom I have worked with since 2005 have articulated this perception to me very clearly, always when discussing how their 'involvement' with crime had reached a certain level. Those who died had, in almost every case, already crossed this threshold. There is, as such, no 'banalisation' of lethal violence; it responds to criteria that have a regular and specific distribution.

At that moment, if there is nothing to lose, there is also nothing to fear. 'I wasn't afraid of dying anymore, my family didn't care about me anymore,' says Pedro. It is also very common, at this stage of involvement with 'crime', of greater distancing from social dynamics deemed legitimate, that fear of death practically disappears. The 'courage' of these boys therefore makes them highly qualified to perform risky criminal acts. The subcontracting of adolescents for such acts is a phenomenon I have identified in numerous situations in the field. The exploitation of young labour in the 'world of crime' is also fuelled by myths surrounding the Estatuto da Criança e do Adolescente (Statute of the Child and Adolescent) – adolescents are convinced that, because they are 'under age', they cannot be legally prosecuted in the event of arrest.

At this point, and without noticing, the initial factors that attract adolescents like Pedro into crime – the access to consumer goods, the sensation of power and freedom, of being an adult, the women – have also disappeared from the narrative. Pedro no longer refers to the pleasure he gets from consuming what he gained from robberies, he no longer uses positive adjectives. Designer clothing, trainers and status in the group, or even income used for household necessities, seen as justification by those outside the boundaries of the 'world of crime', now give way to motivations internal to it, to a relentless cycle of criminal acts, with no pause for enjoyment. Relatives and friends outside 'the crime' disappear from the testimony, the home disappears from the daily routine and turns into a distant horizon ('I only go to sleep'); work now translates as profits made through criminal acts; social spaces of consumption and leisure are no longer frequented in the narrative (although they may still be in real life).

Professional to institutionalised thief

I was fifteen, sixteen years old at the time [*when he first went to prison*]. At fifteen I was more ready. I was going to turn sixteen. My godfather went with me, I went there to the prison. I ended up staying there for two days. In prison, in the DP [*Delegacia de Polícia*, police station] in Santo André. I can't remember the name. From there, I went to the UAI [*Unidade de Atendimento Inicial*, the unit for first time offenders at FEBEM [Secure Centres for Young Offenders]. I stayed a month, right. I signed [article] 157 [Armed Assault], Gang Membership – everyone was underage, at that time, all kids, and

Carrying a Dangerous Weapon. Then I stayed in FEBEM for a month and left. I went to the Forum, my relatives were there too. We took an LA [*Liberdade Assistida*, Assisted Freedom, to undergo socio-educational rehabilitation in an open institution], and then I started to sign the LA.[3]

First prison: beaten during the arrest, two days in the police station with adults, one month in the adolescent internment unit. Immersion in the 'world of crime', but now seeing its institutional face. A pre-trial hearing, with the family present. There is now state mediation between Pedro and his family, as between him and all his social ties outside of 'the crime'. The first arrest is always a moment of major change. Members of the extended family are obliged to communicate with one another in order to process what has happened, and think about what to do. The boy is really 'in the crime', he's in prison, everyone suffers. Solidarity is mobilised. Gossip around the neighbourhood confirms suspicions and reaffirms the status of Pedro's social existence: he is 'becoming a *bandido*', has already become one. The police create their record, take photographs, assemble a folder, he becomes someone with a criminal record, thus changing his status in relation to the state. The first experience of institutionalisation is another rite of passage in the lives of peripheral adolescents who, like Pedro, pass through 'the crime'. Pedro's age has also reconfigured his position within the social universe of his neighbourhood. Now he had become one of the 'older guys'. Their only relationships that are not (heavily) mediated by state institutions during the period of internment are horizontal ones with other interned adolescents. Through this strengthening of horizontal ties, the 'community of crime' is strengthened. For Pedro, as for every dedicated member of a community, the world that matters ends at the boundaries that circumscribe it.

That's when I first encountered CEDECA. My brother already knew CEDECA more. My brother wasn't involved [in crime] anymore because of CEDECA, I think.[4] Then I met Lucas [case worker], those guys, and I went with them to the football at Arlindo [*escola pública do bairro*], where I studied, played football, played games there in the pitch, and I got to know them.

It was the Assisted Freedom order that broke this cycle for the first time. By judicial decision, Pedro returned to his home and his neighbourhood, and had to participate in activities at CEDECA. He met his 'social educator', spoke to him and participated in sports activities on the school grounds. His process was to be monitored by a lawyer, who informed him about his rights and who had a basic understanding of the places he frequented in the neighbourhood, of his family trajectory and so on. Since his first robbery, this was the first time that Pedro had become engaged in social relations – albeit characterised by very fragile bonds –outside the 'world of crime'. It is once again a moment of crossing boundaries, but this time in the opposite direction. But things are not as simple as that. Pedro had been back on the street for a month when his friend, who had been arrested with him, was also released. They soon met up.

> That same day he was arrested with me. He said, 'I have a job, I just got out of jail.' I had already got involved with those guys already, big guys, some good jobs, lots of money. He stole a car, put a licence plate on it, was going to make a '*bode*' [literally 'a goat', or falsification of a licence plate]. Then I called some girls I knew who were a kind of involved too, and they said it was a lot of money. I said, 'Okay, I'll drop by your house.' And we went to their house. There were just the girls and some guys, with some weapons, I said: 'Wow, how beautiful! How beautiful!' I had never held one like that. I learned to use them.
>
> And my friend said: 'Let's go to the 45 [45th Police Station], near São Rafael', to get his documents. He had just got out of prison, and he went with me, with the stolen car. He took his papers from the police station. I asked to drive the car. I had not driven in a long time. Like this: 'Will you let me drive? It's been a long time since I've driven, I just left FEBEM.' I got in, drove the car, and he was arrested because of me. I was coming down, gun in my hand, as-yeah, and I had a car. And I let the car stall. The vehicle stopped,

like this. So I turned, the car stopped. I turned on the ignition [makes a noise imitating a slowly moving car]: 'That's it, driver!'

I moved out slowly and the police came to mess with us and told us stop: [noise of a car speeding to escape]. But it was a '*bode*', a stolen car, and he said, 'We can't stop, I was just in prison, I just got out.' And I said: 'I don't want to either, I just left FEBEM. Let them shoot! Let's go!' I started to accelerate and we were hit by one [in the vehicle], and another one. The guys shooting at us were five vehicles. We went up an avenue in Santo André and started: we kept going, going, going, when I looked around there were seven cars behind us, and I couldn't drive very well. I went up an avenue, the traffic light was changing, and we hit the two side-view mirrors and when we looked ahead, there was a car. We hit the car head on: whack!

It smashed the door, hit my face and everything; I didn't faint, but I went blank, then I snapped out of it. My friend had just run from the car, I leaned on the door like this [makes a gesture of jumping out of the window], and I managed to get out. When you're terrified, I think a hundred can fall on you, when you think you're going to die, I don't know how, you manage to ... I started to run, I ran a lot.

Then I saw an abandoned car – to this day I don't know how I managed to – inside a [petrol] station. A worn-out car, and I got underneath. There was nowhere else, it was crawling with police. Then I went downstairs. (...) Then they caught my friend inside the supermarket, then they came and picked me up. Lucky for me it was a woman [female police officer]: 'Oh! Listen up, try and get out of there, turn around!' And I had to try and get out, and I got all scratched up, I don't know how I managed to get myself under the car. I managed to get out. When I got up, I got out, a big black guy [another police officer] came, picked me up and punched me in the belly. But he saw that I was all cut up, all dripping with blood, and said, 'If I hit that bastard, they'll think it was me who beat him up. I won't even hit you anymore!'

All messed up, scratches all over my face, you know? Then a lot of cars showed up; I looked one way, I looked the other and ... I was never going to escape. The guys were all armed. And I saw my friend, and he was 'an adult'. Then he looked me in the face: 'Alright, Pedro?' [I said]: 'I'm a minor, don't worry about me!' He went in one car, I went in another, and the guy [police officer] said to me: 'Listen up, blame everything on the older guy.' I looked at his face, like this: 'But it was I who stole [the car]! The big guy had nothing to do with it'. He [the police officer] punched me in the chest. 'Go on, you can beat me, kill me, I'm all broken anyway, do whatever you want!' He pistol-whipped me in the chest. Then I said, 'Aren't you stronger than that, officer?' I looked at his face: 'Then you have to do more to me, because it was me who did it.' He went and punched me in the mouth. Then I said, 'Alright, now I'm really broken.'

We arrived at the police station, the victim arrived, and ended up not recognising either of us. Then the cops: 'You're going straight to SOS [slang for the Secure Centres for Young Offenders], *neguinho*.' I went to a cell that had a couple of thieves in it. Then my friend was arrested and the staff began to mock: 'It's the people that likes our food! They leave one day and come back the same day, man!' Hell, I started to laugh. I had another friend in the same place. He said: 'Alright, Pedro, the victim didn't recognise you. Soon you'll be back on the street, don't worry! I don't know about him as he just left and came straight back, but you …!' I said, 'That's okay.' That guy was, like, I rated him; now not so much, but then I really rated him, he'd done five spells in prison. I respected him like hell and he respected me.

I made friends with some people inside, people greeted me: 'So you're Pepê?' Then I started making friends with people on the outside, lots of them (…) talked about me. The 'thieves' spoke about me because I'd been stealing the whole year, and I'd earned myself a name, friendship. The people were like, 'Look, a little kid of that size and he has a bigger appetite than a thief.' The guys: 'Let's take you to SOS.' 'Yeah? Let's go. To do what?' Half an hour [later]: 'I'm going to take a shower.' The policemen looking at my face: 'Fuck! You really are lazy!'

I was taken to the UAI again, and the official from there said: 'Damn, again!' And the dogs: 'You already know how it works. Hands on your head, "no sir", "yes sir"'. I stayed there for two months again. I went to UAP 8 [The acronym stands for *Unidade de Acolhmento Provisório*, Provisional Reception Unit, but in fact Pedro goes through a UAP and is referring to the UIP 8 – *Unidade de Internação Provisória*, Provisional Internment Unit in Brás, where he spent his period of internment.]

Legitimacy in dispute

My sister came to visit me once and I said: 'I'm here because I want to be, I wanted this for myself. I don't want visits! My family had already seen me stealing like that, had suffered with me and come to visit me, it was too much.' My sister had a daughter already. I sent her away, she got nervous. And the clerk: 'Hey, you're out of order! How can you treat your sister like that?' And I said, 'I'll treat her how I want, she's my sister.' Then he said, '*Neguinho*, you're really out of order!' Then I said; 'I really am, you prick!' Then he came and punched me. 'If she was your sister, would you want her coming to visit you here?' I asked him. I stared into his face without saying a word. I never had visits, not I never wanted any. My sister went, but I said, 'No, I don't accept visits!'

I made friends with people, with some of the staff. And I got semi-release,[5] I had to stay in the house to sleep. Then I made some friends, there were some bad kids, some little black guys who got in a lot of trouble, and I ended up running away from there. (...)

Then I was fugitive, being hunted and nervous. And I got involved again. Like this: one of my friends died, then another died. I saw it, I had never seen a guy die in front of me; the guy was in a robbery, he died in front of me and I ran away. That was the scene, and I said, 'Wow, I went, the guy didn't come back with me.' (...) Then there was a policeman who I hit, and he came to look for me here, but he couldn't find me. I ended up being hunted by the police, getting in fights with thieves, and I started making friends with some serious people. Then I took part in a robbery, a friend of mine also got shot, another got one in the neck and couldn't really speak, but he escaped. I didn't escape. Man, then things started to get worse.

Instead of me getting better at home, I wasn't bringing any more *reais* home because I could not get hold of any more money. Then I went to FEBEM, things got worse at home, and my older brother was looking after things (...) I can't say why it had been better before, to this day I don't know. A lot of things just went right. I think I ended up getting involved with some guys that had already been in prison, it was real *zica* [bad luck], as they say, too much *zica*. I ended up joining them and got targeted by the police, they saw me and already knew me. They ended up getting to know me, I'd be going somewhere and the police would circle me: 'Where's your friend?' And I ended up being targeted, and, because I had bought a motorcycle and a car, the police said to me: 'The kid is *growing*, he's making money.' I ended up losing my car and motorcycle. Some kids died, the police followed me, wanting to know who I was, and I ended up calming down. Then I got more involved with CEDECA, and I started to distance myself.

The scene shifts, quickly, between meeting friends, cinematographic pursuits by police and living at edge of life and death. Next, his second experience of institutionalisation is treated as natural. In this section of the testimony, it is no longer the criminal acts that structure the story, but only those that resulted in him returning to these institutions. His sister reappears, representing the family. She was emphasised in this role. But the justification Pedro uses to avoid these visits demonstrates how specific his codes of honour have become – his sister is expelled because the relatives had already 'suffered with me and come to visit me, it was too much'. The comings and goings strengthen his 'friendships' with peers, Pedro earns a 'name': 'So you're Pepê?'

Returning to the internal boundaries of crime, and to the institutionality surrounding it, Pedro describes what become his social networks: individuals who are institutionalised or recently released from prison, police and state agents in the criminal justice system. The mediation of these ties, needless to say, is almost always violent. This is because institutions that deprive people of their freedom (or socio-educational institutions, in the case of minors) end up exacerbating the sense of social rupture from the 'legitimate' world and, in this way, reinforce the 'world of crime' as a reference in individuals' trajectories. This apparatus is erected between the space of internment, in which horizontal relations are always with others who have committed criminal acts, and the judicial process, where all relations gravitate around the act committed. This monothematic circuit, which serves only to strengthen the identity of the 'criminal', appears precisely at the point where the state begins to mediate social relations. From this perspective, the 'world of crime' expands to social contexts far beyond the urban periphery, taking root in the institutions themselves: one need only recall the 'PCC attacks' in São Paulo in May 2006, for evidence of these connections (Adorno and Salla, 2007).

The original motivation for joining 'the crime' reappears: 'I had a car and a motorbike.' But these possessions are no longer evoked with the same justifications and enthusiasm. Now the car and the bike generate envy, exposure and danger. Envy because he is visible and everyone wants what he has. Exposure and danger because the police know the boy now he has crossed the boundary, they know his friends, and when they see them in a car, on a motorcycle, they approach (to arrest them, or simply to 'harass' them). 'It was real *zica*, too much *zica*'. Pedro uses this expression, which means 'bad luck', in a concrete way: he knows well that having a 'name' means that both 'thieves' and 'police' are watching him. Each new 'job' is a shoot-out. Friends and accomplices are being shot. One dies in front of him. Another one. Things get much worse. It was all 'illusion', another category that is continually deployed.

Way back

There was a friend of mine who almost killed me because I stopped stealing, a little. And my friend: 'Let's go and rob?' He had just robbed a pizzeria. I said, 'No, I'm not going.' 'Come on, you asshole!' 'You can curse me as much as you want.' Then he just began to joke around with me. Then there was a day he went, he cocked the gun in my face: 'Let's go! Otherwise I'll kill you now!' 'Kill me if you're a man!' And he was my friend, he was walking with me ... I looked him in the face, like this: 'Friend? Bastard! You're lucky I don't kill you now 'cause I'm not armed.' Look in my face: 'Yeah, lucky because there are a lot of people on the street.' I went home, got a gun, and waited, watching. The kids saw me armed and said, 'Pedro's got a gun.' Then he saw me from above and started shooting. 'So, it's on!' I started shooting at him too, and hit him with one in the arm. 'Either you kill me or I'll kill you, just because you did that to me.' He left for the countryside and I stopped stealing after I got into that scrape. He committed a homicide in Curitiba, killed a guy, a policeman, I don't know. He got out and said he was coming here. I said it was either me or him.

He committed one more robbery and is still in prison today. I distanced myself, joined CEDECA and started with Lucas. He was my LA case worker, and he said at Nasce: 'Stay there and look after the children'. I said, 'Yes, I'll go.' I was super shy at the time. I arrived super shy, I met Neide, who is a colleague [of the Nasce technical team], who is from the church, Juliana, and they welcomed me. With trust, because no one would trust a boy who has such a precarious record, looking at his record and knowing his past. They don't know everything, because I've never told everything to anyone. You can't tell … There were things I told you about today … Before I didn't have the courage. Today, thank God. I'm alive because of God. The only one that protects me to this day is God, only Him.

CEDECA reappears, accompanying a new Assisted Freedom order. Again, this puts Pedro back in touch with other spheres of his family and neighbourhood, as well as monitoring his judicial process. Now, however, the moment also comes with the threat of death; Pedro is effectively on the threshold between a tragic outcome or a reconversion to the world of legitimate coexistence. He decides to try to make his way back from being a *bandido* to being a 'worker' again.

But crossing the boundary and leaving the 'world of crime' behind takes great effort. Narrated without much certainty, the scene of the fight with the friend is summarised to demonstrate the difficulties of leaving 'the crime'. The quarrel ritualises this passage and thus is described in Manicheistic terms: all or nothing, inside or outside, with me or against me, him or me. There is no fluid transit between these worlds, their boundaries are policed. The 'world of crime' is not an 'engagement regime' (Thevenot, 2006), which an actor moves in and out of. An individual may move between different action regimes on the same day – leaving his house, buying a baseball cap, going to school, and at night taking part in a criminal act, before returning home afterwards – but the boundary of identity which circumscribes the 'world of crime' cannot be crossed. This boundary delimits 'worlds' and controls the relationship between them.

For this reason, an individual 'conversion' is required. One has to 'exorcise' the thief within, remove this identity from the body. As studies have shown, conversion to neo-Pentecostalism often appears as a viable route of escape from the 'world of crime'. Having received many new converts since the 1980s (Almeida, 2004, 2009; Machado, 2018), neo-Pentecostal churches have specialised in providing passports and visas for those who wish to leave the 'world of crime' without becoming a 'clandestine' presence across the border. As mediators of such migrations, these institutions maintain diplomatic relations with illicit actors and their forms of organisation. At the same time, they maintain a clear distinction of conduct between one side of the boundary and the other.

In looking at the 'other' side, other people also appear in the testimony: Luke, Neide and Juliana, CEDECA educators who accompany Pedro's journey. A job opportunity arises: 'Stay there and look after the children.' 'Yes I'll go.' Pedro became an office assistant, then an educator, and began to receive a salary, a possibility created in agreements between the organisation and the municipal and state governments. At the time of our interview, he had been working at Nasce for three years. In 2008 he completed six years at the institution. The narrative re-enters the 'legitimate world' and the space in which we were sitting, around the rigid plastic table. At this point, the flow of the description shifts again. In a rapid inflection, Pedro's testimony takes up the same original parameters of justification. He rediscovers family, religion and work; he's once again in the 'legitimate world'. Pedro takes deep a breath and finishes his testimony like this:

I've never stolen anyone's pen. The only thing I wanted was to earn money and I started stealing to sustain my family. But my mother taught me one thing: if you see a pen on a table, you don't take it because it's a lack of respect. I only stole because I was in a lot of need at home, and I robbed others, from outside ... who had it [money], and not those who didn't. I helped people who didn't, I gave them money ... To this day, I help wherever I can. I got involved with the people [at Nasce] and I liked the children. I had never seen children suffering like this, like different, with walking disabilities, depending on others to eat, to use the bathroom ... My cousin is disabled, but I was never involved with my cousin. She can't walk and can't speak. I didn't have that contact with her. I have it today. Here I learned to have contact with children and to know how to live. How do you say it? My difficulty, which I have at home, which is financial, isn't the only kind that exists. Here, I learned to see children who can't walk, or who can walk, but can't talk, who have difficulties, Downs children, who are hungry too, and don't steal, don't need to steal, who live in a different way. The mother suffers like hell because she has such a child like that, who's ill. And I keep remembering that. The staff explained to me how to feed them, I went, I started; I was really scared, but I calmed down. I think God gave me a new life, I've managed to almost have a family, I consider it a family here. More than a school.

Now, today, I did a course before being registered as a Youth Agent and it helped me a lot. Because it had theatre, recycling, communication and computing. And I learned a lot. I had contact with things I'd known when I was little and that I'd abandoned, thrown away, because of the hatred that I had. I think the problem was more my mother, never in my life had I thought about losing my mother. Nowadays I say this: 'Yes, but one day everyone will. She died in a way, sick ... God, religion, I don't know ... Religion, each one has a style. I always go in for religion, but I'm not one of those [who is very dedicated]. I only know that I believe in the word of God. Everything He's done in my life to this day, I only believe in Him. My mother's flesh I lost, but her spirit became a heart that entered into my heart. And I think her strength, from above, made me stronger and made me wake up to life. Others people can talk bullshit, but she's my soul, what most protects me. The soul of my mother and God protect me, even today. I tell you that I'm not afraid to get into a fight today, I can't do that, but I don't go looking for it either.

Legitimacy in dispute

There are some people who look at me and scowl, but I've always respected to be respected. I think what matters most in the world is that you have respect for others. I think that with that you gain the trust of thieves and workers. I think that's right.

Coexistence of regimes

Back in the world of 'workers', Pedro can say, 'I've never stolen a pen from anyone.' But, perhaps due to the expressions he saw on the faces of his interviewers, he realised that it would be necessary to elaborate upon this a little more. It is at this moment that religious conversion and the value of legitimate work reappear. The testimony becomes a religious 'testimony'. And, as an epilogue, Pedro elaborates a synthesis of what he has learned in his transit back and forth across the boundary: 'what matters most in the world is that you have respect for others'. As a result, 'you gain the trust of thieves and workers'.

This phrase is significant. If by following this rule one wins 'trust' on both sides of the boundary, it is because in both domains this is a *shared* organising principle. And if this shared principle is 'what matters most', it is because in order to live it is necessary to earn respect from both sides. The moral-religious code seems to organise 'non-deviant' sociability in general, defining the criteria by which actions and subjects can be considered legitimate on both sides of the boundary. It is no wonder that the expression 'world' reappears with another meaning in this context: no longer as an expression of circumscribed universes (of 'crime' or 'worker'), but as something more all-encompassing, containing them both. In this moment of synthesis, the dispute for social legitimacy, which runs through the whole narrative, appears even more clearly. For the first time the 'thief' appears to hold the same status as the 'worker' and Pedro knows that, in order carry on, he must be a respected interlocutor for both. As such, even if he is back in the world of 'workers', he is still guided by his knowledge of the boundary. 'I think that's right.'

In fieldwork it was not uncommon to hear this synthesis. I have met many other young men and women who have crossed back and forth across the boundary of the 'world of crime', expending a great deal of energy in the process. The trajectories of these young people are almost always similar to Pedro's: there are invariably fluid daily circuits between family, work, the criminal justice system, social policies and 'crime', alongside the presence of a bipolar distinction in identity between 'workers' and *bandidos*. This is why the specialist literature that narrates these life trajectories is highly repetitive. Singular as they may be, and even if they have multiple outcomes,[6] the set of plausibilities that structures the trajectories of the 'boys of crime' is patterned. There are always money and consumer goods circulating freely across the boundary, although the transit of individuals is much more regulated. Illegalities are continually being converted into 'political merchandise', as described by Michel Misse (2006a, 2018), while at the same time delineating social hierarchies. There are always churches handling conversions like exit passes and entry visas, and there are always state institutions, weapons, victims and shootings at the inflection points of trajectories. There is, therefore, a lot of regularity in the boundaries that circumscribe the 'world of crime', in São Paulo and in the urban peripheries of other Brazilian cities. There is regularity in the relations between these boundaries and the totality of social relations.

During field research I have noticed that even young people who had never entered the 'world of crime' – representing the vast majority of the population – could not avoid referring to it. The ways that the boundaries of 'crime' are positioned relative to their families and social circuits are varied, but always self-evident. Sometimes they were school friends, cousins or brothers who 'got involved' in illicit activities, especially drug trafficking; in other cases, parents, uncles and aunts, or they themselves were invited to participate in criminal acts; mothers invariably expressed pride in having 'resilient' children. Boys and girls born to low-income families in the outskirts of the city in the 1990s know that the 'world of crime' is a domain that, whether you want to or not, you have to deal with. Coexistence between the 'legitimate world' of workers, and the 'world of crime' of the *bandidos* is an constitutive condition in their lives.

At an ethnographic level, it is quite clear that the social ordering internal to the 'world of crime' has expanded its capacity to shape the wider parameters of social organisation, and that the circulation of goods, services and discourses across the boundaries that delimit it is increasingly intense. On the other hand, the fact that the flows that cross the borders of the 'world of the crime' are more intense today does not make these boundaries less operative. On the other hand, the increased flows crossing them also call for increased selectivity and control of these boundaries, a control exercised mainly in the flow of people, and which has been contested between dominant actors in the 'legitimate' social world and in the 'world of crime'. In this way, the frontiers of the 'world of crime' become spaces of contestation for defining what is socially and publicly legitimate. They thus become implicated in strategies for managing territories and populations, especially in urban peripheries.

This dispute over legitimacy is already clear from an empirical perspective. Depending on the problem he faces, a young man from Sapopemba might, for example, file a labour suit or demand justice in 'courts' of the PCC; he might seek the services of a social organisation or ask a trafficker for help. He might get a job delivering flyers or start selling drugs. Depending on the interlocutor, these actions will be considered more or less legitimate, and, discursively, will appear more or less valid. But in everyday life any one of them might compose a repertoire of actions that it is possible to legitimise. I have argued above that urban conflict in São Paulo is not confined to the contestation of power in the institutional domain, but presupposes a prior conflict, within the social fabric, that defines the criteria by which social groups may be considered legitimate. With this perspective in mind, the boundaries of the 'world of crime' in the peripheries of São Paulo take on much broader political meanings.

3

Coexistence

Ah, my family … it's complicated. My brothers, I have three brothers in prison. In total, we're eight children in our house. Five brothers have already been arrested. Now there are three who are in
prison and two who are free. Lázaro even ended up giving volleyball
lessons in the neighbourhood, but it ended up not working out. He
didn't help himself, either, stealing and getting arrested. One, Raul,
who comes before me, was the most right-on in the house, the most
hard working. He married young, has a young son, worked, it was
all going well. But I think he couldn't stand to see himself working,
working, working and never having anything, and a lot of people
who didn't work having everything. He couldn't resist and ended
up stealing too. He was arrested. There was an escape, he ran away.
When he ran away, he was already regretting it. So he went to work
in a company, he got there. The boss was very annoying. He was one
of those people who doesn't know how to respect employees. He
shouted at everyone. He stayed three months, I think, and then left.
Then he started stealing again. He was arrested again, and is facing
two separate charges. He said he'll change when he leaves. Anísio is
about to leave too, he's already setting up a business. And the other,
Fernando, is a minor, the youngest, he's in FEBEM [Secure Centres
for Young Offenders, today *Fundação Casa* / House Foundation].
[Neto forgets Marcela, his sister who is also under arrest at the
time]. And we're waiting. I think by the end of the year they'll all
be together again. They haven't been for a long time. (Neto in 2005)

Despite Neto's expectation, 2005 ended without his family being
reunited. To this day it has not happened, and the hope of one

day reuniting the family ended in August 2009, when Anísio was murdered. Ten years on, in 2019, the second generation started to be arrested and shot. This chapter presents ethnographic research with the family of Ivete, Neto's mother, living in the favela of Jardim Elba, Sapopemba, in the East Zone of São Paulo.[1] I describe how the cleavage between workers and *bandidos* operates differently in three dimensions of the family trajectory: (i) within the domestic group; (ii) in the family's relationship to the favela and the neighbourhood; and (iii) in the contextual ways that the family – and its members – are represented in the public sphere. After that, I discuss some of the political implications of the radical opposition between workers and *bandidos* in public discourse, when compared to the transformed relationships between work, family and crime in contemporary peripheries. It seems to me that it is within this equation that the legitimacy enjoyed by the PCC in the district's favelas – and not only in them – becomes possible.

Neto, a twenty-five-year-old black man, was introduced to me by a coordinator at CEDECA when I started my research in the neighbourhood. With her hands on his shoulders, she said she wanted to give me an example of a special boy. In 2005 Neto was a capoeira teacher in the organisation, and he personified the ideal type of the 'rescue' of boys from the favela through cultural projects. He took advantage of the opportunity given to him and, unlike most of his siblings, was able to chart the trajectory of a worker. In 2007 he migrated from capoeira to working at a store in Tatuapé mall. In 2008 he was promoted to security leader of the same store and he now coordinates a team of seven employees. He even bought an engagement ring, but decided to postpone his marriage until later (having children would get in the way of his ambition to leave the favela). It was better to wait until he had more stability. Neto wants to have a different destiny from that of his brothers; that was the main theme of discussion from the first time we met.

At home it's us and my mother. There are six sons and two daughters. Of the six sons, I'm the third, the two oldest have children,
the two girls have children, and two of my younger brothers have
children. There are two who don't, and I'm one of the two. It's
because I'm very young, I just finished studying [high school], and
I plan to go to college. (Neto)

Neto always returned to the contrast between his choices and
those made by his brothers. In the first interview above it was
involvement in crime that defined this cleavage. Now the criteria
were gender and whether or not they had children. The distinctions generated further qualifications: studying and university
were always the stated objectives. I wanted to analyse this cleavage
further; I asked Neto if I could meet his family. 'Of course!' A few
days later I called him to schedule an interview with his mother,
Ivete. Neto met me at CEDECA and took me to his house. We
entered through a small, iron gate, that was always open, facing
the road. This was the boundary of the favelas in Madalena. The
easy access left me unconcerned, I could find my way back later
on my own.

Between the gate and the front door of the house there is a
cemented space. One of Neto's brothers was cutting a friend's hair
there with electric clippers. It was Alex, who used this cemented
area as his source of income: he had set up two video game
machines there, and from late afternoon small favela children
could have fun with five- and ten-cent chips. At night, it was the
teenagers who showed up. In the following years the area became
a garage, and then the foundation of a small bar was built.

Ivete was waiting for me in her room, combing her hair. There
was a living room with a kitchen and a bedroom behind. Upstairs
was another room, with a separate entrance, where the eldest
daughter, Ivonete, lived with her twelve-year-old son, Vitor. The
prospect of the interview generated excitement; several residents
wanted to tell their stories. I sat down on the couch. Ivete's
face was sombre, almost absent. Her arms and legs trembled

involuntarily, her appearance seemed to confirm the information I had received that she was very depressed. We spoke for almost two hours that first day. When she felt she'd finished her testimony, Ivete proceeded to call each of her children present to record quick testimonies. Then also the grandchildren, and finally her daughters-in-law. Sitting next to each of them in turn, from time to time she interrupted the conversation to add what she considered to be important information and reflections. Ivete told the stories of how she came from Salvador to São Paulo, of how drug traffic had greatly helped her family, and gave some examples. She asked Marcela to describe in detail what life in prison was like, how she had survived there. She interrupted Alex to tell me about the kidnapping that Lázaro (another of her children) had committed in the neighbourhood itself. The afternoon ended.

At the end of almost four hours of conversation, Ivete was much more relaxed, she had stopped shaking, she was a resolute woman. The transformation of her appearance, mediated by her narrative to me and Ana Paula, caught my attention and moved me. The day was over, and its impact on me had been enormous, though I had the feeling I had understood very little. The testimonies had a logic that for me, at that moment, mixed different things: family, community, crime and prison. The demarcation of family morality and what was considered to deviate from it was not regular. It was as if the family had placed these worlds in relation to one other, not in a watertight opposition.

At the same time, it was clear that this was not a family that shared the values of crime. It was not. Ivete's testimony is clear in this respect: it was precisely because of the children's adherence to a life of crime that Ivete had fallen into depression and, in recent years, that had been her biggest problem. The accounts of her suffering caused by the *decision* of the children to enter the life of the crime were, and are, always constant. I had the same sense with two other families, also favela residents in Sapopemba, whom I got to know in some detail in the following years.

Coexistence

When it's not easy to understand what's going on, it's time to describe. Putting together field notes and transcribed interviews, I assembled a general picture of the dynamics of the family at that time. It required a lot of cross-checking between the huge number of names mentioned, the key elements of each trajectory and their turning points. I visited again several months later. So much new information emerged that my map had to be redrawn. It was like this for two years. In the middle of 2007 I tried to organise everything, and the family story opened up so many issues that what was supposed to be a scheme to simplify things ended up being a complex web that I would try to decipher before each new visit. By 2010 it was no longer necessary to consult it – I felt like I was part of the domestic dynamic. By 2019 I was organising a second-generation scheme. The categories are the same. Ivete sends me a WhatsApp message telling me that 'it seems to repeat'.

Over those years, I heard many stories of violent crimes committed by Ivete's children and grandchildren. The invariably polite way in which I was received at their home and the ease of the boys' smiles, the beauty of their faces and the leisurely Bahian accent did not fit the stereotype of the *bandido*. When I walked to their house, entering the favela, sometimes the thought that I was going to visit *bandidos* affected me, and sometimes I even felt afraid. But the moment I shouted Ivete's name at the door, I felt bad about feeling afraid, it was absurd. Of course, the criminal acts of the brothers involved are understood as work. As paradoxical as it may seem, that is the case. And so, they are restricted to 'working hours'. The internal codes for criminal activities were always contained within meetings, planning and executing robberies, and sociability with peers. The space of the house and daily life were usually neutral to any conversation or reference to these activities. There, those who are *bandidos* in the social and public world are simply Ivete's children. To this day I still have contact with the mother and children. With each new visit a ritual unfolds: whoever is at the door greets me and invites me in to sit down, warns me that there is no coffee and starts telling me about what has been happening with the family. I ask about each of them, I tell them about my family, there is always a lot of news. Before we arrive, however, it is necessary to summarise how this family arrived in Sapopemba.

Ivete: from Salvador to São Paulo in eight years

My life there in Salvador was very painful. There was … as much suffering as here. [long pause]. There was a lot of suffering. My children and I were in a lot of need, I had a husband who beat me, he mistreated me a lot, who is the father of my children. So that's why I ran away from him. And I came here. I fled. (Ivete)

Ivete arrived in São Paulo in 1987. She left behind her husband and seven children. The oldest was ten years old and the youngest, the twins Alex and Lazarus, were two years old. An acquaintance of Ivete's already lived in São Paulo; she stayed with the friend for a few days, but couldn't remember where the house was. She recalled, however, that she had been mistreated there. She lived on the street and in other places she could live for free. Five years passed without her seeing her children. A sister of Ivete's, who had stayed in Salvador, had a telephone. But it was expensive. Life only improved a little when Ivete met a 'guy' and went to live with him. This man gave her a house in the Elba favela, where she still lives today, and gave her her eighth son, Fernando. 'The only one I wanted.'

Ivete tells me that she had fourteen pregnancies: four miscarriages and ten births. Eight survived to early childhood and were alive when I met her: 'I thank God every day that all my children are alive.' Her new husband worked, and her life in the favela, where she didn't have to pay rent, finally allowed Ivete make some plans. It also allowed her the possibility of helping those who lived nearby and building networks of reciprocity with her neighbours – called 'familiarity' ('*conhecimento*') in the favelas – which helped her to adapt to São Paulo. Familiarity brought odd jobs as a cleaner, and in 1992 Ivete had enough money and courage to try to bring her children from Bahia to São Paulo. She travelled to Salvador and learned that she had already lost legal custody of the children years earlier. She returned to São Paulo without the boys and spent three more years without seeing them. In 1994 she finally got a stable job on an assembly line at a metal parts factory. She sought out a lawyer to help her win custody of the children, and at the same time she received a phone call from Salvador. It was Marcela, her second daughter, who had been diagnosed with breast cancer and was close to death.

She decided to go and see her. She came to a redundancy agreement with her employer, as she needed the severance money to pay for the trip. When she arrived, she saw that the children were in a much worse situation than she had imagined, and much worse than they had been a few years earlier. Ivonete, at the age of eighteen, was subject to regular sexual abuse by her own father. Marcela, aged sixteen, had invented the history of breast cancer in a desperate attempt to bring her mother back. Having succeeded, she mutilated one of her breasts when Ivete arrived to prove the illness was real. The father had been unemployed for some time, he drank too much and was very violent. He beat the boys often. Given this terrible situation, it was at least possible that the court would grant Ivete custody of the children. And indeed it did. The migration was completed when Ivete and her seven children arrived in Sapopemba.

Eight years after the mother's arrival, and for the first time, her eight children were reunited. Everyone was happy except her second husband. Ivete's second marriage ended there. And that was no small thing. Without the job, and now without a husband to provide, with eight children to raise, Ivete realised that things would be complicated.

Strangers in Sapopemba: the search for protection

Oh, it was very difficult. Because I was unemployed, a single mother, I had them [to look after] … the streets were unpaved, my kids were the only black kids on the street. A friend came to me, who lived opposite, looked at me laughing and told me that I was going to raise my children to be *bandidos*. 'How are you going to raise your children all by yourself?' I told her that I had faith in God that they wouldn't go that way, you know? (Ivete)

The year is 1995, Ivete was unemployed and caring for the children on her own. The extended family had remained in Salvador. The accounts of the period emphasise both material deprivation and family estrangement. There are many references to the neighbourhood street market, which was the source of the family's livelihood. The boys guarded the cars of shoppers for small change. At the market they bought fish heads, carrot and beetroot leaves and other leftovers. With the small amount of money they earned, Ivete bought flour and made *pirão* and soup, which would have to last the week. She tells me that on Tuesdays and Wednesdays a small chicken farm in the neighbourhood discarded chicken carcasses, and poor families would gather there to receive them. It was humiliating, *too humiliating*, as they compared their poverty to the circumstances of their peers. But Ivete had only her second husband's pension – a little more than half a minimum wage, about R$600 (US$150) – to live on and a few days' rent from her eldest daughter, who was working as a cleaner.

At the end of the week, the boys went to the market to look after the cars. There were boys down here who beat them, took their money. […] One day the traffic knocked on my door, because I'd called the police on these boys. The trafficker came to my door. Then he saw that I was alone, it was all dark here … he saw that I was alone, they only threatened me, right? That I would have to leave if I called the police again. […] But I'm a determined woman, the next day I went to work and on my way back from work I went to look for the traffic. I went to look for him. […] I got there and explained my situation to him, the situation I was in, and the situation of my children at the market, you know? That I went to work, and when I came home, my children were locked inside the house, because the boys from the street beat them, they threw stones at the house, because it was open here at the front. And they were all small, the oldest was Ivonete and she was very shy, you know? So they understood. But they just asked me not to call the police any more, that when I needed to, I should go and look for them, that would deal with it.

And I really needed them, days later they came back. […] Then my daughter called, she said that those boys were messing around here at the house again, throwing stones. Then I told her to go and look for the guy. Then she went there, she looked for the guy, the guy came down here, he sent someone down, he didn't come himself, he sent someone down … and he warned him, right? That if they continued to bother the family, my family, that they would come down again and this time it wouldn't be to talk. […] And from that day on, I came to have, so … a … how can I explain to you? A dialogue. (Ivete)

A guarantee of security, in a situation like Ivete's, made all the difference. In this case, the police were not the most appropriate security force. In the favelas of São Paulo, since the early 2000s, much has changed. Year by year, I came across ever more testimonies that framed drug trafficking and local crime as part of the community, rather than opposed to it. If, in 2000, when favela residents referred to the community, the churches and organisations that coordinated collective action were the main point of reference; now it is a broader territory, in which several actors are represented, with the 'world of crime' in particular standing out. The explanation for this transformation is simple, and it was provided by rapper Mano Brown in a television programme: 'Who protects the community? Does the police protect it? It doesn't. So it has to protect itself.'[2]

As the case here shows, the state monopoly of legitimate violence is a fiction; the traffickers (or small businesses, as Mano Brown described them in the same television programme) and thieves gradually assumed the role of the armed force that regulates the rules of coexistence (what is allowed and what is forbidden) and provides justice, through constant debates about what may be considered inappropriate, illegitimate and immoral. Ultimately, the debates established by the crime to analyse such situations may resort to violence, including lethal violence. However, this violence will always be legitimate at the local level because it is supported by collectively accepted arguments, albeit ones based on a lack of alternatives.

Thanks to her 'dialogue' with the traffic, Ivete begins to be respected by the neighbours. The stigma attached to a single mother from a poor, black family from Bahia begins to be reversed. From there, she is able to access other spaces of sociability and, through these, obtains a job as a 'community health agent' in one of two teams of the Family Health Programme (Qualis) linked to the Unidade Básica de Saúde (Primary Health Centre, UBS) in Madalena. She gained the job through a public selection process which considered her voluntary engagement in community activities (linked to CEDECA) and with the UBS. It also took into account the respect that *workers* and *thieves* had for her within the favela, and the fact that she could visit any favela house, access any family. The minimum wage did not guarantee a change in the family's circumstances, but Ivete's network of contacts in the neighbourhood increased significantly. When I got lost in the favela, all I had to do was ask where Ivete lived, and anyone could point me there.

The kids' work: from licit to illicit

The late 1990s were a paradoxical time. Ivete's family earned two and a half minimum wages, paid no rent, and all the children were enrolled in school. Looking in from the outside, it seemed that things were starting to work out, soon the boys would be able to help a little more, life would gradually to improve. Ivonete, the eldest, had already got a better job in a family home and lived in a neighbouring area, still contributing to the budget. Neto got a job at CEDECA, Lazarus was also trying to follow the same path. However, it was in those years that the boys' involvement with crime became consolidated.

Marcela had already formed a relationship with the traffic while still living in Salvador, doing small services for them; by the time she was seventeen she had become addicted to crack. Her five younger brothers, all aged between ten and fifteen, also grew up close to the crime, which had a booming market at that time. In the 1990s drug trafficking established itself in the peripheries as the centre of gravity of a range of highly profitable transnational illicit markets that also included arms trafficking. As the years passed, the boys' lives were more and more affected by the violence surrounding the relationships that structure this world in the peripheries. At that time, São Paulo's homicide rate exploded: 'the violence was too much', Ivete told me. Many close friends of Ivete's children were murdered in the favela. 'Binho, Ze, Marquinho, o Bola …'. It is shocking to hear them recite the names as if they were discussing accounts. Ivete knew that at the point when the boys began to get involved, she had to try to find other work for them; and, as we have seen in other chapters, everyone has worked from an early age.

> I studied until fourth grade and then stopped to go to work. And I didn't get a vacancy [to study] at night. At that time up to a certain age you couldn't study at night. So I worked and didn't study. (Neto)

The market was enough for the children when they were young, but as they grew it provided diminishing returns. But, because they were there, five of the brothers (Neto, Lázaro, Alex, Raul and Anísio) were offered another opportunity: they were grouped together to help unload bundles of sugar cane from trucks at a warehouse nearby. The work provided a more reliable income, as it could be done every day and not just on weekends.

> There was a sugar cane depot up there. So we stayed there and we earned tips from the customers. Some time passed, then I started to work. [Question: Didn't you have a salary at the beginning?] Not at first, but later I did. I know that five of the brothers worked there at some point. (Neto)

When the boys started to be paid, it was calculated based on production: R$25 per thousand. That is, 1,000 *bundles* each containing a dozen canes, each unloaded from the truck, peeled, cut and gathered ready to be sold to the mills. This is the kind of remuneration offered to favela families for outsourced activities even today. The contractors were also residents of the neighbourhood. Again, we see the weight of the symbolic and objective distance between those who live in '*the houses*' and those who live in *the favelas*. The adolescents worked there for three or four years. It was a family business and they got to know their employers well, and received various kinds of assistance from them. They tell many stories about this period.

For a while a semblance of complementarity was maintained between these families, across their material, working and symbolic relationships. Flavoured with regular gossip, the interactions of familiarity between employers and employees produced a degree of harmonisation between opposites – a recurring trope in the history of relations between different social classes in Brazil.[3] However, in São Paulo at the turn of the millennium it was no longer possible to manage class conflict using the Freirean model of complementarity between elites and blacks. If Ivete appreciated the relationship with their supportive employers, Lázaro referred to the period in another way: 'slavery, man!' The relevance of the two points of view is the difference between the generations. It is not surprising that it was Lázaro who made the first explicit break with the ordering of family relations around work. At the age of fifteen he kidnapped the boss's teenage daughter, with a gun in his hand. They said he was in love with her. The story deserves quoting at length.

At the time that [the kidnapping] happened, I worked there, I was an employee of the family. And I've never been one to mess around, but my brother … I don't know how it happened, but they [the bosses] got the impression that some of my brothers were going to kidnap one of their kids. That was about fifteen days beforehand. And after a fortnight, the kidnapping actually happened. So she [the mother] immediately said that it was my brothers. I was near her house at the time. I went to meet my girlfriend at school, who is now my wife, but when I came around the corner I heard the screams. I came back and saw the car in front of her house. So I came here, I got my mum and I said 'let's see what's happening'. By the time I got there, her nephew was coming to speak to me. Then I got in the car and we went to look. But at that point I still didn't know what had happened. Then he explained to me … Oh, they kidnapped Érica, let's go back and see if we can find them. We walked everywhere, but we couldn't find them. Then we went back and stayed at their house. My mum told me that they thought it was one of my brothers … I stayed quiet. (Alex)

At the very moment it [the kidnapping] happened I wasn't sure whether or not Lazarus was involved, but then Alex came running, saying that the police were there at the boss's house. And that was on Av. Agua Espraiada. That I should go and see what was going on. […] We got there, the girl's mother was saying it was Raul, that Raul had kidnapped their girl. Except that Raul had been arrested eight days earlier. He said: 'It was either Raul or Lazarus.' So I went to look for Lazarus when I got here, but I didn't find Lazarus, and Lazarus usually came home early. That's when I got suspicious. Then I spoke [to the other boys] standing by the wall, I asked them. Lazarus arrived, and he spoke. And the boys said: 'It was him, with Teco and so and so.' They named the boys. So we went after them. I called a boy who was from the traffic and asked for help to rescue the girl. Because I couldn't get to the other guy, and they had already talked to them on the phone, 'look, give the girl back', they already know that Lazarus was involved, 'you're going down'. Then he [Teco] said, 'I'll only give her back when they give me the money', that is, he wasn't going to respect the girl. I had to ask for help from the traffic. The guy from the traffic helped me. (Ivete)

Turning point. In a quick shift, the whole frame of reference of the family's social existence is altered. Lazarus was an employee and suddenly becomes a kidnapper. Alex was friends with the children of the family and their cousins, and at a stroke he is suspected of complicity. The family of workers, on good terms with their bosses, becomes a nest of *bandidos*, a threat to order and peace. More than that, a contract has been broken. The rumours had already circulated, the teenagers' plans were already known to some. Lazarus had spoken to friends of his in the neighbourhood, the action had been prepared, one of his accomplices worked for the local trafficker. The unfolding of the story is exemplary of the plurality of authorities that favela families seek out in such cases: first, Ivete resorts to her direct personal patrons (even though they are the victim's parents); second, she asks for help from an authority in the 'world of crime', a normative body responsible for solving such cases.

> So I asked for the help of the trafficker, because I found out that the other kid involved in the kidnapping worked at his *boca*, that he worked for him. He [the trafficker] took a risk, he asked to keep the police out of the case, because the police were already involved, right? He took a risk, he went there with me, it was me, him and the mother [of the abducted girl]. [...] We went to get the girl, we rescued the girl. They respected the boss. They were afraid of the boss. We got there, the girl was there, she was fine. [...] If it hadn't been for the trafficker, he [Lazarus] could have either ended up dead or in prison because of this kidnapping. (Ivete)

Lazarus was neither killed nor imprisoned, but was punished by his boss. Above all, he owed him for the opportunity he had been given. Publicly, it was a small problem, a crime reported to the police that was later retracted. In the favela, the episode was widely commented on and, like many others, reinforced the legitimacy of crime as an authority in resolving conflicts. Ivete saved the girl and her son, but could not avoid the gradual firing of all the other boys from the small sugar cane company.

> Some time passed, and the guy fired me … I asked him if it was
> because of what my brother did, you know? He said no. But I think
> it was. […] I don't really blame him. (Alex)

It was clear that this extreme event had ruptured the previous agreement. 'I don't really blame him.' This breakup didn't
happen only in Ivete's family: the conflict between *houses* and
favela in everyday language and sociability seems to be the product
of such stories. The ordinary event is not news, the exceptional
is commented on for days and constructs meanings. The boys
lost their source of income. After a short while, however, this
would no longer be a problem – the logic of getting by on the
street (Gregori, 2000) had been learned early on, and the boys
knew that if licit work paid little, there were lucrative opportunities in the increasingly dynamic illicit labour markets that the
neighbourhood offered. Some of them had become accustomed
to committing petty crimes since their days working at the market.
Furthermore, if everyone already considered them to be *bandidos*
anyway, they should at least be able to gain something from this
reputation. From then on, their entry into the world of local crime
was gradual, ultimately encompassing four of the six boys.

> You get involved. You grow up and start getting involved. You end
> up getting involved in real crime, someone gives you a gun, you see
> the guys coming back from the job, with loads of money, and you
> want it too. […] I got to know the guys, I got involved. (Lazarus)

Lazarus repeats the standard testimony that I have heard several times during fieldwork: the need at home, the presence of
close colleagues in the 'world of crime', the amount of money that
comes back from a 'job' (a robbery or other criminal act). The
familiarisation with weapons, the ritual of the first criminal act and
the immediate reward in status and recognition. Things work out,
let's try again. As in the case of Pedro, in Chapter 2, we can see that,
usually (though not exclusively) among lower-income families, the
small proportion of boys and girls who enter find that crime is a

risky and highly challenging paid activity that, if performed well, opens the doors to consumption and recognition. This is no small thing for those who have never been able to consume and never saw 'the system at their feet', as rap group Racionais MCs put it in their song 'Tô Ouvindo Alguém Me Chamar' ('I Can Hear Someone Calling Me'). Remuneration for criminal work is highly varied, but is always attractive when compared to licit activities, and grows according to the individual's level of involvement with the structure of the business. In Sapopemba, if the 'lookouts' (usually young children or addicts) spend nights in the alleyways to earn up to five *reais* or a small amount of drugs, a seventeen-year-old boy can earn R$100 a night, selling drugs in a *boca* (or *biqueira*). His manager will receive R$200 to R$300 a night. 'Sometimes R$500.'

Access to firearms and insertion into this community facilitates the association of trafficking activities with other types of crime, which further expands potential income. In Sapopemba there are organised networks of robbery and car theft, where adolescents are subcontracted with fixed payments. If a boy earns R$200 to deliver a stolen car, the reseller can earn R$10,000 for a single vehicle. Pedro tells me that he even got invited to participate in the robbery of a mansion for R$40,000. Among the youngest and lowest paid in the business, the money obtained is a guarantee of immediate enjoyment of the basic consumer goods typical of the social life of young people in the peripheries: nice trainers, the latest cell phone, branded clothes and, if possible, motorcycles and cars with accessories and sound systems. Of Ivete's children, Lázaro and Anísio began to take part in house robberies from fourteen years of age, later in car robberies and, finally, in robberies of automated teller machines (ATMs). Fernando and Raul also stole, but mostly sold drugs. Marcela was the only one during this period who was already in the crime and getting only a small residual income: she used crack, she was a *'noia'* (crackhead), and therefore somewhat of an outcast.[4]

Coexistence

Ivete knew a good deal about the children's criminal activities, and she suffered greatly with this knowledge. She suffered in particular with the difficulty of trying to keep them on the path of workers, and with the risks which she knew that they faced. She reflected on their arrival in São Paulo. She believed it was just a phase. But, as they became the most well-known thieves and traffickers in the neighbourhood, Ivete's five boys started to be targeted by the police. A recurring story: the boys and their bosses settled many accounts with police officers, but at a certain point this was no longer possible – they started getting arrested.

Imprisonments

> I went to commit a robbery there in Jardim Santo André, in a pizzeria. I was fifteen years old. I was caught by the police and arrested. I think it was the third one I'd done, in that area. And then, I started to work a little, then I stopped for a while, was unemployed, but didn't mess around. Because the situation was bad, I started to get involved in the crime again. (Lazarus)

Lázaro was sent to a juvenile internment unit for the first time aged fifteen. The year was 2000, the family had been in São Paulo for five years. The first prison sentence always represents a fundamental shift, modifying the individual's status vis-à-vis both their primary sociability groups and the political system. Shortly after Lazarus, Anisio was also arrested for robbery. Marcela was the third, holding up bus on Sapopemba Avenue. Then Raúl, and finally Fernando. All had been through detention facilities and prisons several times since then.

With the arrest of one family member, domestic dynamics and networks of sociability in the neighbourhood change, as we saw in the previous chapter. The family is seen differently by neighbours and distant relatives; but above all, by the police. Another recurring scenario: Ivete's house becomes the target of frequent police raids. Beyond the everyday effect of the transformation of all the group's social relationships, they must deal with the subjective impact:

> When my first [son] was arrested, I had a major crisis, but I was still clear-headed. I was very nervous, very shaken and everything, but ... I was lucid, I continued to work and everything. When my second child was arrested, I still held on. Now when the third, my daughter, was arrested ... because of the fact that she used drugs, that she'd left home, that I fought a lot, a lot, to get her off the drugs ... I went several times to the *boca* to get her, to know that she was robbing buses, the risk she was running, that I had fought [for her] ... and I looked after her two children ... so I guess that's when I started to have my own crisis, right? [...] And that left me bedridden, it made me really bad.
>
> I had a mental disorder. I went ... as they say ... I went mad. I didn't recognise anyone, didn't eat, I didn't drink water ... And I went twenty-five days without recognising anyone. Not even my children. They went into the room, they went out again, and I was under the covers. Either I was crying or I was sleeping, either crying or sleeping. I got to the point of losing all clarity, all clarity. (Ivete)

The intensity of suffering experienced in cases like Ivete's belies any interpretation that would paint violence in the peripheries as something that is trivialised. As can be seen, nothing about it is trivial. During fieldwork I encountered numerous cases of nervous breakdowns and diagnoses of depression and mental disorder associated with similar situations. In the case of Ivete, the crisis was further intensified following the arrest of Raul – the 'most right-on', as Neto had said – and, finally, when Fernando, the youngest, was first interned in FEBEM.

> I told him [Fernando] that he was my only child who had received everything I could give. And that he was the only son who I could afford to give trainers that cost R$200, because his father pays alimony. It's a little, but it's enough. That he did not need to steal, that if he studied I would give him 50 *reais* every month, from his pension, for him to take ice cream with his girlfriend, to walk ... but that he would not enter this life, that this life would lead him to nothing. So the next week he was arrested, arrested for stealing

a car. So I do not blame myself, right? I suffer a lot because he was there … because I had him, I had a lot of affection for him, because he was the only son I really wanted, that was from my second marriage. The other children was on the basis of suffering, which I had. I suffer a lot today, I'm very sad about it, but I'm accepting it. (Ivete)

The earthquake caused by the first three imprisonments lasted more than a year, the most difficult phase. Then two more children became *bandidos*. In 2005, when our interviews began, Ivete had begun to qualify her despair: 'I am very sad, but I am accepting it.'

Polarity and composition

Fernando was deprived of his liberty in 2003. He was released only in 2008, and Ivete returned to the favela to work as a community health agent. Eight years after Lázaro's first detention, therefore, the internal cleavage between the working children and the *bandidos*, the basis of Neto's narrative, had stabilised. The situation was no better – Marcela had spent months in the area known as Crackland [Cracolândia], in the centre of São Paulo, and had returned to prison. Raul had been in prison for four years and was sentenced to six more. Anísio continued to commit robberies, which were increasingly specialised and risky. Lázaro sold drugs in the neighbourhood and Fernando alternated between months in licit employment and periods in the traffic. Everyone was well known to the police, they frequently had to 'settle accounts' to avoid arrest. However, at least there were no more surprises: the same five children 'caused stress' to Ivete, the other three continued their lives as workers. And, in the end, she accepts it.

These days I no longer feel guilty about them. While some have opted for the life of the crime, there's Neto, there's Alex, there's Ivonete, right? The three did not enter the life of the crime, they didn't take drugs. I'm so proud of Neto: he's going through great difficulties, […] but he remains firm. He even said to me: 'I'll fight to get into university; you have eight children here, here at least four, four should have gone to university. But no, they all chose the life of the crime … because they wanted to. It wasn't because you wanted them to. It was because they wanted to. You didn't make them go. If you had made them, I would have gone too, Alex would have gone, Ivonete would have. But no, they went because they wanted to. And there's no use, you can't change that. You must now take care of yourself.' (Ivete)

In the division of labour within the family that contrasts the working children to the *bandidos*, a specific type of nexus is created between them. Neto and the other two working children maintain their mother's stability with narratives like the one expounded above – they alleviate her sense of responsibility for their siblings' trajectories and reaffirm their commitment to honesty and work. If 'there's no use, you can't change that', all that is left is to live with the fact that the family is in the crime. 'The neighbourhood is like this', after all. As the research proceeded, this discursive polarisation within the family and the ways in which it provided relief from the family's broader dynamics became increasingly clear. However, something unsuspected also increasingly came to my attention: it was only the working children who spoke about themselves, contrasting their experiences to those of their siblings. They were always emphasising the resilience they had needed and the difficulties they had encountered in trying to stand firm and stay on the right path. It was they who always struggled to differentiate themselves from those in crime. And they harshly criticised their siblings' choices.

It's like this: a worker can't buy a shoes that cost … now it's cheap, but that costs R$500. Or a car that costs R$5,000. A worker, in order to buy something like that, he will have to work ten, fifteen years, to be able to buy that. And in the traffic, you work twelve hours, what you earn in twelve hours in the traffic is the same as fifteen, twenty days of work, depending on your salary. So many boys get recruited. (Alex)

From my point of view, it's better to be a worker than to be a drug dealer. Also because the traffic only gives money to the bosses, the workers [in the traffic] never get much. The worker [in the traffic], lots of them manage to buy a car, to buy clothes, to buy furniture for the house. But you never have peace. You go to sleep, and sometimes the police invade your house. That's how it works. Like if you're a drug dealer, or a thief, there will always be someone or the other with their eyes on what you have, so you start attracting enemies, and there comes a time when people who want what you have come and kill you. It's not worth it. So it's better not to have anything ... and the real boss doesn't even live here, does he? You wouldn't stay here ... he'll be somewhere far away, somewhere nobody knows. And he's just collecting money. (Alex)

If everyone worked, had a good job, registered, do you think it would be necessary for this house to be the way it is? I didn't even need my mother to work; if everyone contributed, we would have a good life, wouldn't we? A good salary for everyone, right. But no, they want to stay in that easy life. You sleep, wake up at noon. [Ivete interrupts: 'the life of a thief'; Ivonete continues:] Yeah ... not a thief. Of a sucker, because I think like this, and it's not because I'm Evangelical, because I always lived like this: if I was going to go down the wrong path, I would have to make a lot of money. [...] Because that's it, the guys steal, they sell drugs, they're trapped and they don't have a towel to carry, they don't have a bedsheet, they don't have underwear. [...] If I wanted to, I had plenty of opportunities to get in [to the crime]. [...] Look, and it's not a problem with their heads, these things. It's their own behaviour. Because if it was a problem in the head, I'd have the same problem. If anyone should have a problem it's me, because I suffered the most with my father. I always had the most problems of anyone, I always had more difficulties, and despite that I never went into the life of the crime, I never used drugs, nothing. (Ivonete)

As we can see, Alex says that trafficking gives money only to the bosses, that workers in the traffic don't get what they want, that it's an illusion. Ivonete says that if her brothers earned real money, the crime would pay, that the person who has a real justification for entering crime is her, as she suffered more than anyone else with their father. In the workers' argument, therefore, the central problem is that crime does not yield what it promises, as much as it promises. Compared to what common sense might dictate, the burden of justification is thus reversed: it is Ivonete, Alex and Neto who are forced to find justifications for not having opted for the life of crime. The recurring need to reaffirm their arguments, and to make them more sophisticated, only confirms the strength that the alternative option presents.

Maybe for this reason the five family members who live in the 'world of crime' don't need to say much. None of them makes the slightest effort to create a counter-argument to dispute the arguments of their worker siblings; nor do they strive to form a group of thieves to challenge the workers in the house. Each one always speaks only for him or herself; only to justify their entry into crime with standard responses, when encouraged. They always emphasise, however, that no one goes hungry anymore in the family. The time of making *pirão* out of fish heads begged for in the market is over. The interaction between the groups of siblings thus represents a recomposition of the parameters of solidarity of the family group, which allows the internal coexistence of workers and *bandidos*.

A situation which I observed seems to me to be paradigmatic of this new code. I was at Ivete's house, accompanied by Almir, a friend of the family, when Lazarus arrived. By car, music playing loudly, baseball cap to one side, 'thief style' (as he told me). The boy stopped in front of the house and left the car open. But he turned off the sound and took his cap off before entering. At the gate, he took a huge bundle of money out of his pocket, which he counted and recounted several times, displaying it. Seeing the scene, Alex immediately asked for R$50 for the gas; and Lázaro promptly handed it over. They quickly commented that a friend, an acquaintance from the Elba favela, had been murdered. Alex left, with Lázaro's car. Almir asked him to keep the money, it wasn't right to show everything on the doorstep like that. If the police arrived, everyone would be arrested. A minute later, Lázaro opened his mother's purse and placed some R$10 bills in there, without her noticing. Another R$10 went into his own wallet. He then walked to the front of the house; called over a boy on the corner (who must have been about ten years old) and gave him the rest of the money. The boy ran to make the delivery to his boss. Lázaro continued the conversation with Almir, they are old friends.

For the five children involved in crime, therefore, there is no need to provide discursive justification for their presence in the house. Their function in the family finds a different form of validation, with their financial contribution being the central element. In order to provide greater comfort for their mother, to somehow repay her for the stress and pain they cause her, to help with household costs, collaboration over the family's budget seems to have become a structural factor maintaining the cohesion of Ivete's family. It is through this polarity between the workers and the *bandidos* that the condition of reciprocity between them arises within the family. The internal disagreements, producing specialisation of their different functions, maintain the family's internal and social cohesion.

Here, the paradox initially identified by Neto finds resolution. It would not be possible to say that the crime has overwhelmed the morale of the family: within the family home they do not speak about cars, motorcycles, music and women, themes and objects at the centre of their sociability with friends. That's why, when he gets home, Lázaro turns off the sound, takes off his cap and takes the money out of his pocket. However, the working family has not defeated the crime either: no one demands that the boys stop their criminal activities, partly because they help to support everyone, they are fundamental to the domestic routine. And this is not only in Ivete's house.

[There's a case here that] the whole family is involved with the traffic. The mother is alone and even she's involved. You see her life situation, it's just like mine. [...] And I can't change it. I try, even try ... I try to give advice to one or another: 'Ah, why are you in this life? Get out of this life.' But the money is a lot of money. It's a lot of money. And [without it] we would go hungry, right? (Ivete)

The working children support the structure of the group symbolically. They are the mother's pride and joy. On the material plane, however, the household's livelihood is guaranteed by the children in the crime. The family thus has both symbolic and material providers, which allow it to be maintained in both spheres simultaneously. Once this new condition is in place, the crisis tends to be resolved, albeit only provisionally. Between the discursive patterns relating the period of the first prison sentences, which had left Ivete in bed, and those during the last visits before Anísio's death in 2009, I noticed a clear displacement. In 2008 Ivete made a joke about the 'comings and goings' of the children between prison and the favela: 'I'm just waiting to see who will be the next to be the governor's guest,' she would tell me, smiling, resigned.

Ten years ago, by 2009, I had known the family for nearly five years and I was particularly close to Ivete, who had picked herself up from the crisis of the previous years: she had gone back to work, she cut her hair every fortnight, she thought about travelling and started to believe that she could marry again. Neto had bought a car in instalments, Ivonete had set up her salon in a house in Madalena and Alex had stopped working with video games and was leasing a bar in the favela. They showed that it was possible to build their lives through work, they showed that their mother had given them values. But they could not help her materially.

Anísio, who specialises in ATM robberies, had paid for the renovation of Ivete's house and had even hired Alex as a builder. That was where the idea came from of building a bar at the entrance to the house, so he could stop paying commercial rent. Lázaro continued to bring in money to the house, for petrol, the comings and goings of the siblings; and Fernando, still young, was able to support his ex-wife, his girlfriend and his son with what he earned in the traffic. Marcela and Raul remained in prison. The refurbishment of the house, paid for with money from crime and carried out by a working son, symbolised the reconstruction of a project which held Ivete's life together.

This was a project in which individual choices were clearly tolerated.[5] After a few years, the crisis and the remodelling of the house gave rise to an individualisation of life trajectories, albeit subordinated to commitment to the family group. The prisoners did not request visits within this configuration, nor did Ivete feel it necessary to visit them.[6] The family resumed its condition of protecting the individuals in the larger group, although it no longer expected model participation from all members. Cooperation and mutual protection for the survival of individuals persist as central to the code.

The emergence of crime in the peripheries thus reconfigured survival strategies, attitudes towards work and what is legitimate, and even affected the domestic universe of families like Ivete's. This reconfiguration of the structuring pillars of social dynamics in the urban peripheries is still underway, and what will emerge from them is still uncertain. If, publicly, worker and *bandido* are opposites, in the interior of numerous families living in favelas and peripheries in São Paulo today, both licit and illicit activities are articulated, both in providing subsistence and for inserting individuals into broader social circuits. Under adverse external circumstances, the group maintains solidarity: it doesn't matter how; what matters is that they protect one another. The moral crisis is dealt with rationally, condemnation of criminal activities ceases. This is an option like any other.

Crime and work become represented as an individual choice – and each choice produces a set of consequences, a lifestyle and so on. Everyone knows the codes of both, and both can be accommodated within the family. Between them, crime and work can guarantee the functioning of the house. The first more clearly contributes financially, although it makes the family vulnerable to the police and eventual tragedies; the second is less profitable, but is socially legitimate, more sustainable over time. In this nexus of practices – none of it is purely discursive – workers and *bandidos* are not opposed.

Fracture

Ivete's family passed through a new phase of hope in mid-2009. The boys' income was more steady, all were grown up, Ivete was feeling better. Ivonete had moved house and planned to get married. But, as might be expected, tragedy was around the corner. In early August 2009 I when to meet Ivete at the health centre where she worked. I was pleased to see her again, we always got along well. She hugged me, asked me to sit down and asked if I knew what had happened. I didn't know. She told me that Lázaro had been expelled from the favela and had been told he could never return. 'He did what no thief can do: he grassed.' She wept uncontrollably and said she would never see him again. She described how it all came about – so as not to be arrested again, Lázaro had made a deal with the police. Since June of that year he had been informing for them. The scheme was discovered and two debates were carried out by the crime to determine his future. Miraculously, Lázaro escaped with his life, but was beaten almost to death and placed, an hour later, on a bus to a city in the Northeast. He runs the risk of being killed there and was warned that he could not return to São Paulo. Anísio participated in the discussion and was told that he would have had to take part in his brother's beating. Ivete cried a lot, at some points she seemed to lose consciousness. I hadn't seen her in years.

I returned home, and the next day Anisio was murdered with his friend and neighbour, Orelha, in a criminal act. The story was told in the following terms by a friend of the family: 'Anísio, he died. Murdered. Ivete is devastated. He who was the one who was paying for the renovation of her house, who most helped her out.'

Misfortune never comes alone, they told me. Ivete spent months bedridden, cared for by friends in the favela who had also had children murdered. Ivete left her job once again and went back onto the psychiatric medication. Since then, Anísio's photo was on the wall, and there was nothing sadder than seeing it. The situation became worse still in December 2010, when her youngest, Fernando, was found dead in the favela.

4

Crime and punishment in the city: repertories of justice and homicides in São Paulo

When faced with everyday situations that they consider to be unjust, residents of São Paulo's peripheries may appeal to different sources of authority in pursuit of justice. The choice of which authority to approach depends on the type of problem in question. For example, if a man has a job and for years has not received the overtime to which he is legally entitled, he will go to a labour tribunal. If a mother does not receive the alimony owed by her ex-husband, she will contact the civil justice. If she has had a child unjustly imprisoned, or if she has suffered police violence in the favela where she lives, she will try to appeal to the press and, if that doesn't work, to human rights advocates. Where all else fails, there is always recourse to 'divine justice'. But if someone has been robbed, beaten, coerced or killed (and the perpetrators were not police officers), a complaint will be made to a local authority in the 'world of crime'. If necessary, through the intermediation of '*irmãos*' ('brothers', or members of the PCC who have been baptised into the organisation), a 'debate' will be arranged that can arbitrate the dispute and pass sentence to ensure that justice is done.

Thus, in addition to the state and the law, a resident of São Paulo's peripheries will also tend to identify a range of other authorities as legitimate sources of justice: (i) participants in 'crime' and, above all, in the PCC, who have gradually been legitimised as caretakers of the 'law' (also called 'ethics' or 'proceedings'), based on customs that govern the conduct of the *bandidos* wherever they live; (ii) the mass media, in particular television (from popular and police programmes to the television news, where individuals can seek to publicise the tragedies and injustices they have experienced and, in this way, appeal for some kind of restitution); and finally, hovering over them all (iii) divine authority, the supreme force that offers redemption to those wronged – in the afterlife for Catholics, and as worldly prosperity for followers of neo-Pentecostal denominations. Among the latter, which have grown steadily in the territories discussed here, conversion can lead to very real worldly benefits (Birman and Machado, 2012; Almeida, 2019a).

Contrary to what might be assumed, the existence of this repertoire of different justice authorities does not make the rule of law, or official legality, irrelevant in the eyes of these subjects. Residents of the peripheries are perhaps the social group that is most active in pursuing the law to guarantee their formal rights, which always remain under threat. The pursuit of justice across different channels that we observe in this context is much more a question of instrumental decisions, grounded in everyday experience, than one of idealised normative principles. As it is very difficult – at times impossible – to access all of the theoretically guaranteed rights by recourse to the state and legal system, individuals appeal to other authorities that they perceive as complementary to them.

This chapter does not address the entire repertoire of authorities and forms of justice, nor the social order that coexists in the peripheries of São Paulo. I do not examine the use of the media or of churches, nor methods and forms of justice pursued by civil society organisations defending social or human rights. Rather, I focus on describing and analysing the norms of conduct that prevail in the peripheries of city, and the mechanisms of arbitration established to deal with cases of noncompliance. It is these 'debates', overseen by criminal factions (particularly the PCC), that have helped to entrench these groups' legitimacy and authority.

Studying these mechanisms is important because the internal logic that governs the mechanism is radically different from the logic of democratic rights, and yet it has taken root in the peripheries of the city since the 1980s – precisely during the period in which a democratic legal justice system was created in the country. This last paradox interests me especially, because it is central to the key question that has driven my research in the peripheries of São Paulo for more than ten years. This can be summarised as the attempt to understand the ways in which peripheries appear in public spaces, and the ways in which these appearances have transformed since the late 1970s, including the distinctly political meanings that have emerged.

In this research agenda the notion of politics is central. I have always understood it, in a broad sense, as the set of conflicts implicated in the construction, maintenance and transformation of public life. In social contexts exhibiting great asymmetries of power, and reproduced in the structure of the state, politics is not limited to the disputes carried out between actors constituted in institutional spaces, but also presupposes a prior conflict: that, played out within the social fabric itself, which determines the criteria by which social groups come to be considered legitimate or illegitimate.[1] Thinking about politics in the urban peripheries thus implies studying the ways in which the legitimacy of actors and actions is constructed in the social fabric, in public debate and, finally, in state institutions. The dispute for legitimacy in each of these spheres constitutes a fundamental condition for the construction of a subject or public space, which is also a constitutive dimension of political conflict.

This chapter is organised in three parts. In the first I outline, along general lines, the radical transformations in social dynamics that have occurred in the peripheries of São Paulo since the 1970s. Based on this context, in the second part I analyse the 'justice of the "world of crime"' by describing different 'debates' that I have collected in fieldwork and documentary research. In the third part

I analyse correlations between the implementation of mechanisms of justice internal to the 'world of crime' and the reduction of São Paulo's homicide rate, developing an analytical argument about the necessary structural symmetry of analyses of justice, crime and politics in contemporary Brazil.

Displacements

From the 1970s to the 1990s the debates relating to urban peripheries were clearly established in the Brazilian social sciences. The study of low-income work, syndicalism and the emergent industrial working class in these territories developed over three decades, accompanying the (radical) transformations that unfolded over the period. The scale of migration to the Southeast of Brazil, the impacts of the constitution on the urban popular classes and metropolitan implications, as well as the specific characteristics of the working-class family and transformations of Catholic religiosity in urban environments, were common themes. The questions of favelas, urban infrastructure and the metropolitan housing deficit were key concerns both for intellectuals and for militants. The effervescence of the mobilisations in these territories during the 1980s shifted the debate onto themes of urban social movements and, in the following decade, to reflections on the construction of democracy, participation and public policies.

Underlying these analyses, therefore, was the recognition that the social dynamics of the peripheries centred upon the categories of work (especially industrial), family, migration and religion embedded in the promise of regular Fordist wage labour. The project of intergenerational mobility within the working family, which was the contextual synthesis of these categories, constituted the nexus of meaning that linked the peripheralisation of the great industrial centres to the project of national modernisation. The prospect of integrating these masses became, as it were, the founding myth of the social dynamics of these territories. A common

129

perspective among older generations even today, this narrative had sufficient strength to maintain the social cohesion of São Paulo's peripheries until the 1990s.

Since then, analyses have followed empirical transformations in each of these spheres, which came to be understood as representing a crisis. If labour continued to be the central category structuring sociability in the peripheries, the crises of structural unemployment and flexible accumulation permanently displaced the centrality of the 'project' of the Fordist worker. If Catholic popular morality was still very present, neo-Pentecostalism grew ever stronger. If social movements continued to act, their representativeness had begun to be questioned, both in public space and in the social fabric (due to the appearance other actors claiming to represent the peripheral population). The generation born in the 1990s were no longer migrants, could no longer dream of the stability of industrial employment, as had been the case for two or three decades, and, therefore, no longer saw the possibility for family mobility. Under these conditions expectations for a better life, when they existed, had become individual.

In my fieldwork it is fairly common to hear the narrative of these displacements, in individuals' testimonies and life trajectories, linked to the growth of violent crime. The transformations of work, family and religiosity have regularly been described to me as something that rubbed up against the boundaries of the 'world of crime', which undermined 'community' and even 'family' coexistence. 'It wasn't like this before!' The theme of 'violence' and the references to a criminal universe have emerged, in my own and many other studies in the peripheries of São Paulo (Marques and Torres, 2005; Telles and Cabanes, 2006; Almeida, D'Andrea and De Lucca, 2008), as spheres closely linked to the displacements of fields that structured everyday life. Violent crime, according to this perspective, is linked to displacement throughout the social world.

When I began to study the young people involved in the 'world of crime' in Sapopemba – one of São Paulo's ninety-six districts, with a population of some 300,000 and bordering on the municipality of Santo André in the so-called 'ABC' region – I became aware that, for them, the 'crises' of work, family and Catholic religiosity, which had led to the breakdown of their parents' collective projects of social mobility, were already considered a constitutive element of their being in the world. That is to say, these were no longer 'crises'. These young people's trajectories were already so heavily shaped by the inevitability of the new scenario that they already engaged with a new repertoire of possibilities for individual and collective action founded well beyond family, industrial work and Catholicism. This displacement, which I have explored recently in other works, made a series of arguments to legitimise the 'world of crime' as a space of legitimate social relations like any other, albeit among a small minority of the population. However, this 'world' plays specific roles: it is both a source of income generation (which therefore is in symbolic competition with the world of work) and, as is of particular interest here, a normative locus for social dynamics and the pursuit of justice (which symbolically contests the status of the law and the justice system). It is with regard to this last aspect that I shall continue.

'Crime' as protection

In the situation that Ivete's family faced, in the previous chapter, having protection made all the difference. She needed some kind of support and 'the traffic' provided it, at the same time relieving the police of this responsibility. Analytically, 'the traffic' drew Ivete's family, like so many other residents of Sapopemba's favelas, into a regime whose normative ordering was distinct from the legal order and responsive to a different authority. As we can see from Ivete's account, the norm of protection that was made available to her came attached to the condition that she would not involve the police, i.e. official legality. Essentially, the trafficker told her that not bringing police into the favela was the condition both for the family to be allowed to stay in the area and for it to continue to receive protection.

It so happens that, from the perspective of the family, this new arrangement works better than the first. And in this way it becomes legitimised: the police came to investigate the violence against Ivete's children, but the problem was not resolved. However, once the trafficker intervened, the matter was settled definitively. Ivete tells me this story to explain how, from then on (a period of fifteen years), she has maintained 'dialogue' with 'the traffic' in the area where she lives, with the latter guaranteeing the protection of her family.

During the 1990s, when Ivete first talked to the traffic, there was no PCC and Elba favela was the scene of bloody conflict between rival groups. The violence 'was too much', in Ivete's words. But eventually it stopped. The so-called 'pacification' of relations within the 'world of crime' began at the beginning of the 2000s and became consolidated in 2003 when, according to successive reports from the field, the 'brothers' took over the task – which had previously fallen to the main local trafficker – of ordering the 'world of crime' and making its internal operations and negotiation function without conflict. With the success of this initiative, and with various drug sale points coming to obey the same 'law', a single 'command', armed disputes between them disappeared.

Due to this, I observed a clear shift in the testimonies of residents of the peripheries regarding the 'world of crime'. Something that had previously been alien to 'families' and distant from 'workers'' lives became part of everyday life for a new generation. Modes of organisation that had emerged in prisons, and initially remained restricted to them, became part of the social fabric of favelas. Norms that were previously exclusive to those considered *bandidos* also began to creep into forms of sociability among young people not involved in illicit markets. In this way, dynamics that had been external to the 'community' gradually became constitutive of it.

The use of armed violence is, of course, the ultimate source of the legitimacy and authority of the 'world of crime' and the 'brothers' in the peripheries of the city. However, at the level of the everyday, these groups also oversee much more subtle aspects concerning disputes over norms of coexistence. These include claims about what constitutes acceptable behaviour, the 'attitudes', 'disposition' and 'procedures' that can protect these, and the offer to provide 'justice' for those who need it. In what follows I shall explore the complexity of this 'justice' system, based on empirical examples.

The 'justice of crime'

The 'world of crime' in São Paulo has its own 'ethics', 'law' and, in order to judge deviations from these, specific processes of enforcement that have been instituted since the beginning of the 2000s. In my field experience, in dialogue with other researchers working on similar themes and in reading journalistic accounts (especially those published after the May 2006 attacks), cases of conflict mediation by 'brothers' of the PCC – both among favela residents and among individuals involved in crime – have been a recurring theme.

Although somewhat arbitrary, for the sake of description and categorisation I think it is possible to analyse the complexity of this everyday apparatus at three different levels: (i) there are debates that deliberate on 'minor infractions' that can be solved by a quick 'chat' between individuals in the area where the incident occurred; (ii) there are cases of medium gravity, which have to be arbitrated by consulting other 'brothers' who are more highly respected in the 'world of crime' and who are not present in the locale, via cell phone; and (iii) there are cases of life and death, which are decided only after 'debates' that are much more complex than the first two cases, in which several individuals occupying positions known as '*torres*' (towers) reach a consensus (Biondi, 2016).

Sentencing is carried out in line with the PCC's ethical

principles, and is based on the performance and statements of both the accused and the victims. There is room for wide-ranging arguments to be made by the accusers and, above all, by the defence – in which the virtue of the individual must be demonstrated (Marques, 2007; Feltran, 2018). The debates are agonistic and deliberative. Ultimately they can determine who may live, kill and die. Below, I present cases from the field and documentary research in which these three levels of arbitration and implementation of sentences have occurred.

Minor infractions

The boys who stole the money from Ivete's children at the markets in the example outlined in Chapter 3 did not even have to receive a 'corrective' or beating. In fact, they did not even receive a direct warning: it was enough for the '*dono*' (boss) of the drug sale point to simply send a warning that he would personally come to resolve the problem if necessary. At that time there was no PCC in the area, but today the 'brothers' would probably do the same thing. More recently, problems which have come to the local 'crime' have been dealt with using the codes. Some concrete examples include: a couple who often quarrelled in the Madalena favela in the middle of the night, and whose screams bothered their 'working' neighbours; an incident where some teenagers stole a car near the favela and attracted the police, who chased them in; in the same favela, a boy who stole the bicycle of an acquaintance of the manager of one of the '*bocas*'. In another episode, a case of female marital infidelity surfaced, and the husband declared his intention to kill his wife. All of these situations demanded intervention by undermining the expected norms of conduct.

In all these cases, therefore, 'the crime' immediately responded. Quick 'debates' were convened to arbitrate the cases and impose appropriate measures, aiming to provide satisfaction to the injured parties without the need for violence. As I was told, these debates decreed that: the husband and wife were forbidden from shouting loudly during the night, so as not to disturb the neighbours, and the problem was resolved; the boys who stole the car near the favela, attracting the police, received a verbal warning and told that the next time they would face serious consequences; the boy who stole the bicycle had to return it and apologise to the victim, and it was made clear he shouldn't mess up like that again; the betrayed husband was allowed to give his wife a 'corrective', but was denied 'the right' to rape or kill her.

In all of these cases, it was a first offence, there were attenuating factors and a second chance was offered to the 'deviant'. In all of the cases, even if there had been 'debates', it was on the local level (in the '*quebrada*') that the dispute was resolved. In all cases, the 'law' invoked was local norms; however, it ultimately rested on a broader principle, which is shared across many '*quebradas*': the need to resolve conflicts in such a way as to avoid the injured parties resorting to the use of private violence, which would launch a cycle of revenge and an escalation of lethal violence among favela residents.

More serious infractions, but which can still be redressed

Young people involved in drug traffic who misappropriate money earned from drug sales, act irresponsibly and cause trouble, commit an act of insubordination or generally fail to observe the principles of '*crime*', when they are judged in 'debates' are generally sentenced to punishments more severe than verbal warnings. Jorge, a boy I met in 2005, when he was eighteen, went through a 'debate' in 2006. He had been in charge of a drug and arms deal which, due to either incompetence or deception (I was never able to confirm which), produced a loss to the 'firm'.

> What happened was this, he ended up getting involved in a situation where merchandise and a weapon were stolen. It was he

who was in charge, and it seems he'd trusted a guy who ended up screwing him over. (Luiza, Jorge's friend)

If the 'vacillation' had occurred at the end of the 1990s, it is almost certain that Jorge would have been summarily killed. But in 2006, under the new 'law' of '*crime*', he was tried, with a right to defend himself, and his arguments counted as much as those of both the accusers and defenders. The prosecution suggested that he had sought to benefit by appropriating money from the traffic (which would entail paying back the money, a beating or expulsion from the favela). The defence, meanwhile, argued that he had been deceived by the supplier. He conducted himself according to the proper protocol and did not 'chicken out', which counted in his favour. The rumour circulated around the neighbourhood, many people showed up to attend the event, and the main trafficker in the area came personally to follow the proceedings. Some of my research respondents attended, in order to defend Jorge.

> They debated whether to kill Jorge. […] We went there, and when we arrived, we saw the guys, saw Jorge, he was being bold, there in the middle of it all. They decided they were not going to kill him, but that they were going to give him a corrective. […] They gave him a beating, man, they really smashed him up. And after that he was like a pariah in the crime, there was no way to return. And this guy showed up, I knew this guy was the biggest dealer in the neighbourhood. […] When I saw this guy, I said, 'Man, now it's gonna get ugly.' But this guy was more relaxed, so I knew they weren't going to kill Jorge, he wouldn't let it happen. (Luiza)

Jorge's courage and arguments in his own defence, along with the protection he received from the main trafficker in the area, a 'brother', saved him from a worse fate. He was found not guilty of the accusation of betrayal, but it was not the first time he had caused trouble: years before, Jorge had already received a warning and even a suspension (a 'hook', as he called it) of thirty days' work.[2] Because it was a repeat offence, and in light of the loss caused, the boy was beaten and fired from the local traffic, which had the long-term effect of shaming him in the eyes of the 'community.' He could no longer sell drugs, and therefore also lacked the source of income that had sustained him since the age of twelve. Nonetheless, Jorge knows he was lucky that the punishment wasn't worse.

In this case, as for the minor infractions, it was also a 'brother' from the '*quebrada*' who judged the 'debate'; this time, however, he appeared in person to mediate the discussion. He had to manage the situation skilfully, on the one hand, to avoid unnecessary violence and, on the other, so as not to compromise his authority – if he appeared to be protecting someone against the 'law of crime', or if he seemed indecisive when it came time to pass sentence, he might himself have been questioned. The 'law' applies to everyone. Although there is a lot of local autonomy in decision making, in cases considered 'life and death', a death sentence cannot be passed without the approval of a 'tower'.

Cases of life and death

Pedro was twenty-one years old, and told me that his cousin had been murdered after a 'fight'. The story is controversial, and involved a 1,000cc motorbike – an object of desire for any 'thief'. Pedro's cousin had the motorbike stolen by a young man, whom he killed a few weeks later in revenge without the authorisation of the PCC. A 'debate' was called to rule on the case – Pedro's cousin had to explain why he had committed a homicide without first seeking permission.

> My cousin, my cousin, had already killed … And he died in an ugly way, at the hands of a thief. Except it was in the debate. […] It was in the debate with the 'thief', face to face. And he said: 'I'm right', and he was well respected, 'and that was it!' Then the guys said: 'No, I'm from such and such a place, I'm from this street' [they introduced themselves] and began the discussion. […] We went along [to attend the 'debate']. You go there. If you're right you can

leave. If you're wrong, you die. My cousin was right [Pedro was among those who defended him], but he died. (Pedro)

In these cases, the 'debate' is scheduled in advance, defenders and accusers are summoned, a virtual communication network is set up and it is no longer the 'boss of the *quebrada*' who decides. Nor is it a simple question of the judge consulting with a superior for approval of his decision. In cases where a death sentence might be passed, there needs to be consensus among several 'brothers'. Homicide, although established as a possibility, is highly regulated. In order to get an idea of the level of sophistication that these 'debates' can sometimes have, I will now turn to a case publicised in the media in 2007. A television network presented a special report, based on wiretapping by São Paulo's Civil Police, in which the 'debate' that resulted in the execution of someone accused of murder was described in detail.[3] I went to Pirassununga, where it had happened, and read all the official documents about the case. In the transcript that follows I present the entire television news report, before commenting on it.

> Presenter (Janine Borba): This week, police released a new wiretap that reveals the frightening details of trial held by the *crime*.
> Presenter (Paulo Henrique Amorim): A judgment made via cell phone: in defiance of the state and of justice. [background music]
> Narrator (reporter Raul Dias Filho – RD): March 27 this year. The scene is Pirassununga, in the interior of São Paulo state. The builder, Adriano Mendes, 33, leaves motorcycle school with his wife, Daiana Ponsiano, and a friend, Vânia Alves. When passing a speed bump, Adriano loses his balance and falls. Three boys, who are passing by, mock Adriano. They begin to argue. One of them, Fabrício do Nascimento, takes out a gun and fires two shots at the builder, who dies instantly. Adriano's brother, ex-convict Agnaldo Mendes, who has served time for drug trafficking, demands justice and a week after the crime, the trial over the death of the builder begins. The process followed all of the steps of a normal trial, with defendants, victims and witnesses. The difference is that the rapporteurs and judges of this summary trial are prisoner and gave

their verdicts via teleconference. According to police, this parallel court was run by the criminal faction the PCC, at the request of the victim's brother.

Deputy (José Henrique Ventura): Everything was so fast that, while we were still working on the case, we discovered that there was a trial in progress.

RD: Police recorded the conversations of members of the faction, monitored via wiretaps. It was almost 24 hours of recording. The discussions revealed in detail how trials of the crime work. The two women who were on the bike and Agnaldo, the brother of the murdered builder, are taken to a farm in the rural part of Pirassununga. Also present are the three accused, Fabio, Marcelo and Fabrício, who fired the shots. The trial will begin. The person in charge is the PCC member known as 'Mais Velho' ('Elder'). Those who will judge the case are far away, hundreds of kilometres from the farm. There are seven prisoners. Each one in a prison in different regions of the state. Communication is guaranteed by cell phones interconnected in a teleconference. The trial begins, with some prisoners defending the accused:

Prisoner 1:[4] Fabrício has already set himself straight, man, asking for an opportunity, you understand, brother?

Prisoner 2: If he already arrived asking for an opportunity, he knows he made a serious mistake, and totally went against our ethics. And now he's, I don't know, asking for an opportunity of life.

Prisoner 3: I have the same opinion as you there, man, because the kids are young, brother. Shit, man …

RD: Inmates discuss the possibility of applying only a 'corrective'.

Prisoner: Give him a serious *'cambau'* [beat him], the kind that'll send him to intensive care, you know brother?

RD: The prisoners ask to hear from Daiana, the wife of the murdered builder.

Daiana (wife of the victim): We were leaving school. Then Adriano rode over the middle of the speed bump and he couldn't regain control of the bike and fell. Then Adriano lifted the bike, and the guy said to Adriano: What happened, what happened? Then Adriano said: was that you? Then I said: Adriano, let's go, let's go. Leave it, let's go. Adriano was getting on the bike to leave, and he kicked Adriano in the ribs, he kicked him.

Prisoner: And was it clear they were 'laughing'?

139

Daiana: Yes, they were making fun of him. They were making fun of him and the guy pulled the gun.

Prisoner: But did he pull the gun out and point it or did he just stay with the gun in his hand?

Daiana: He pointed it. As soon as Adriano had got back on the bike, he fired.

Prisoner: Adriano did not lay a hand on any of them, didn't give any of them a slap?

Daiana: No. He got shot, then I grabbed him and went into 'panic', seeing Adriano with blood spilling out in every direction. Then he grabbed me, pulled me by the hair and started calling me a whore and said: do you want it too, bitch? You want it too? And he gave Adriano another shot in the head.

RD: During the testimonies, a person is making notes.

Prisoner: No, no, no, no. There you skipped a part. Here you put it like this, [reading loudly, slowly]: A-dri-ano was lift-ing the bike when he looked back, saw Fabrício with a re-vol-ver.

RD: The trial took a break in the middle of the night. It started again at 11 in the morning.

Prisoner 1: Hey Saddam!

Prisoner 2: Hey brother!

Prisoner 1: Let's go, kid.

RD: After hearing the version of the witnesses, the prisoners decide the fate of the boys. But they announce the sentence only after consulting with the faction's leadership.

Prisoner: The others stay, but the boy who took Adriano's life, he can't come back, no, brother.

RD: The prisoners are concerned someone will seek revenge.

Prisoner: Now we have to give a checkmate. We can't put anything at risk, man, it has to come in tomorrow or afterwards. It's reflecting on me, on Aquário, on you, on our brother, there, Saddam. Because automatically, it's the same on the internet: one channel pulls everyone together, and everyone is a single body, it's a bond, understood brother?[5]

RD: The prisoners communicate the decision to one of the defendants, Fábio, the brother of the murderer.

Prisoner: You are getting a chance at life, understood Fábio?

Fábio: Yes.

Prisoner: If any situation occurs with the family of Adriano, who died, with the family of his wife, the one who was on the bike, or even with the other girl who was on the bike, if you are involved, we will make sure you pay the highest price.

RD: Agnaldo, the brother of the victim, does not agree with the sentence. He wants the death penalty for the three involved.

Prisoner: So, listen carefully: you're only going to punish, you know, the guy who took the life of your brother. Did you understand, man?

Agnaldo: But the other two will go unpunished, brother?

Prisoner: Kid, the point is not that they'll go unpunished. The point is that the other two did not 'take' your brother's life. Alright, they were on the spot, but they did not 'take' their brother's life. Got it, man?

Agnaldo: Got it.

Prisoner: So we're being fair and correct. Do you understand, kid?

Agnaldo: Yes.

RD: It is time for the jurors to communicate the decision to Fabrício, the boy who shot the builder.

Fabrício (defendant): Hello.

Prisoner: Is that Fabrício?

Fabrício: Yes.

Prisoner: Are you aware of what you've done? You took a life, man, right? And you haven't even provided the right to defend himself.

Fabrício: I understand, brother.

Prisoner: So, look, Fabrício. We don't accept that anywhere, do you understand, man?

RD: The group of prisoners also decides who will execute Fabrício: Agnaldo, the ex-convict who wanted to avenge his brother's death. A problem arises: none of the criminals has a weapon that they call a '*chuteira*' (shooter).

Prisoner 1: The boys who are there, the other ones there. Is there a *chuteira* there, brother?

Prisoner 2: I don't know. You have to check with the boys there, brother.

RD: One of the people in the farmhouse goes out to get a gun. Shortly after, Agnaldo executes Fabrício. The sentences passed by the parallel court operating in São Paulo's prisons are carried out quickly and ruthlessly. Just 20 minutes after being convicted by the trial, Fabrício was killed in this place [pointing to an open area of the farm], executed with five shots at point-blank range. The police did not have time to prevent the crime, but Agnaldo was arrested days later. He denies committing murder.

Agnaldo: I didn't do it, I didn't. Justice with my own hands, never.

Deputy: During the assessment of this case, we were contacted by a guy [civil police] from Campinas, dealing with a similar case to the one here, asking how to proceed. So I have the impression that it is not restricted to our region [of Pirassununga]. I have the impression that it operates across the whole state, since there were prisons from several regions participating in the conference call. [...] What's concerning is the ease with which they, from within the prison system, are able to communicate by teleconference, something that sometimes even the police are not able to do. (End of video)

There are many perspectives from which this could be analysed. I will limit myself here to three comments. Firstly, the news report demonstrates the sophistication of the 'debates' – the use of teleconferences via cell phone, simultaneous coordination across seven prisons and in a farm prepared for the event, twenty-four hours of recording, a specialisation of tasks (witnesses, arguments by accusers and the accused, roles analogous to those of judges and clerk, performative procedures around sentencing). It also reveals an articulation of various levels of authority (the consultation with the leadership) and the efficiency of the execution. This sophistication not only suggests but empirically demonstrates both the breadth of the apparatus and the legitimacy among the different actors involved of the process of justice performed by the 'world of crime'.

Secondly, if, on the one hand, it has already been made clear that not all 'debates' are as sophisticated as this one, and that not all end in a death sentence (on the contrary, the norm is to avoid, as far as possible, 'the poor killing the poor'), on the other hand, it is important to point out that there are infractions that are judged even more summarily – in particular, cases of proven rape, paedophilia or confessions of betrayal of the faction's principles.

Of course, the network of relationship and protection surrounding the defendant, as well as the level of controversy generated by the crime that has been committed, also play a part in the way the trials are conducted, their level of sophistication and the sentences passed. The son of a 'brother' of the PCC would certainly not be judged in the same way as a '*nóia*' (crack addict) or a 'Jack' (rapist).

Thirdly, it is worth mentioning the multiple meanings of justice present in the transcript. In addition to its 'demonstration effect', we can also perceive that the deliberative process and the sentence passed have at least three purposes: (i) to demonstrate the firmness of the criminal faction in observing the rules of conduct, listening to all parties, and punishing deviations: 'you took a life [...] without providing a defence', and 'we do not accept this anywhere'; (ii) to demonstrate the fairness of the process, based on argumentation and, ultimately, through the demonstration of authority: 'we're being fair and correct. Do you understand, kid?'; and, above all (iii) to stop the chain of private revenge that such a case would generate if there were no mediation – the victim's brother demanded that the three defendants be sentenced to death, but the 'crime court' decides that it is legitimate to execute only the defendant 'who took the life of his brother'. The legitimacy of the sentence is further supported by the direct threat of 'radical' retaliation in the case of further acts of revenge.

It is precisely by preventing the cycle of private revenge that the apparatus of the 'debates' can be seen to have contributed dramatically to the fall in São Paulo's homicide rate.[6] This question deserves a specific reflection.

'Debates' and the policies of 'crime'

When I asked people why young people in the neighbourhood were not being killed anymore, three explanations were typically offered. The first was: 'because everyone has already died'; the second: 'because they've already arrested everyone'; and the third, more common, answer was: 'because you're not allowed to kill anymore'. It took me quite a while to understand these three statements, to understand that they signalled a radical change in the regulation of violence, and especially homicide, in the peripheries of São Paulo. It took me even longer to understand that this regulation had to do with the emergence of the PCC in those territories as an authority dispensing justice.

From the perspective of the residents, 'everyone has died' meant two things: first, that too many people had died there and that a significant portion of the total number of murders in São Paulo was of people close to them. Those who are constructed as distant and generic by quantitative data – young men, aged from fifteen to twenty-five, black and brown, with or without criminal records – are part of the affective relationships of people who live there; and second, that those young criminal actors who had killed their peers in the 'wars' had also died in the same vendettas. The observation stood, however: if the 'world of crime' was still active and, indeed, continued to expand, one could only conclude that new participants did not kill one another as they once had. Something had changed.

'They've arrested everyone' meant that those who killed, and were not killed, were no longer on the street, no longer circulating in the '*quebrada*' (Malvasi, 2012). The policy of mass incarceration imposed ten years previously had produced results.[7] The growth of prisons took many low-level drug traffickers and young people, who were armed and at war with each other, out of the favela alleyways. Although they were quickly replaced on the streets, given that they were occupying active market positions, in the prisons they became part of much more specialised criminal networks, in which the agreement of 'peace among thieves' was legitimised.

It is not uncommon to hear the claim that the PCC emerged precisely to play a representative role in negotiating with the prison administration and brokering disputes between prisoners (…). The

first role is known as 'war with the police', while the second is
known as 'peace among thieves'. Marques (2008: 289).

This is where the meaning of the third, most common, explanation becomes clear. When people in Sapopemba's favelas told me
that you 'could no longer kill', what was being said was that in the
territories that the PCC occupied around this time the principle
was established that a person could be killed only with the permission of the 'Command'. After this change in the policies of *crime*,
the youth who previously had to kill a colleague for a debt of R$5
in order to maintain the respect of his peers can now no longer kill:
he must appeal to the PCC to claim reimbursement for his loss.
Punishments are given without the need for homicide or, more
accurately, necessarily without homicide.

It is from this perspective that we can understand the impact
of this apparatus on the official statistics. In the example given
above, the victim's brother believed that to gain revenge for his
brother's murder all three of those involved in the murder had to
be killed. However, by permitting the death of only one the 'court'
made a point of ending the dispute there – the 'checkmate' does
not allow the vendetta to continue. It was the legitimate authority
of the 'law' (of crime) that passed and executed the sentence – and
if anyone decided to disobey, they would 'pay the highest price'.

Before the establishment of this mechanism, the three accused
would probably have been killed. And this triple homicide would
have generated new private acts of revenge, and so on. This spiral
of lethality is still present in other major cities of Brazil. Through
the massive implementation of the mechanism of the 'debates' in
the peripheries of São Paulo, however, this cycle of private revenge
has been interrupted. And since the law passes a death sentence
death only as a last resort – there are many other intermediate
punishments – the whole cycle of revenge which had piled up
the bodies of teenagers and young men in favela alleys during the
1990s was greatly reduced.

So, were the 'debates' introduced by the PCC the main cause of the decline in homicides in São Paulo? Undoubtedly, say urban ethnographers and their interlocutors in the field. Viewed from the periphery, other causes mentioned in the public debate (disarmament, underreporting, demographic change, improvements in police organisation etc.) seem, at most, to be ancillary factors in explaining the dramatic shift in the statistics. In a 2009 interview Mano Brown (rapper in the group Racionais MCs) was asked about the 'extermination of young people in the peripheries', and he replied:

> The extermination of young people in the peripheries ... [pause]. I'm from São Paulo, right? That's where I have deeper knowledge about. And in São Paulo today there's a different direction. The extermination has been 'temporarily' stopped. By laws that aren't from the government. They're from another government. And in other states, I fear that will be the solution too. The government was unable to take concrete action on security issues. And organised crime managed to.' [The reporter doesn't understand what Brown is saying, and proceeds like this ...] 'In your opinion, Brown, what has changed in the last eight years?' [referring to the Lula government].]The answer Brown gives is unexpected] 'The emergence of the PCC'.[8]

It doesn't seem possible to ignore – although there is clearly a desire to do so in some quarters – that the fundamental factor explaining the reduction in homicides in São Paulo, from an ethnographic perspective, is the internal regulation provided by the 'world of crime'. The introduction of 'debates' as legitimate mediators of conflict in these environments is central to this explanation. On the other hand, it is not possible to celebrate the logic that makes these mechanisms so efficient: the institution of exceptional spaces, overseen by actors who are not publicly recognised, to arbitrate over life and death.

However, when we analyse the ways in which deviations from the 'law of crime' are judged, and, above all, if we contrast it with 'official law', we see the tension that runs through the dispute over legitimacy. On the one hand, we can see that the 'debates' are performative events in which 'commitment to crime' and the 'willingness' of the individual to 'cooperate with the Party' are questioned before the judges. Based on this performance, a consensus is reached between the judges which is translated into a coherent sentence, within the exceptional nature of the law, that must be executed immediately. In order to formulate this judgment, it must of course be claimed that neither the position of the individual in the social hierarchy of the group, nor his or her phenotypic or personal characteristics, are taken into account. It is a form of justice recognised *by the subjects* as valid 'for all', which underpins the PCC's argument that its form of justice represents procedural 'democracy'. 'All' means all thieves and brothers, of course, but it is for them the universe of human beings (Feltran, 2018).

On the other hand, state justice is recognised in the peripheries as having universalistic normative laws, although the procedures through which it is applied are unequal and inefficient: justice functions slowly, it discriminates against individuals based on their social status, place of residence, skin colour and class position, in addition to being subject to the technical expertise of lawyers. Thus, from the perspective of those living in these territories, if 'criminal justice' had exceptional contents inscribed into its 'law', it would be fair to apply 'equally' to everyone. Thus, the 'law of crime' expands its legitimacy in the peripheries, just as official criminal justice is perceived to be primarily geared towards locking people up. The fact that the 'official law' has democratic content only works to legitimise it among middle and upper classes, who develop the perception of living in a 'consolidated democracy'. The tensions in disputes over legitimacy at the edges of the city are plain to see.

In the introduction to this chapter I posed the question of how we might understand the paradox that the 'justice of crime' became legitimised in the peripheries at the same time that Brazil's democratic political regime became institutionally consolidated. This is what, in my view, helps to understand the paradox: in São Paulo the boundary that marks contemporary social tensions and cleavages is fed by actions of 'fighting crime', supported by a supposedly legal universalism that is, in reality, selective in its implementation. This selectivity, precisely because it is unable to resist social hierarchisation, merely reinforces its adversary – the legitimacy of extra-legal justice and the authorities that provide it. As such, for those who live in the favelas of São Paulo, the 'world of crime', together with the media and churches, come to constitute the necessary repertoire of authorities that provide access to justice. Working on a daily basis, these authorities constitute necessarily reflexive perceptions of justice that offer privileged points of entry for analytically describing the fault lines of social tensions in São Paulo today.

5

Violence and its management

I listened to the sound of my footsteps striking the tarmac for a few seconds before engaging the group in conversation. I had been in Sapopemba for four days, accompanying educators from CEDECA on home visits and to adolescent internment or treatment units that conduct socio-educational measures.[1] That particular day had been spent walking around Madalena, a neighbourhood occupied by workers in the 1970s. It now consists almost entirely of self-built homes, most of them legalised and registered with the council. Commerce in the neighbourhood is predominantly local although sufficiently diversified to satisfy everyday needs. It was 10 a.m. in early January, and the sun began to peek through the clouds for the first time as we passed the small shops.

'Social educator' Sidnei removed his coat and continued walking, carrying it in his hand. I also took off the fleece I was wearing, but tied it around my waist. The asphalt was wet and the fog rose over houses with fences lining both sides of the street. We couldn't yet make out Sapopemba's largest favela complex located in a valley to our west. At the corner of the main entrance to the favelas, I noticed two boys standing chatting, also carrying their coats in their left hands. They were smartly dressed in new clothes and designer trainers and had a characteristic way of walking, incorporating specific corporal techniques. Upon spotting us, they immediately ambled over and broke out in smiles. Extending their right hands, they greeted us with the news that a friend had been arrested and they had missed the AF (Assisted Liberty) hearing, before asking if the sheet music Sidnei was carrying was for the *cavaquinho*[2] to be played in the samba band on Saturday in Vila Prudente, another of São Paulo's best-known favelas. Sidnei informed me that the pair were attending a music workshop he gave at CEDECA, in compliance with socio-educational measures taken due to their apprehension by the police two months earlier for stealing copper wiring from a building site. Kids 'from the community'; Sidnei explained that they had 'got caught up in the adventure of it' and weren't part of the 'world of crime'. Our walk continued. In front of another small shop selling clothes, Sidnei joked as he called out to the teenager behind the counter; later he told me that she had been sexually abused by her father, that the case was currently being decided in court and that it was a group of CEDECA lawyers who had made the formal accusation of abuse after interviewing the girl and her mother.

After covering no more than two blocks, we had already come across two cases of intervention by the government's legal regime in the arbitration of crimes and infractions. In both cases, the judicial measures enacted had generated or would go on to generate rulings that would attempt to redress the situations (by means of socio-educational measures in the youths' case and the possible imprisonment of the teenager's father). In both cases, lawyers working for CEDECA had served as privileged mediators of access to the court, according to an agreement with the Public Defender's Office (*Defensoria de Justiça*). I have come across numerous cases like these during my years of field research in Sapopemba; however, I have also come across several other forms of judicial regime that are commonly employed in the territory.

Based on my ethnography conducted in the region, in this chapter I argue that if access to the judiciary is present in the peripheries of the cities in São Paulo state, thus broadening the distribution of rights that could hardly be described as universal in Brazil, it is not the only normative regime of reference for the inhabitants of such territories. There are at least three *other* regimes for the normativisation (and normalisation) of conduct that *coexist* with the official law and its forms of regulation, and which do not always compete with it. I treat these normative dynamics as different 'normative regimes', since they institute not only principles or codes to be followed in daily life ('laws' or 'rules', sometimes 'ethics', the so-called [way to] 'proceed' [*proceder*]) but also delineate their legitimate operators, as well as the plausible and practical regimes of debate and deliberation. These regimes are also at the basis of the execution of measures for punishment or control defined by these operators.

The first and most striking of these regimes takes the principle of the 'law of crime' that establishes a code of conduct known as the 'due procedure' regulated in discussion meetings between adversaries known as 'debates'. As we had seen in the previous chapter, these 'debates' take the form of highly sophisticated tribunals that somewhat mimic the state judicial system, but differ in several key respects. The 'debates' increased substantially in the 'PCC era' of the 2000s, and have come to occupy a legitimate space for the use of violence previously regulated by practices of 'popular justice' such as lynching and payments to assassins, which were the subject of many studies in São Paulo in the 1980s and 1990s. With the legitimisation of the 'debates' in the 2000s, these traditional practices of popular justice have tended to disappear in the city's peripheral zones.[3] The second regime normativises the de facto actions of low-ranking police officers, who interact directly with the official law as well as with the members of the 'world of crime' and their *modus operandi*. The central characteristic of this second regime is its selectivity: a distinction is always sought to be made between 'workers' and 'hustlers' in order for the subsequent employment of a *continuum* of practices that extends from the strictly legal to the blatantly illegal. The third and final of these normative regimes, conceived of as an *alternative* or *complement* to state justice, is based on a predominantly Christian 'law of God', which is leveraged in a variety of ways by the churches and religious groups that proliferate in the urban world, although I will not deal with this latter regime in this chapter.

I argue here that violence – understood as the use of force or the threat of force – and especially lethal violence, is strictly managed on the periphery of São Paulo. Breaking with the argument that identifies a banalisation of violence in favelas and in the periphery and contrasting with the management of modes of violence operated in other areas of Brazil's peripheries, I present three ethnographic situations from the 'PCC era' that suggest how violence has been strictly managed in these territories. While the selective operation of this repertoire of *normative regimes* that *coexist* on São Paulo's periphery may be verified in the empirical description,[4] I further argue that at the base of the operation of this repertoire lies a dispute over the legitimacy of principles, codes and subjects capable of regulating violence on the city's periphery.

In the first three sections of the chapter I present three situations of interaction between state agents, lawyers and several of my research interlocutors, in this case youths affiliated with the 'world of crime'. The situations allow me to verify how the logics of the three normative regimes in question interact in order to justify the various courses of action taken by the subjects in each situation. In the conclusion I outline the particularities of each normative regime.

Ricardo and his towel

Sidnei and I pressed on. At the corner of Avenida Primavera de Caiena we paused again, this time to take in the view of the city, extending over forty kilometres to encompass the entire eastern side and the downtown region, all the way to the bottom of Avenida Paulista, with the silhouette of Jaraguá Peak in the background. We carried on for another 100 metres and arrived at an iron gate, where, upon seeing us, a small boy ran to call his mother to let us in. Side-stepping the dog, we made our way inside, asking for news of her oldest son, Ricardo. Janete invited us to take a seat; she had known Sidnei for a long time. As they began discussing Ricardo, seventeen, I became aware that there was yet another complex story at hand. A look of exhaustion must have flashed across my face as Janete asked me, 'Doesn't this work of yours get to your psychological mind?' 'All the time', I thought to myself, smiling and reassuring her of the contrary. We continued with some small-talk on the image of the saint on the wall, her clock featuring an emblem from Palmeiras football team, her husband's job (which he would lose the following month) and the small, crocheted doily on top of the television.

Ricardo arrived and I could tell Sidnei was pleased to see him – he didn't often find him there. As he emerged from the bathroom at the back of the house, wrapped in a towel, I noticed he was very thin, with whitish skin and prominent bones. He quickly nodded a greeting, heading towards the bedroom. From the sofa where I was seated, I could see him remove the towel and dry himself, while in the foreground sat his teenage sister, attempting with difficulty to place an orthopaedic brace on her thighs. In the dim yellow light, I felt like I was invading the intimacy of their home. The young girl then came out of the room on crutches, and was helped by her mother to the kitchen. This kind of disability is domestic; you don't see it in public.

It was, however, the image of Ricardo drying himself that had struck me, with his silhouette reviving the image of a dead youth I had seen in a favela a year before. He had also been a 'crackhead', I thought to myself. 'Rock and coke': crack and cocaine. A 'crackhead's' face typically takes on the angles of the skull, with sunken eyes, dull hair and a prominent jawbone. Ricardo's skin was pale, with no colour except for the dark green tattoo of his mother's name on his forearm and small purple wounds spread across his legs and back. He asked his mother for the blue shorts. 'The blue ones?' she answered, 'They're in the wash!'

153

He returned to the back of the house, whistling under his breath, an old towel almost doubled around him. He came back with a comb and went back into the bedroom, once again leaving the door open, as his visitors were men. He put on a pair of black shorts and came and sat down beside us, topless, wearing flip-flops. He greeted us again, this time extending his hand and looking us in the eye, taking the scene in more slowly. Sidnei introduced me by explaining: 'Gabriel is one of us, Ricardo, he can be trusted.' It was only then that I saw the first living details: a gold chain around his neck, a carefully combed spiked fringe, and a toothbrush in his hand. He began to converse and had plenty to say. His image improved to me as he began to appear as a person with all his own unique traits, breaking my stereotyped image of a 'crackhead', and allowing me to see past the generic idea of an addict's body. The eloquence with which he expressed himself surprised me; in reality he was highly articulate in the lexicon used by the 'brothers', spinning a loose narrative of highly moving stories with fluency and humour. Within ten minutes we – Sidnei, Ricardo's mother and I – were laughing along with him.

Two 'framings'

The first story that Ricardo told us was as follows: while joyriding around the neighbourhood in December, he stopped to give a lift to a friend named Joana, whom I had met before and who would turn up later on that day. At this point he claimed that he had never dated Joana and had only 'taken' her. Upon Sidnei's protests at the use of the verb ('she isn't an object!'), Ricardo switched to claiming to have 'screwed her', to their mutual amusement. When the car was stopped by the police, both Ricardo and Joana were arrested and their parents were summoned to the police station. It was only once they had been beaten up and charged with armed assault that they were allowed to go. (Ricardo said that the car had been loaned to him by a friend who had stolen it, but wasn't able to prove it.) Joana, who had been on her way to buy nappies for her son when she accepted the lift, felt mistreated. It was Ricardo's second arrest, making him a 're-offender.' On hearing about the socio-educational measures he had been subjected to, I recalled that Ricardo was only seventeen, and therefore still a minor. Despite the fact that I had heard stories like this one hundreds of times, they still interested me. Listening to them is very different from understanding them. Sidnei expressed concern and offered advice as though from a position of authority, his advice being endorsed by Ricardo's mother. 'Haven't you noticed how much weight you've lost?' she chided. 'I know I look like skin and bones but I've really cut down. I'm cleaner these days ...'

The second story referred to the eve of our visit on 6 January 2009. Ricardo had been caught by the police again, the third time in two weeks. Claiming he felt like he was 'in the police firing line', he said that he was 'flying a kite' on the corner at eleven o'clock in the morning when a patrol car had stopped and a 'big black' plainclothes officer had stepped out, cornering him and announcing, 'This is the police'.[5] Pulling him by the shirt, he had asked him various questions, such as his age, criminal record, proof of identity (ID) and about his friends etc. He had then handcuffed him and taken him 'down there' into the favela to where 'the boys' were, a reference to the other teenagers working at the *boca*, where drugs were sold and where Ricardo also worked. At first, Ricardo resisted, telling the police to take their hands off him and pleading with them not to rip the silk shirt he was wearing, before finally agreeing to accompany them to the station. All the boys were 'corralled' together, but only the two 'already with a police record' were put into the patrol car.

Ricardo was ushered into the back of a Blazer jeep with a friend who, he claimed, was not a minor. They were photographed by one of the officers with a cell phone, Ricardo retorting that the 'neighbours' had also photographed the patrol car, and that if the police officers didn't free him and his friend, they 'wouldn't free them either', with their 'allies' going after the police officers ''til the end'. *Using psychology, eh.*[6] According to Ricardo, the police officers continued patrolling the area with Ricardo and his friend still in the vehicle for almost an hour. After that, the vehicle pulled up at one of the local police stations and they were asked, while still in the car: 'Do you still not know what's going on here?'[7] The 'deal' proposed was the payment of R$50,000 for their joint release, with Ricardo describing them as 'crazy'. After negotiations and calls to other business partners, the price soon dropped.

It was agreed that the 'brothers' would pay the amount agreed for the boys' release. According to the rules, Ricardo and his partner would now be indebted to the 'brothers', although Ricardo didn't want to say how much was paid. The details of the deal, like others of its kind, were not to go beyond those immediately involved. As is common in these cases, neither of the two minors was officially charged by the Civil Police, one instead being released on his own 'conditionally', in order to fetch the sum demanded, this strategy serving to guarantee the deal. Ricardo returned to hand over the money at the agreed time of 4:00 p.m., handing over what he'd been able to rustle up, along with a phone number of the contact who would pay a second instalment the following day. With the boys released, Ricardo went back to the *boca* 'pissed off', heading straight to meet friends and smoke a joint to 'calm his nerves'. By ten o'clock that night he was home. 'And that was my day yesterday,' he said.

The 'boy from crime'

After recounting these two tales, Ricardo signalled that the conversation was over. The house had a low ceiling, and he wasn't comfortable on the bottom bunk. The earlier laughter was substituted by advice, with Sidnei assuming his role as a 'social educator', trying to set commitments with Ricardo to 'get him out of crime.' From that moment, we began to feel that we shouldn't outstay our welcome. It was already eleven o'clock in the morning, and the other kids would be at the corner, expecting Ricardo to join them.

The boy skilfully started to bring the conversation to a close, and got dressed to leave. He said that he would try to enrol in school and that he had only just missed the deadline. We all knew he wouldn't. He got up, placing first one arm, then the other, into his short-sleeved, white denim, baggy shirt, with a pattern and an enormous hole from a cigarette burn on the back. It was the 'silk shirt' he'd been wearing the previous day. He then decided against it, 'in case it attracted the police again', instead selecting a very baggy grey and white striped T-shirt. He then pulled a pair of red tracksuit bottoms over his shorts, and put on white cotton socks and a pair of Nike Shox trainers. Finally, he added another silver chain around his neck, a baseball cap and sunglasses. His skinny 'crackhead' body was well concealed. To be a 'crackhead' means losing the respect of your peers, and Ricardo knew that to keep his status among his friends, he needed to stop using the drug. He mentioned this a few times. Now that he was dressed, Ricardo's body resembled those typical of kids from the São Paulo periphery in the 2000s, which another adolescent referred to me as 'hustler style'. While observing him getting dressed, I realised that the 'crackheads' recognised as such in the streets are at a more advanced stage in their dependency than Ricardo. Wearing baggy, colourful clothing, he hid his condition well. The tattoo on his forearm took on aesthetic coherence, completing the 'style'. When Ricardo was ready to join his friends, we left the house together. The dog kept quiet this time. At the gate, his mother shouted 'Be good!' and Ricardo smiled, adjusted his baseball cap and turned right. Sidnei and I turned left; we were going to visit another family.

From then on, I carried my folded jacket in my hand, my arm outstretched, like the rest of the men there. I met Ricardo two days later, in another favela in the neighbourhood. He acted as if he didn't recognise me; he didn't want to talk to me in front of his friends, who were also teenagers. He was arrested again the following week and detained due to the lack of a deal. Luckily he was still a minor. I visited the internment unit where he was being held and continued to ask about him during the months to come. By July 2009 he had suffered health problems, including a sexually transmitted infection, and claimed to have converted to Pentecostalism. Other interns referred to him as 'the pastor'. He tried to cure himself of his crack addiction.

Into the 'world of crime'

March 2009. After a long day spent in two government intern-ment units, I returned to Sapopemba tired but wanting a chat, and so decided to visit Ivete's family.[8] First I searched for her at the favela health centre where she works, but was out of luck. I then went to her house, but only her grandson was at home. Thinking she might be at the house of her eldest daugh-ter, Ivonete, I made my way there. 'Who is it?' she called out. 'Gabriel!' 'Gabriel who?' she asked as she opened the curtain, smiling. 'Are you busy?' I enquired. 'No, come on in!' 'You're not busy with a customer?' I asked, knowing that Ivonete works from home as a hairdresser. 'Well, actually yes, I am!' she said, gestur-ing to her mother in the chair in front of her. I was happy to have found them. I feel close to their family, an affection having grown between us over the years. We exchanged news. Ivete's children were all much the same, with five of them 'in crime' and the other three 'working'. She told me that her second daughter, Marcela, who had been addicted to crack for ten years, had been arrested again. 'It was God's will, Gabriel ... she was going to finish her-self off.'[9] I asked if Ivonete was going to church that evening and she said yes, inviting me to go with her. While we were arranging for me to go home and shower and return straight away, Ivete's grandson came running into the house, breathless: 'Grandma, grandma, Anísio's been arrested! The boys told me! The police are at your door!' he exclaimed. Aged thirty, Anísio was Ivete's oldest son.

Outlaw family

Ivete jumped up, pulling out her hair clips in one swift move. Everyone grabbed their ID cards and left the house. 'Let's go,' she said to me. I asked if it would okay for me to join them. 'No problem,' she responded. Ivonete went ahead with her son, while Ivete and I tagged along. Running to catch up with us was Humberto, Ivonete's fiancé. Seeing that Ivete was worried, I tried to console her as we walked along. But I noticed that she was resigned: she already knew what had to be done, as nine years had passed since the first time one of her children had been arrested, and the arrests had been numerous since then. Gradually she quickened her step and moved to the front of the group, before realising that she had forgotten her cell phone. I said that she could use mine if needed.

We quickened our pace. Ivete asked again if we all had our IDs on us. Humberto didn't, so he was told not to get too close to the police, as dealers' relatives are always potential suspects.[10] We turned the corner to get to Ivete's house, and saw that there was no longer a patrol car parked at the gate. I was feeling tense. Were the police inside the house? The street felt completely different to how I had found it half an hour ago when looking for Ivete. The neighbours had come out of their houses, due to the commotion, waiting for Ivete in order to gauge her reaction and see how her kids interacted with the police officers. Ivonete exclaimed, 'What busybodies!' as we quickly passed by.[11]

When at last we entered Ivete's house, the atmosphere was very tense. The police were no longer there, but the children were there discussing what had happened. Fernando (the youngest son), Vilma (his girlfriend) and Alex (another of Ivete's sons) were talking loudly among themselves. 'They took Orelha and the cars!'; 'He's at the police station'; 'The lawyer'll already be there,' they shouted, as they tried to work out which police officers had arrested Anísio. Knowing who they were would help them to decide on which game to play with them. Alex turned to Fernando and asked him why he had let the police in without a warrant. Fernando replied, 'What else could I do?' Alex probed him further, 'You said that you knew Orelha!' Fernando kept quiet. I felt wholly out of place.

They all knew me, however, and they nodded a greeting, consenting to my presence. They carried on talking nervously among themselves, as if they felt like the family had been invaded. Ivete asked them to explain calmly what had happened and to tell her everything. The boys started to repeat what they had been saying before, this time in a more organised fashion. Ivete made a point of including me in the discussion, leading me by the hand to the circle in which she spoke with her kids. Fernando's explanation was the most coherent. He said three civil police officers in plainclothes had arrived in a silver Golf. They had come looking for Anísio and Orelha, a neighbour and partner of his in the assaults he committed. A military police patrol car then arrived, a Palio Weekend (pronounced 'palio kend'), providing back-up to the operation. The plainclothes officers approached Anísio's car, which was parked in front of Ivete's house, with the specific purpose of arresting them. Because they were known 'hustlers', Anísio and Orelha immediately had an arrest warrant read out to them, before being handcuffed. The police then entered the house to 'collect proof'. Until that moment, everything had seemed to be in order, the police merely enforcing a court order.

Modes of interaction: the police and Ivete's children

Once inside the house, the police told Fernando that the car had been reported stolen, with its number plates switched. It had then been used in other robberies known as *saidinhas de banco*.[12] They said they weren't saying his brother was responsible for the robberies, not yet, but were looking into it. With respect for the rules of law, the investigator then directed dozens of questions at Fernando, the youngest brother, who was also known to be the most 'loose-mouthed' among them. At the age of twenty he had already been held in a youth detention centre once and shot twice, and had been 'traumatised by the police', he later told me. The police asked about each of the brothers, with one of the boys recognising the officers, as they had confiscated the slot machines from Alex's bar the previous week. It was evident that the whole family was under investigation. Fernando answered all the questions, as usual, saying that he knew nothing and trying not to get involved. But he didn't know what to say when the police asked what Anísio did for a living. When the family heard this, they shouted out the agreed-upon answer in unison: 'He installs sound systems!'

With the police's questions over, Fernando told us that he had stayed put while his brother and partner were escorted to the patrol car. Outside the house, the police officer said to him: 'Son of a bitch of a cock, you trying to play the guilty one for that bum? Trying it on, are you? This place only makes crooks! I've a good mind to take this to the Command and leave them to solve your problem!' Fernando said he hadn't done anything and that the police had said they were going to call the PCC, 'because they know those guys'.[13]

I wouldn't have picked up on the meaning of this interaction if I hadn't been alerted by Ivete and Alex as to what was going on. The police's explicit reference to the PCC demonstrates that the officers were not merely relying on the normative legal regime, but also referring to another one. The police who patrol the favelas are aware of the codes of the 'world of crime' and may select the regime of justice in accordance with the situation, leveraging official laws for formal 'workers' and the codes of 'crime' for *bandidos*. When they became aware that they were dealing with a 'family of *bandidos*', they chose the second mode in order to reprimand Alex. Furthermore, the references which the police made to the members of the PCC in the region showed that they knew them personally, thus making it implicit that they had financial connections to the '*Partido*' in the area and that they might therefore be interested in a monetary solution to Alex's problem.

After entering the house on a warrant and confirming that they were dealing with a 'family of hustlers', the police then abandoned official normativity and began acting according to other codes, known to those involved in 'crime'. The reference to the PCC made this change explicit and demonstrated that the police officers – individually recognised by one of Ivete's sons – knew of such a fact. Although the selling of drugs in that specific territory wasn't entirely regulated by the PCC, the group had the power to regulate the actions of the individuals affiliated with illicit local activities. Fernando did not act like a 'thief' who deserved respect and was therefore reprimanded by the police in a way that the PCC would approve of. Moreover, by publicly stating in the street that he 'knew the guys from the Command', the police officer subliminally affirmed that he was involved in the circuit of relations between the police and the faction, opening up the possibility of another 'agreement' between them. This was all too encoded for me, but entirely understandable to Ivete's children.

The meanings inherent to the interaction in question became even more explicit when the police asked about Anísio and Orelha's lawyer. Together with another two kids 'in crime', both of them paid a monthly fee to a private lawyer who defended them against criminal accusations, providing emergency legal assistance in situations such as this one. Anísio had informed the police that the lawyer would already know about their arrest, as Alex would inform him immediately, and that he was waiting for them at the police station. This information had made the police officers feel that they were dealing with professional 'hustlers'. By the time we arrived at Ivete's house, the lawyer had actually already phoned the policeman who had made the arrest and been to the police station.[14] The police officer would have asked Alex where the lawyer was from (wanting to know who they were and therefore if he should leverage the official law or the already instituted form of normalisation enacted via financial deals used in the 'world of crime' for the release of detainees).

Alex told us that at first he pretended not to have heard the question, as he didn't want to let the police know such information about the lawyer. He tried to stay out of the interaction, turning his back on the police officer without answering. The officer became angry, shouting 'You asshole, you son of a bitch! You turning your back on me?' Alex turned round as a sign of respect for police authority and said, 'No sir, I answered your question, sir, the lawyer is from Santo André, I don't know his name … and if you're calling me an asshole, sir, it's because I am, sir, I am.' And then he really did break down into nervous tears.

In the interactions between Ivete's sons and the police, the possibility was therefore already configured of utilising an extra-legal regime to give order to the situation, in the form of a financial deal preventing the young men's arrest. A specific mode of managing the use of violence in interactions between the police and 'crime' was thus established. There was no physical aggression, no exchange of gunfire and no confrontation, just a conflict contained within the sphere of discursive interaction steered toward financial deals. The doors of the patrol car finally closed, before the cars drove off and the arrested youths were taken to the police station in the east.

The police station: trajectories of coming and going

The family members present decided to head to the police station to see how Anísio was being treated. 'Let's go in Neto's car!' one of the 'working' members of the family suggested.[15] The route was known to the family, as several of Ivete's children had already been there before.[16] Ivete asked me if I wanted to go, and I said it was up to her. Since I was the only one of us with an official driving licence, I took the wheel. Aside from Ivete and me were Fernando, Vilma and Caio (Fernando's son and Ivete's youngest grandson, who was two years old). From the back seat, Fernando continued to narrate every detail of the scene with the police, while Vilma remained silent with Caio on her lap.

It was raining and I found myself driving at night through busy streets full of cars, in poor visibility. I had no idea where we were going. The Palio had a very stiff steering wheel that moved around a lot, despite my best efforts, even when we were going straight ahead. There was almost no petrol in the tank, so we stopped to fill up and I offered to pay. It took a lot of force to turn the steering wheel and the whole car shook. When I commented on this, Fernando said 'Yeah, it's still not that great.' I knew that the car had been in a very serious crash the year before and had been fixed in a neighbourhood chop shop. We soon arrived at the police station, but discovered we were at the wrong one. The mistake set us back twenty minutes. Upon arriving at the correct police station, we discovered that this would prove to be decisive.

Ivete went up to the counter on her own, while we hung back some ten metres behind her in the doorway. She asked about her son and was told he wasn't there. She understood the message straight away. I heard the officer from where I was standing and also clocked what was going on, but Fernando didn't and went up to the counter to protest that the lawyer had said Anísio had already arrived with him. Ivete glared at her son and the police officer behind the counter got angry, raising his voice: 'I'm telling you – and whoever else is interested – that there are no Anísios here! There's a Jonas, who's been arrested, anyone here a relative of his?'

Ivete apologised for her son, thanked the officer for the information and left. We all went out to the yard and made our way towards the car in silence. Ivete asked to borrow my cell phone and called the lawyer again, who confirmed that he had just dropped Anísio off at home. Relief rippled through the family, and I felt it too. I then felt a strong urge to find out exactly what had happened. I asked Ivete if she could confirm that a deal had taken place, and she nodded in the affirmative. Fernando disagreed, claiming 'My brother doesn't like giving money to the police, see? I don't think there was a deal, it was the lawyer that got him off.' But everything had happened so quickly that there wouldn't have been time to take a statement and complete all the legal paperwork requesting a release etc. The lawyer would never have got him out so quickly via the official regime. Not least because Anísio, at thirty years old, had already spent a total of five years in prison in two separate stints. Another arrest under the circumstances of being 'caught red-handed' wouldn't have been so simple. Hours later, I found myself back in the favela talking to Anísio at Ivete's house while he watched the national news. I found out that he had agreed to pay R\$16,000 for his release (R\$15,000 to the police and the rest to the lawyer).

Debates: another legal order?

August 2009. I visited Ivete again one Friday afternoon, this time at the public health centre. When she saw me she hugged me and offered me a seat. She asked if I knew what had happened. I didn't, so she informed me that Lázaro, another one of her sons, had been 'banished' from the favela three weeks earlier. 'He did what no thief should do: he informed,' she said, before bursting into tears. She was afraid she would never see him again.

Lázaro was twenty-six and was the manager of a local '*biqueira*' (a small point for drug dealing). He'd been 'in crime' since he was fifteen, and had already been arrested three times. On the run from the law for a year and a half, he used a fake ID (his twin brother's) and sold crack and cocaine. He had a good car and was earning a reasonable salary. He had told me months before that he'd paid R\$30,000 in a single year for the police to allow him to keep his drug point up and running. He was also protected by one of the area's leading dealers, although he was not very popular among men his own age in the favela. Rumours had abounded recently that he had been baptised as a 'brother', although I never managed to confirm this with his family.

Ivete told me that Lázaro had been detained in May, striking another kind of deal with the police in order to evade another prison sentence. He accepted the invitation to become an *informer* for the detectives, and for some months had been informing specialist police officers on the workings of the trafficking business and other spheres of 'crime' in Sapopemba. However, this secret arrangement was discovered in July 2009. In situations like this 'the crime' organises discussion meetings known as 'debates', in order for both the defenders and their accusers to judge the arguments and punish the guilty.

The course of the 'debate' that decided on Lázaro's expulsion from the favela is highly instructive of the way such a regime works. José, the main drug trafficker in the territory, who had known Ivete for fourteen years (ever since the family arrived in the favela), immediately called Lázaro for a serious chat. Only José and one of his subordinates took part in the 'debate'. He had heard from one of the police officers that Lázaro was an informer. According to Ivete, José asked Lázaro in no roundabout fashion whether he was part of the police informant scheme, which he vehemently denied. The accusation was extremely serious, but there was no proof. Lázaro had been known by many there since he was a child and, although this transgression deserved death, José respected Ivete too much to order the death of one of her sons without being certain. José therefore intervened directly in the case, asking Anísio to take Lázaro to the bus station and put him on a bus for somewhere far away, completing his immediate 'disappearance'. This offered Lázaro a 'chance to live' before the news reached the ears of the 'brothers'.

They left within half an hour but, on the way to the bus terminal, Anísio's phone rang. The information that Lázaro was an informant had already reached the 'brothers' and they had the power to override José's decision. Despite having received many reports that the PCC 'controls' the entire Sapopemba region and others throughout the São Paulo periphery, I have obtained information about the existence of other criminal factions in the district. There also continue to be 'independent' traffickers and criminals. José was one of these. However, the hypothesis I have been working on is that the PCC 'brothers' control only a part of the illicit markets, although they are the normative final authority in deliberations over the order of the entire local 'world of crime'. This means that a youth can rob a car on his own and not hand it over to anyone in the PCC, but his conduct in relation to other members of 'crime' and the police is guided by the normative regime controlled by the PCC. In Sapopemba all individuals enrolled 'in crime' are guided by this 'legal structure', as are all the favela residents at large (whether or not they engage in criminal activities).

The 'brothers' phoned José and asked for Lázaro to be returned for a second 'debate', this time in their presence. Anísio brought his brother back, and Lázaro was then submitted to another discussion, this time under much greater pressure. Some of the 'brothers' wanted to summarily execute him, considering him to have 'bedded down with the police' and judging this to be a cardinal sin worthy of the death penalty. Others taking part in the debate weren't sure about the decision, and execution is conducted only when there is a consensus. Perhaps out of respect for José, who was an older and well thought-of dealer, or perhaps to avoid the bad feeling that might be generated by 'overturning' his decision, the 'debate' voted to 'banish' Lázaro from the favela. He would never be able to set foot in Sapopemba again.

Before making it back to the bus terminal, however, Lázaro was beaten up and left with broken bones, his brother being forced to participate in the mob that attacked him. Anísio dragged him back home, and no less than an hour later, he was placed on a bus for a major city in Northeastern Brazil. He ran the risk of being killed there if other 'brothers' disagreed with the sentence. His mother sobbed as she told me the story, even appearing faint at some points. She told me that the following day she had been to see José, and later paid the 'brothers' a visit to thank them for letting her son live. I hadn't seen her so distraught in years.

I returned home and the following day heard that Ivete's anguish had been compounded by the murder of Anísio, aged thirty, on Saturday 22 August 2009. My first thought was that it had had something to do with Lázaro's informing, but everyone roundly denied it, claiming that he and Orelha had been carrying out an assault and were shot by police when making their getaway on a motorbike. Orelha, who was driving, died from a gunshot in the back, while Anísio died from the crash at over 100 kilometres per hour. Details of the story were confirmed to me by their brothers. I returned to Sapopemba a week later to find Ivete in bed and surrounded by other favela residents who had also lost children to murder. She had taken leave from work and was once again taking psychiatric medication. A family friend told me, 'Anísio died: he was murdered. Ivete is very sad. He was the one paying for the renovations to her house; he was the one who helped her out the most.'

Normative regimes and the management of violence

I have affirmed that when confronted in their daily lives with situations considered to be unjust, residents of the São Paulo periphery turn to a variety of instances of authority in their search for justice. The choice of which instance to activate depends on the type of problem confronted. If a man in formal employment fails to receive the overtime owed to him, for example, he can turn to the Labour Court. If a mother doesn't receive child support payments from her ex-husband, she can activate proceedings in the Civil Court. If one of her sons has been unfairly arrested or has suffered police violence in the favela where he lives, she may try to appeal to the press and, if this doesn't work, to entities involved in the defence of rights. In extreme cases there will always be those who appeal to divine justice. However, if someone in the family has been robbed, assaulted, beaten up or killed (and the agents of the criminal acts were not police officers), a complaint may be made to a local authority from the 'criminal world' if needs be, in order to activate mediation by the 'brothers' in the form of a 'debate' organised to arbitrate the contention and execute measures in the name of *justice*.

Thus, from the perspective of my research interlocutors, and especially among those that live in the favelas of Sapopemba, at least four different sets of *law* (understood as normative codes of conduct) may be recognised as legitimate and said to be in operation on a daily basis. For this same reason, four different forms of legitimate normative regimes may be recognised, delineating four different instances of justice and their specific operators which inform everyday life:

(i)   the state's *legal justice system*, operated in the courts through state lawyers, agents and civil servants, and which is based on the Federal Constitution;

(ii)   the *justice of the 'world of crime'* operated in the 'debates' promoted by criminal factions, especially the PCC, sustained by a code of conduct known as the 'law of crime' or 'procedure';

(iii) the *justice of the police* at the hierarchical base of the corporation, operated *in loco* during patrols and stormings of the favela and its residences, which can vary from strict compliance with official law to much more obvious illegality, depending on the status of the individual in question;

(iv) *divine justice*, operated by religions based on biblical (or Afro-Brazilian) references, priests, pastors or *pais de santo* (the figureheads of Candomblé, an afro-Brazilian religion), who invoke codes of conduct particular to each religion.[17]

The press also acts as a fifth instance, which may be turned to in the case of injustice; however, it is viewed more as a mediator heightening the probability of access to formal legal channels through the greater publicity it affords.[18] The ethnographic situations described above seem to me to allow the characterisation of at least three of these normative regime which *coexist* in the territories researched and which are differentiated by contrast. As I have mentioned, recourse to divine justice calls for a specific approach that will not be dealt with here.

My sole intention in analytically delineating these regimes – which evidently appear mixed in the situations presented – is to conduct a less normative reflection on the dynamics of criminality and the management of violence on the periphery of São Paulo, which naturally favours comparative analyses, with the field research allowing for an analysis of a repertoire of instances and procedures that I provisionally refer to as normative regimes.

It must be noted that, although they differ from one another, the reference to the official state law is not insignificant in any of the regimes. Being of legal age and possessing criminal antecedents, for example, modifies the course of daily interactions and forms of criminal action, with a case in point being the contrast between the situations experienced by Ricardo at the age of seventeen and Anísio at thirty when they were accosted by the police. The normative action displayed by the police officer involved in the interaction – as a reference that should be seen as a successful operation – varies as much in relation to the official legal reference (that distinctly frames the direct interlocutor of the operation) as in relation to the modes of operation of the justice system. If the police officer perceives that a boy of sixteen working in drug trafficking will not be held even if arrested (for being a minor, or due to the lack of evidence etc.), in many cases the boy will not even be escorted to the police station. Punishment for his conduct will then be issued by means of aggression or extortion, even at the time of the operation.

Violence and its management

The regimes involved in the normativity informing daily actions are multiple. The official law will punish deviations in the case of the individual being taken to a police station, and from there to a court. Before that, however, *other* instances may be activated that are authorised to instil codes of conduct and punish transgressions. Ricardo and Anísio were able to avoid imprisonment by paying for their freedom; as Anísio had a lot more to lose, he paid a higher price. Lázaro was judged by another 'law', however, and the punishment has a validity that goes far beyond the legitimacy of official law – he was 'expelled' from the favela forever.

Since the official regime is not the only one that operates in the city's peripheral areas, it must be said that the police are also not the only entity to patrol the behaviour of the residents in these neighbourhoods: the 'world of crime', lawyers, local associations and churches also play their parts, like various threads of the same network. Among these actors, however, only the 'world of crime' has the ability to implement a regime capable of offering codes of behaviour and of establishing operators and instances for the legitimate surveillance, judgment and punishment of transgressors. The case of Lazaro's judgment and punishment is an example of the several spheres in which this order works and of the type of law that it establishes, in which, however, homicide is avoided in so far as is possible.

In sum, if the 'legal justice' system claims to be democratic and universal, favela residents are aware that its application is actually rather unequal and selective. Space is opened up to legitimise the regime of 'criminal justice', which does not deny exceptions but claims to be 'fair' because it is applied equally 'to everyone'. The normative regime applied by police officers in peripheral areas is a manifestation of the hybridisation of the two previous regimes, serving as an institutionalised manifestation of the de facto selectivity of state justice, operated according to codes internal to the 'world of crime'. The procedural justice of the 'law of crime' thus expands its legitimisation on the city's periphery to the same extent that the official legal regime reveals its selectivity – a phenomenon continually affirmed by police actions.

When Ricardo was accosted by police officers whom he didn't know, he was first requested to state his age and whether or not he had a police record. Such questions are common in police dealings on the periphery and evidently serve to identify the individual's situation in relation to age criteria and their previous affiliation to the 'world of crime' which, together with their corporality (the set of diacritic signs of individuals and groups, combined with ways of dressing and speaking etc.), offer parameters for the sequence of police action in relation to the 'suspect'. After this initial attempt at identification, official ID is requested in order to check the information provided and, depending on the case, allow the police to 'access their record'. Nevertheless, if such criteria are relevant for the police officers – and the cases studied above are clear in this respect – it is because they discriminate (in terms of the normative police regime) between the different roles that individuals like them can occupy as 'workers' or 'hustlers' among a myriad of variations of positions of *status* within these categories. Once the accosted individual or group's situation has been defined *in situ*, a specific type of action is then decided on: a 'worker' is normally frisked, searched and released without question, while a 'criminal' will be kept in the interaction for longer, sometimes having their personal belongings stolen and being forced to reveal information on colleagues 'in crime', and, more often than not, paying to avoid arrest.

In all cases, the framing of the action depends on the performance of the different operators, whether individuals in 'crime' and their peers, police officers and their peers, lawyers and operators of the law or religious followers, and of the regimes these parties leverage to produce agreements. It was such in the police's interactions with Ricardo, Anísio and Lázaro in the situations presented above. The discretion shown by the police officer on the street means that his action swings between what is legal and illegal, depending on the framework of actions that the situation permits, and more particularly on the identity of the target individual or group that the force of order is intended for. It is this discretion that, as Veena Das has discussed in her research, upholds the state's regulatory ability in contexts of illegality and extreme violence.[19] In each interaction with 'crime', even when acting circumstantially under non-legal principles, it is the prerogative of the state agent to decide which normative regime, whether the official law, the 'law of crime' or financial 'deals' etc., may be best used to frame the individual or group accosted. The agent's definition (which is always contextual) prevents the accosted individual from defining the rules of the game. This plasticity in the definition of the situations at hand is the *modus operandi* of the state's agents power acting in the periphery.

In the 1940s one interpretation was that 'the main function of the police department was not to guarantee compliance with the law, but to regulate illegal activities' (Whyte, 2005: 154). This affirmation foresaw the thesis of 'the differential management of illegalisms' later developed by Michel Foucault and enthusiastically reappropriated in contemporary Brazilian debate.[20] Even if this dynamic of interaction between the law and illegalisms on the margins of the social was not created by the PCC, the practices of the regulation of violence that it suggests are new to São Paulo.

In 2000 a youth from a favela might have been forced to kill someone who owed him money (even if the debt was extremely small) in order to maintain his honour and *status* in 'crime'. Such an attitude was unthinkable in São Paulo's peripheries during the 2000s. It would still be very unusual in 2019. In another sphere, the price paid by 'crime' to maintain business operations has undergone considerable inflation. The situations analysed above are rare in that sense; there was never such a high concentration of capital among the agents or as much stability in the ways of dealing with the law and illegalisms as in the 'PCC era'. The regulation of lethal violence (achieved by the political hegemony of the faction) in the urban territories under focus is central to an understanding of this concentration and order. Lázaro paid R$30,000 in 2009 to keep his drug sales point up and running. Anísio and Orelha paid R$16,000 to police officers and lawyers for their release after a single arrest. Ricardo didn't reveal the amount paid, but the negotiation began at nothing less than R$50,000.

Since people began talking about the PCC in Sapopemba, a little before I began my research there, homicides and police violence have entered into a marked decline at the same rate at which the financial 'deals' between 'crime' and police officers have expanded. According to my sources, the resources for these deals are 'loaned' by the 'brothers' and paid back by the beneficiaries in instalments. If the possibility of a deal between the parties emerges, the need for an armed confrontation between the police and the 'world of crime' is reduced. Thus the law, punishment and violence regimes are managed by other means.

Contrary to what one might imagine, in the favelas where I conduct research the business dealings of 'crime' are numerous, with an emphasis on car theft, specialist assaults and drug trafficking, although armed control of the territories does not exist. Drug dealers have worked unarmed for several years. The PCC emerged in the area in 2001, and has operated a hegemony in the regulation of violence since the final months of 2003. Since then, the violent actions of 'crime' have been restricted to those related only to their line of business (assaults, robbery, kidnappings etc.) and to the punishment of deviations from the 'procedure' agreed on in the 'debates'. The former are invariably carried out outside the territories studied. By means of the latter, 'unnecessary violence' is avoided if possible and homicide is strictly regulated.

It is this regime that explains why in São Paulo the aggregated homicide rates have fallen so much, especially in the city's peripheral zones, while the rates of armed robbery and other violent crimes remain the same or have increased. Violent confrontations are restricted to criminal events (such as the assault that ended with Anísio and Orelha's deaths) or to episodes like those of May 2006, which are undesired by all those involved, but necessary in establishing parameters of adjustment among them (including the rates to be paid). The territorial dynamics of violence on the São Paulo periphery, strictly managed in these processes, are therefore far from banal or chaotic. Moreover, as the situations demonstrate, these dynamics have been rigorously managed in the interaction between the various subjects, by using much less armed force than in other major cities in Brazil (although the PCC evidently possesses very heavy arms for its criminal activities, and is also present in other major cities). The study of these normative regimes seems to me to constitute a highly effective way of analytically describing the frontiers of contemporary social tension and the ways of managing it. Although seen here from the periphery, the construction of these frontiers suggests much broader implications for the research of urban and political scenarios in contemporary Brazil.

6

Government produces crime, crime produces government: São Paulo's apparatus for homicide management

This chapter offers a situated analysis of the specificities of São Paulo's urban conflict, charting more than two decades of conflict between government policies and criminal policies in the management of lethal violence.[1] In Chapter 4, I discussed the repertoire of normative regimes that pluralise the notion of justice in the peripheries of São Paulo, and of ways in which, over the years, a justice system overseen by 'crime' has come to coexist with regimes of state and divine justice, hybridised through the practices of low-ranking police officers and criminals. In Chapter 5 I described the relationships between these regimes in different everyday situations in the peripheries, focusing on the question of how they produce a specific way of administering violence – understood as the use or threat of force. Clearly, this has direct implications for the question of São Paulo's homicide rates.

Following these arguments, this chapter offers a relational analysis of how these different regimes manage lethal violence, and thus life itself. It begins with a description of the policies implemented specifically for this purpose by both government and 'crime' from 1992 to the end of the 2000s. The chapter is divided into three chronologically organised sections, which between them trace the evolving relationship between the policies of the state and the policies of 'crime'. The first section (1992–2001) shows how the 'Carandiru Massacre' represents a turning point for both state policies (leading to the inclusion of human rights in the organisational structures of police forces and security ministries, an emphasis on prison reform and the beginning of the project of mass incarceration), and those of 'crime' (the creation of the PCC and the beginning of the hegemonic construction of its proposals – war against rival groups and the system, prohibition of rape and homicide between members) during the 1990s. In the second section (2001–6) I analyse the period between the 'mega-rebellion' in São Paulo's prison system and the 'PCC attacks', interpreting the ways in which the PCC expanded its presence in the peripheries of the city, at the same time as the state established the Differentiated Disciplinary Regime (RDD) and deepened the policy of mass incarceration. In the third part (2006–11) I analyse the 'crimes of May' as a critical event (Das, 1995) that rearranges the routine relations between government and 'crime' in São Paulo, producing a truce between them that served the purposes of both and was responsible for the steady decline in the state's homicide rate by 2011. It is during this period that, analytically, a single administrative apparatus of lethal violence, with specialised regimes for governing different populations, becomes more clearly established between the policies of the state and of 'crime'. Before these three sections I clarify the meanings of the notions of government and crime as adopted in this chapter.

State and crime regimes as sources of understanding

The expression 'government', as used here, refers to a source of normative discourses and practices relating to the management of urban conflict. It is a matrix of plausible meanings that is enacted in the routines of executive institutions and in the day-to-day activities of the legislative branch and the judiciary, that is to say, the three formal levels of the management of public security, as well as market and civil society institutions which are also involved. The expression 'crime' or the 'world of crime', on the other hand, refers here to the reference matrix of discourses, the identification of subjects, practices and meanings produced around illegal activities of drug trafficking, car theft and specialised robbery in the peripheries of São Paulo. Crime is also the matrix of a collective subject that is central to the problem addressed in this chapter: the PCC. There are other spheres that are relevant to São Paulo's apparatus for homicide management, such as religion and the media, which are sources and promoters of forms of morality that are heavily implicated in the issue. Here I restrict myself to a relational analysis of government and crime because these are the discursive matrices that produced explicit policies for the control of lethal violence in São Paulo during the period analysed.

To begin, it is necessary to clarify the fundamental parameters within which these expressions will be used. The first is to avoid the assumption that government and crime, although they sometimes give rise policies of direct confrontation with one other, are analytically separate with regard to the production of order. The apparatus works precisely in the tensions between them, and it is this apparatus that in practice regulates a large part of the homicides in São Paulo: namely those concentrated in the city's peripheries, which are my focus here. Thus, it should be clear that I do not distinguish between the security policies of the São Paulo state and federal governments, their political parties or the civil associations linked to one or the other. This is not because they are not different in some respects, nor because I do not have specific value judgements about them. Above all, it is because, from the observational point from which I reconstruct this history, they contribute to the same heterogeneous matrix of discourses: government, the normativity of which is based on a belief in the universality of the law. I also try to avoid representing government and crime as reified subjects or spheres, as might be the case for formal institutions and organisations, interest groups etc. Instead, government and crime are, above all, the moral matrices for the justification of the practices and beliefs of these subjects and institutions, that update the apparatus of the management of urban order both in the peripheries of the city and in the offices of state bureaucrats.[2]

The value statements that subjects perform in the world always refer to some sphere of justification, even if the content of these differs drastically (Werneck, 2009). Government and crime are, in this chapter, presented as spheres that confer meanings – existential, political and moral – on the life and death of different subjects and groups. Both the alterity that places government and crime in radical opposition in the discourses of both, as well as the functional contiguity between them in the management of order, can be captured in ethnographic situations. The relation between the two must, therefore, be understood as shared – something that divides the parties absolutely and at the same time joins them in a common whole (Rancière, 1996a, 1998, 2005). Therefore, although these regimes coexist empirically, especially in the peripheries, at the level of significations they tend to consider themselves as absolutely opposed, and hence to read the subjects inscribed in them as essential manifestations of the other (Misse, 2010). A young man might work in a store and, on weekends, take a joint for his imprisoned brother, maybe a little more so he can sell it in jail. The conceptual capture of this subject as a 'worker' or *bandido*, however, depends on the situation in which it is constructed, which triggers a set of judgements that, because they are understood as being in radical opposition (Zaluar, 1985), obscure the other matrices of judgement that might also be mobilised (Feltran, 2008, 2010c). Thus, for example, it is assumed that the administration of a prison is carried out by the government; however, although it is known that crime is present in the administrative routines of any prison, this still tends to be treated as a deviation from the norm, something absolutely illegitimate, that should not happen and that could never be written in official documents (Das, 2006b). The opposite is true. In order to deal with this problem I try to give symmetry to the analysis by denaturalising the analytical assumptions of both matrices of discourses and show, based on my field data, that government and crime are intimately related to one another. This is a relationship that is, on both sides, morally indefensible, creating a radical polarity between the meanings of the two categories on both sides. It is the homologous presence of this cleavage, constitutive of both the government matrix and the crime matrix, which allows us to think of the sharing between them as a political dispute according to the criteria of meaning making in the world.

Following the trails of authors who have addressed this question (for example Das, 1999; Foucault, 1997; Machado da Silva, 2008), my research suggests that in São Paulo the 'work of time' structured a sharing between government and crime, through the inscription of values and criteria for judgement of the world that became dispersed in everyday routines. On the one hand, the radical distinction between the different territories and populations that characterise the division has crystallised; on the other, a common mechanism for managing the lives and production of the social order in the city has emerged between them. This shows the importance of ethnographic research in contributing to debates about this difference in relational terms; Veena Das states that ethnography is a form of knowledge in which I am led to recognise my own experience as alterity (Das, 2012). Thinking about crime ethnographically implies, therefore, thinking about its modes of naming, constructed from the matrix of the government. Equally, thinking about the government implies to consider its relationship with crime.

In daily life, however, the vast majority of subjects do not live their lives relativising existence. Thus, government and crime are not in general perceived, among those subjects who are seen to be representatives of them, as fluid networks of meaning that are mutable and historically and relationally constructed. It is more common to see essences and truths in the world, and to read these into institutions and people: as good or bad, allies or enemies, whether or not they are known personally. It is more common not to negotiate one's values, and instead to see one's particular world as the only one that truly exists, or at least that is valid for offering universal parameters of evaluation of the world, and therefore of other people. My ethnography shows that in São Paulo there are distinct discursive regimes, each of which offers arguments that legitimise the practices for managing life and death that they perform. These regimes, although they coexist at the level of practice, are seen as autonomous and morally opposed. Even though, analytically, they compose a single apparatus, the respective social conditions within which they seek legitimation are radically different.

The 'time of wars': from 1992 to 2001

The date 2 October 1992 marks a generational shift in the policies of both the state and crime for the management of violence in São Paulo. According to official data, the police occupation of the state's largest penitentiary, following a rebellion by prisoners that began in Hall 9, resulted in the execution of 111 prisoners (Brown and Prado, 2002; Salla, 2006, 2007; Teixeira, 2009; Biondi, 2010; Dias, 2011). The 'Carandiru Massacre' gained national and international attention and caused great controversy. Subsequently, groups within the government who were opposed to dominant policies – that had been centred on torture – gained sufficient legitimacy to get the country's best-known prison shut down. Years later, the '*Casarão*' ('Big House') was demolished with explosives, in an act designed to symbolise this change. Human rights organisations, victims' relatives and law makers were involved in this transition in government policy. From the point of view of the policies of crime, the massacre was also a turning point. If, until that point, organisations such as the Pastoral Carcerária ('Prison Pastoral') and Centros de Direitos Humanos (Human Rights Centres), with origins in the popular struggles of the 1970s, had sufficient legitimacy among prisoners to vocalise their demands to government, the massacre made evident, for at least some prisoners, that their lives could no longer be trusted to human rights advocates alone. During this period at least two forms of everyday conflict inside prisons were intensifying, which such organisations were ineffective at addressing. These were: (i) injustices in relationships among prisoners themselves, including rape, homicides considered to be 'unjustified' and the violation of minimal norms of coexistence (Dias, 2008; Biondi, 2010; Marques, A.J., 2010; Dias and Darke, 2015); and (ii) oppression of prisoners by the 'system', such as the restriction of visits and humiliating rules surrounding these, beatings and punishments considered excessive and delays in criminal proceedings. The following year the PCC was created, purportedly as a response to this situation.

Hegemonic construction

In this way, by presenting itself as the defender of the prison population against internal and external injustice and oppression, and breaking with the associative tradition of the social movements of previous decades, the PCC gradually expanded its legitimacy within the penitentiary system in the following years, implementing specific policies. Its members, called 'brothers', started to be baptised through rituals in which they committed themselves to crime (Biondi, 2016; Feltran, 2018; Manso and Dias Nunes, 2018). During this period, the original motto of the group, 'Peace, Justice and Liberty', served as a banner for wars that were waged by the 'Party' in the prisons of São Paulo against other groups of prisoners and the '*bandidões*', those who used force to subjugate other prisoners. Some factors seem to have been decisive in the process of PCC expansion, among which the group's success in legitimating its discourse among the prison population appears to have been fundamental. This was certainly a violent process, as shown by the PCC's common practice of decapitating its opponents. However, legitimacy does not seem to have been achieved solely through the use of physical coercion but, rather, above all, with the claim that violence should be just. Legitimacy was based, therefore, on the establishment of policies based on the law of crime, whose normative principles – what was understood as 'right' – the PCC claimed to represent (Marques, 2008). The relationship between normative principles and concrete actions in the management of routines by the PCC is therefore analogous to the relationship between law and government, but one in which the law is recognised as being based on the principle of respect for all.[3] This is how the PCC were able to implement policies prohibiting rape, murder, disrespect for basic rules of coexistence – and, later, also the use of crack – in the prisons they came to dominate. Using a mixture of violence and persuasion according to the situation, the PCC constructed an objective capacity to hold a monopoly over the legitimate use of force in each prison territory. Once the wars of movement against rival factions and the war of position in the formation of conceptions of the world had consolidated the 'Party' in a position of authority in most of São Paulo's prisons, the hegemony of the 'Command' in the prison system was marked with another key event that acted as a kind of ritual of PCC consolidation: the 'mega-rebellion', which took place simultaneously in twenty-six prison units across São Paulo in 2001.

State policies: tension between matrices

Alongside this unprecedented legitimation of crime as a pole of political power among prisoners, in the mid-1990s two other sets of discourses regarding violence, murder and justice – based on alternative criteria of peace, justice and freedom – were publicly legitimised in the State of São Paulo. Paradoxically, how the social world invariably presents itself. The first of these matrices was that of human rights discourse, which gained influence in the public security sphere, among a new generation of state managers and in training courses for police and prison officers. The 'massacre' would not be repeated: public policy reforms, bolstered by the deepening of democracy, would more effectively regulate prisons and youth detention units. However, a second discursive matrix of the government proposed the opposite: that it would be necessary to crack down on crime even more decisively.

The 1990s were characterised by the renewal of public security discourse in government departments and by a growing feeling of insecurity in Brazilian cities, fuelled by an explosion of homicides among young people in the peripheries, almost always in cycles of revenge killings by peers or by police that were referred to as 'settling accounts'. Fortified enclaves, ever more private security, twenty-four-hour surveillance cameras (Caldeira, 2000). The fight against 'impunity' became the focus of public security policy that diffused through the social fabric. If the first of these new matrices emphasised universal rights and citizenship, the second portrayed society as oppressed by its own laws – the rights of some were seen as constantly threatened by others; the repression and the elimination of voices defending the latter would permit the former to live in peace.

The latent conflict in government between these different conceptions of security tended to be resolved through a division of labour between groups. Managers and consultants heading official policies were socialised in the language of human rights; the lower echelons continued their normal everyday practices in the peripheries, supported by punitive 'public opinion' (read: the elites who control the mass media). The continuation of rebellions in FEBEM units, as well as in state prisons, and the negative publicity they revealed were highly damaging and revealed a crisis in the government proposal of defending human rights. On the one hand, they scandalised national and international human rights organisations; on the other, many believed that the government had been weak to allow them to occur in the first place.

In the midst of these conflicts, economic liberalisation and restructuring drove professionalisation, globalisation and flexibilisation in the management of all markets operating in the country, including illegal and illicit ones. Structural unemployment, which reached 22% in the São Paulo metropolitan region in the late 1990s, the informalisation of markets and the high rates of profit in illegal markets have increased violent crime rates. Competition for control of these emerging markets generated an arms race and, effectively, open warfare in the peripheries of the city. 'A lot of mothers cried' in the early hours, in hospital waiting rooms, medical-legal institutes and cemeteries. Even today, the generation who lived through this period still bears the psychological scars. Given its centrality in the news, crime became the subject of more systematic investigation, although always from a distance. In the peripheries, it is common for the 1990s, especially the later part of the decade, to be remembered as 'the time of wars'; in other public debates, it is commonly referred to as the moment of the 'consolidation of democracy'.

During the period, the public security complex both increased incarceration, with the aim of reducing homicide rates, and at the same time promoted training courses on human rights for police and prison officers. Although this appears paradoxical, these could be seen as two complementary sides of the same policy associated with the distinction between 'repression' and 'prevention'.[4] The modernisation of security policy followed the logic of all sectoral policies at the time: of attempting to increase efficiency and effectiveness. The war on crime had the drug war as its central ally, and it equated the trafficking of narcotics with heinous criminality. New anti-riot designs for prisons were drawn up; the reinforcement of Provisional Detention Centres and their decentralisation to the interior of the state put an end to the precincts of Police Delegacies; criminal proceedings were streamlined; small towns benefited from jobs created by these new public facilities – prisons also became a site of private investment, making those unintegrated into the labour market profitable, a trend that continues to grow. The policy had the support of many well-trained human rights experts, and it was believed it would turn the page following the era of massacres. The project was successful in the view of managers, and for this reason remains active to this day. This is certainly not because it reduced crime or rehabilitated prisoners, of course, but rather because it succeeded in hiding the structure of the conflict from public view. On the one hand, it satisfied demands for the punishment of the poor, widely viewed as the cause of disorder; on the other hand, it responded to the diffuse demand for a modernisation of public security, centred on the notions of rights and citizenship.

The point here is not to claim that the government produced a discourse of guaranteeing rights in order to then deliberately promote practices that contradicted it. Such contradictions are constitutive of every government, rather than being necessarily problems of political will, intentions, conscience or ideology, precisely because the margins are a precondition of how the state functions (Das and Poole, 2004). The argument that interests us here is, rather, a pragmatic one (Breviglieri, Lafaye and Tromm, 2009; Cefaï and Terzi, 2012): it is important consider the knowledges that are constructed at the level of practices, in the interstices of these official discourse, that is, those that are routinised as resistance in government departments and their consultancies, in the day-to-day of prisons and internment units, in everyday life in favelas and peripheries. For these are the knowledges that, clashing with official normativity, construct the matrices of justification of lived experience. As the mismatch between routine situations and institutional ideals is immense (much larger than is commonly believed), the beliefs in human rights and in the renewal of public security practices in the prisons of São Paulo in the 1990s gave way to endemic practices of abuse.[5] Meanwhile, the policies of another government, the PCC, became legitimate among prisoners. Low-ranking officials and administrators were forced to deal with two regulatory regimes, in different situations. In the corridors of prisons the 'human rights' proposals brought by government advisors were not implemented; but neither was the system 'dominated' by the policies of crime. The tension between these different normative regimes comes from the way, in the practices of public security, it constructed a matrix of practical knowledges that are put into action. It is these knowledges, therefore, that any analytical framework for understanding the problem must take very seriously (Cefaï, 2010).

Of course, those who knew the everyday world of 'violent sociability' (Machado da Silva, 2004) in the prisons during this period were not waiting for redemptive proposals coming from experts and managers. They were expecting that the war between the system and criminals, long established in their lives, would continue. By contrast, what was new was the enhanced ability of crime to implement its own policies. In this scenario, prisoners themselves believed the means proposed by the government guaranteed their rights much less effectively than others at their disposal. Attempts to 'humanise' São Paulo's prisons produced by the government, therefore, did not work as expected; criminal policies, on the other hand, became more and more diffused during the period, expanding across the prison system. The 2001 'mega-rebellion' was a ritual celebrating the consolidation of this process that strengthened the policies of crime.

It is no coincidence that the period of rising incarceration rates coincides exactly with the period in which the PCC appeared and gained legitimacy: the 'time of wars', which was followed by the 'period of white flag'. That is where the meaning of the third, most common, explanation becomes clear. When people in Sapopemba's favelas told me that you 'could no longer kill', what was being said was that in the territories that the PCC occupied around this time the principle was established that a person could be killed only with the permission of the 'Command'. In order to judge everyday disputes, and in particular major conflicts, the 'brothers' started to hold 'debates'. These could be brief and

187

informal or extremely sophisticated, including mobile teleconferences of up to seven prisons at the same time, as police wiretaps, press reports and studies have shown (Marques, 2007; Feltran, 2010a, 2010b, 2011; Hirata, 2018; Kessler and Telles, 2010; Dias, 2011). As has also been demonstrated, inside and outside the prisons these debates follow the same structure (Teixeira, 2009; Mallart, 2012).

After this change in the policies of crime – which rest upon values of equality inscribed in a popular tradition very different to that of the Enlightenment – the youth who previously had to kill a colleague for a debt of R$5 in order to maintain the respect of his peers can now no longer kill: he must appeal to the PCC to claim reimbursement for his loss. This new form of ethical regulation of crime, guaranteed by the armed force of the 'Command', had a far greater impact on homicide rates than is immediately visible; the brother of that murdered boy would feel obliged to avenge him, and so on, creating a lethal chain of private revenge, still common in other Brazilian cities. Under this new order, by contrast, the vendetta is interrupted: it is 'the law of crime' that judges and condemns transgressions, and is viewed as legitimate in doing so. As the policies of crime, determined in the 'debates', impose death sentences only as a last resort – in cases where PCC members are killed without prior permission – there are many intermediate punishments that can be implemented (warnings, beatings, expulsions, bans, depending on the attitude and performance of both the accuser and the accused). The whole cycle of revenge that had piled up the bodies of young men in favela alleys until the early 2000s thus became outlawed.

Criminal politics and economy: the roles of the PCC

As it strengthened its hegemony in the prisons, the PCC also began to appear in the peripheries as a collective subject representing the declaration of 'peace among thieves'. However, the war between rival groups in the '*quebradas*' had reached such proportions in the 1990s that at first this had little more than a residual effect. From the late 1990s on, however, the PCC's legitimacy grew steadily. On the one hand, the notion of the 'white flag' gained prominence in the discourse of figures who were influential in the peripheries but part of the 'world of crime', such as the rap band, Racionais MCs, who in 1997 sang 'A Fórmula Mágica da Paz' ('The Magic Formula of Peace'). On the other hand, internally, mass incarceration took young men who had been at war with each other off the streets and put them back there again, a few years later, having been socialised in the logic of 'peace among thieves' and 'war against the system'. The increase in the incarceration of low-level – and always very young – workers in the drugs trade, due to the classification of trafficking as a heinous crime, also contributed decisively to this transformation in the behaviour of criminals. As the organiser of these flows, guaranteeing them with force if necessary, the 'Command' became increasingly important as arguments about avoiding murder also grew beyond the prison walls.

It is worth remembering that it was in the first half of the 2000s, and especially after the 'mega-rebellion' of 2001, that the ideal of equality was added to the PCC's motto, so that it became 'Peace, Justice, Freedom and Equality' (Biondi, 2010). It was argued that authority should be earned by example, and not by imposition or by humiliation of others; the normative ideal was of a Clastrean model of leadership, without a single leader, centred in a system of non-personalised leadership positions and operating according to a regime of deliberation by debates, that would now also operate outside the walls. Returning to state policies, the RDD (Dias, 2011) was also established at the beginning of the decade, in reaction to the 2001 'mega-rebellion'. The RDD sought the isolation of those believed to be leaders of the PCC, preventing their contact with other prisoners and also isolating them from positions in which they could fight rivals within the 'Party'. Without them, and making punishment by the leadership sporadic, conditions were created that actively strengthened the ideal of equality within the PCC.

In the urban peripheries, meanwhile, by the beginning of the new millennium it was already common to hear that someone's '*biqueira*' (drug sale point) 'belonged to the PCC', or that the resale of a stolen car would be carried out 'by someone from the PCC'. In Sapopemba it was already being said in 2003 that 'all the drug traffic in the region' was run by the collective. The relationship between political statements about equality and those about the market was not – and is not – self-evident. On the one hand, in my research the PCC has always appeared, whether in criminal practices or in everyday discourse, as a regulator of conduct that, through the institution of 'debates', claims a legitimate monopoly over the use of violence in some territories and situations involving subjects involved in crime. On the other hand, however, the PCC also controls markets and economic dynamics.

However, at the same time that I heard the expression 'here everything is the PCC's', I also heard 'that *biqueira* doesn't belong to any *irmão*'. A twenty-one-year-old boy told me that since he was a teenager he had been involved in crime, and that he stole cars which he would hand over for 'dismantling' in the area, for an average of R$200; but he did not even know who was PCC around there, and he had never paid anything to anyone in the 'Party'. A teenager who had been working as a marijuana salesman near a school for two years said that in his '*biqueirinha*' (little drug sale point) no one from the 'Command' got involved. He paid a weekly amount to the military police to avoid problems, a bribe that had amounted to R$20,000 in the last year; but he'd never paid anything to the PCC. How could everything belong to the PCC, if this was the case?

Based on my own ethnography, but also on dialogue with the work of Hirata (2018), Batista (2012), Malvasil (2012), Rui (2012) and, as well as Telles and Cabanes (2006) and Telles (2009, 2011), I worked with the hypothesis that a small minority of these markets are, even if one looks at the whole productive chain, owned by a 'brother' of the PCC. It is true that a car scrapyard that processes stolen vehicles, a clandestine transportation line, a motorcycle resale, or a '*biqueira*' may be owned by 'brothers' baptised into the PCC. In these cases, we can identify an overlapping of the political-disciplinary functions of the 'Command' and its economic activities. Internally, however, my field data and the bibliography cited above suggest that, strictly speaking, these small and medium-sized enterprises may be owned by such and such a 'brother', but not by the organisation as a whole. What essentially matters to the 'Command' in these markets is not their financial health, but how they are regulated. Profitability matters primarily to the entrepreneurs themselves, who make or lose money with their businesses. To the 'Command', what is important is maintaining certain 'procedures' among the agents that integrate the moral dimensions of sociability, the need for collective agreements, procedures to redress injustices and ensuring the conditions for the proper functioning of market dynamics. These include respect for peers and internal codes of justice, the use of 'debates' to resolve conflict situations, restrictions on the use of arms and the prohibition of homicide without the endorsement of PCC members, as well as an issue that has been little mentioned in the literature, but much discussed by Maurício Fiore: freezing of drug sales prices and payments to the police. Other situations must be discussed on a case-by-case basis.

The vast majority of illegal markets in São Paulo are not operated by 'brothers', nor 'controlled' by the PCC. Unlike the case of Rio de Janeiro, it is not a criminal faction, comparable to a business cartel, that dominates illegal territories and businesses. Empirical research clearly shows that these markets include entrepreneurs – of different scales and social backgrounds – who are not from the favela, much less from the PCC. However, at least until 2010, in the accounts collected in my fieldwork and that of many other researchers in São Paulo, all criminal markets were based on a performative code of conduct surrounding crime that was safe-guarded by the PCC. Again, it is the regulating role that clearly emerges as key. In the peripheries, although the vast majority of illegal markets are not owned by 'brothers', they are regulated by the PCC. Whether because the entrepreneurs respect the moral and economic conduct demanded by the 'Command', or because they fear reprisal if they fail to comply, from 2001 to 2006 the PCC expanded its hegemony to all the peripheries of São Paulo, in the capital, in smaller cities on the coast and in the interior of the state.

The attacks and the routine: from 2006 to 2011

Friday, 12 May 2006. I was finishing another week of research in Sapopemba, having completed about a year of fieldwork. I had spent the morning in the Parque Santa Madalena and, that after-noon, almost two hours in a square in Jardim Planalto. A friend had told me a little about the workings of the '*biqueira*' that teenag-ers had operated in the area. This point, where marijuana, cocaine and crack were sold, had just been moved, due to the recent instal-lation of a mobile Military Police base, which we could see housed in a container in front of us as we talked. Traditional residents of Jardim Planalto – mainly the families of manual labourers and small business owners who had settled in Sapopemba in the 1970s – had requested a more constant police presence in the square. But having the police permanently situated in the square had merely pushed the '*biqueira*' fifty metres down the road, slightly further into the neighbourhood. In Jardim Planalto square, internal divi-sions between the 'working families' and 'bandits' had already materialised and were mediated by the ambiguous presence of the police. The picture was not new; Whyte (2005) had described a remarkably similar scenario in the 1940s.

Late in the afternoon I went on my way: an hour and a half on the bus to Vila Mariana terminal, half an hour on the metro to Tietê and then three hours back to São Carlos. I arrived home by midnight. On Saturday morning I picked up the newspaper on my doorstep. A photo of the very square I had just been in was printed on the front page of the *Folha de São Paulo*. It showed that same mobile police post riddled with bullets, and blood on the ground beneath. As I read the story, I realised that this was not the only one. That morning, which happened to be Mother's Day, at the crack of dawn, dozens of simultaneous armed attacks had been carried out against Military Police posts and vehicles, Civil Police stations, individual officers and public buildings across the metropolis. Even plain clothes police had been killed. Saturday began with an initial estimate of more than twenty state officials killed in what was immediately read by the press as the biggest offensive of a criminal organisation – and it was already known which, the PCC – ever recorded in São Paulo. No sooner had the news begun to circulate than it also became known that at the same time nearly a hundred prisons and youth detention facilities had been hit by rebellions, also 'by the PCC', across the state. The actions inside the prisons were an even larger stronger than they had been in 2001, when the faction had made its first major public appearance. The occurrence of rebellions in youth internment units and simultaneous attacks against agents of the government was unprecedented.

The crisis as seen in public debate

Over the weekend several other armed attacks were carried out against police and public buildings, especially in the east and south of São Paulo, as well as across several cities in the interior of the state. In the heat of the events, some buses were set ablaze, much unsubstantiated information circulated and the sense that order had completely broken down took hold. Official reports and rolling news only made the rumours grow that 'the PCC attacks' would spread without any control, the enemy's destructive potential being unknown. On Monday, 15 May, a 'curfew' was tacitly declared in the metropolis: public and private schools dismissed their students, most shops and public service offices closed, overloaded telephone lines failed to work. The events affected all the city's inhabitants and the press talked about nothing else. It was one of the tensest days in São Paulo's 450-year history. The President of the Republic blamed the prison administration of São Paulo, his direct political opponents, and offered to send federal troops to the state. The Governor, police commanders, religious leaders, government officials and deputies from various parties were all forced to appear before the public. The press amplified the 'talk of crime'. 'São Paulo besieged' was the title of a special supplement on the attacks in the country's largest newspaper. The words 'urban warfare' and 'war on crime' circulated on television, on the internet and in newspapers. In the furore, contradictory and spectacular claims were the basis for the most diverse opinions and proposals: ideas for the reinforcement of security measures, calls for summary executions of prisoners and favela residents, reflections on Brazil's social problems. There was no one who did not have an opinion to share.

On Tuesday, as if overwhelmed by an excess of information, public tensions abruptly cooled in São Paulo. By then, all of the desperation seemed a bit exaggerated. The attacks had become much less frequent and could be assimilated into everyday perceptions of risk. Furthermore, the number of 'suspects' assassinated grew to a satisfactory level. The Military Police had killed a single person on 12 May, before the attacks began; they murdered eighteen the next day, forty-two on 14 May and another thirty-seven on 15 May. The police had suffered forty casualties, but they had won the 'war'. With ninety-seven 'suspects' murdered in three days, it could be announced that once again everything was 'under control'. People recomposed themselves and life resumed its rhythm. São Paulo couldn't stop, other topics once again came to occupy the headlines and everyday conversation.

But in the 'private war', between police and the urban peripheries, it was clear that the conflict had not ended. 'I think that the retaliations haven't ended, they will continue,' Valdênia Paulino told me on 17 May. After the authorities had dealt with the public problem, it was time for accounts to be silently settled between the parties directly involved. Adorno and Salla (2007) have shown that homicides committed by the police remained very high in the months that followed the attacks.

The crisis as seen from the peripheries

On a panic-filled Monday in São Paulo, I telephoned a social worker at CEDECA. During the conversation I learned that the nephew of one of my main research participants, Almir, had been murdered. I returned to Sapopemba on Wednesday, 17 May. Activity in the area's human rights organisations was intense. While striving to make it clear that they did not support or acknowledge the legitimacy of the PCC's actions, they focused on formally denouncing the most serious cases of police violation in the region. I also went to the favelas Elba and Madalena, where I visited some acquaintances and stayed in the house of a friend, Ivete, whose family I had studied a few years previously. There, although people were more attentive than usual, the rhythm of life was normal. For favela families, the attacks had not altered daily life; living under risk was, somehow, normal. Furthermore, no one there condemned the attacks.

They were surprised only because no one knew when they would happen, nor what would trigger them. But they had been sure that it was just a matter of time before there was some kind of reaction against the police, and that the forces of order deserved it. The PCC already had enough strength to show it publicly, to bring the police to the table to negotiate, both inside and outside the prisons. Writing my field journals during this time I was aware of the gulf between the public debate and what I was hearing in my ethnographic work. On the one side, in the news and in conversations with my university friends, even when these were focused on criticising the news, the agenda was focused on counting the number of casualties, the spreading of collective fear and rumours, talking about urban violence and Brazil's social problems, questions about the PCC and its history. On the other side, especially in the accounts of favela residents, what was discussed were concrete cases of violence experienced during those days; those 'brothers' of the PCC, who were known to all, were named. It wasn't simply a matter of differences in the topics that were discussed and judgements reached about what had happened; there was a fundamental difference in the respective places that the events occupied. It seemed to me that in the public debate the events were an 'issue'; in the favelas of Sapopemba they were concrete cases. In short, favelas residents had lived the violence of the week at close hand, and 'from the other side'.

In the news an image emerged of a powerful organisation that had sprung up from the prisons and favelas. Meanwhile, residents in favela Elba saw two Military Police officers scrawl 'PCC' on the walls of an abandoned room (the 'discovery' of a 'hideout' in the favela was widely reported in the mainstream press). The *Jornal Nacional* television news broadcast classified those killed in the 'urban war' as 'police', 'suspects' and 'civilians', while Almir's relatives mourned the death of their nephew. Authorities, politicians and police calculated the number killed in the counter-offensive; Ivete advised her sons to be more cautious during those days. Finally, while on one side there was a public debate about 'urban violence', in the peripheries, and especially in the favelas, people had to confront violence that directly interfered in the most intimate spheres of life.

Even in Sapopemba, however, a clear gap could be seen between what was being said by favela-dwelling families and what was being said by social organisations. CEDECA and the Centro de Direitos Humanos de Sapopemba (Sapopemba Human Rights Centre) adopted a neutral position, seeking to increase understanding of the crisis, criticising the public handling of the events and assuming a position of defending the rights of residents in the midst of 'urban warfare':

> On Saturday morning, we took the car and went for a ride, we stopped at all the police stations in Sapopemba, at the base of the Guarda Metropolitana, at the Military base, offering our solidarity, leaving our contacts, because it was Saturday and Sunday, to get any attention we could. The cops did not have a reserve force, they were alone, tired because everyone's time off was suspended, without even a pot of coffee, abandoned in this periphery. And they didn't know when the transfer would happen. (…) So the state abandoned [the police]. From there we went to the families too. That day I had already said, 'Let's tell the families to be careful, because there will be lead coming in the population's direction' (Valdênia Paulino)

If the role of CEDECA was to mediate, the families living in the favelas took sides. Ivete, in those days, did not fear 'organised crime', the 'PCC', nor any *bandido*. She was afraid that the police would violently invade her house, looking for her children; that one of her imprisoned sons would be executed in a prison rebellion; that one of her free sons would be murdered in a 'revenge' killing by the police. She knew, in short, that the 'war on crime' had identified her family as a target long ago. What was different about the days of the crisis was the way in which routine practices of repression were radicalised. Viewed from the perspective of favela residents, the 'novelty' of the urban conflict was only that it had become intensified and less selective in an already highly institutionalised process of police repression of the favelas and their residents, especially adolescents and young men.

Balance: one week, 493 dead in São Paulo

The State Department for Public Security waited as long as possible before releasing the official list of who had been killed during that week in May. Under pressure from human rights bodies and the press, a partial release was made ten days after the events had begun. The numbers suggested that 168 homicides had been committed: 40 state agents killed during the PCC offensive and 128 people officially registered as killed by the police. There were also twenty-eight arrests. It was not pointed out that individuals killed in 'massacres' and those who had 'disappeared' were not included within the official count. A more realistic calculation was finally reached some six months later. Only the newspaper *O Estado de São Paulo* carried out an investigation in twenty-three Medical-Legal Institutes across the state, which indicated that between 12 and 20 May 2006 at least 493 homicides were committed in São Paulo. Of these, civil society organisations claimed at least 221 were committed by police officers, and the official figures indicated that 52 referred to those killed in the PCC's attacks.

There were, therefore, another 220 homicides committed that week, for which not a single investigative hypothesis has been offered. The critical event made it clear that the possibilities of subjectivation of that generation born in the favelas are already shaped by the public construction of 'urban violence'. Killings by police during their counter-offensive were widely read as contributing to the re-establishment of urban order. On the other hand, it was evident that in the favelas the PCC had already achieved legitimacy in opposition to the police.

The 'crimes of May', from this perspective, rearranged routine relationships in São Paulo along the tense borders between government and crime. In light of the grave repercussions of the events – which were controversial and risky for all the actors involved – and following reflection on them, both crime and government settled, tactically, on a kind of armistice that was functional for both sides and seems to have been responsible for the steady downward trend of homicides in the state until 2011. The parties' achievements during this period were mainly focused on access to 'political merchandise' (Misse, 2006a). In my interpretation, it is during this period that a single apparatus administering lethal violence became stabilised across the state of São Paulo, a single apparatus which nevertheless includes specialised regimes, composed of state and criminal policies and directed at distinct populations.

Entangled governance: from 2012 onwards

From this perspective we can clearly see how the aggressive policies of both crime and government cooled between 2006 and 2011, even if tensions continued, sometimes latently and at other times – like in 2012, when more than 100 police officers were killed by the PCC in São Paulo – more explicitly. The events of 2006 were a key turning point for São Paulo's administrative apparatus for dealing with lethal violence, centred on the relationship between these policies. The great demonstration of the strength of crime in that month of May, coordinated both inside and outside the prisons, was followed by an unprecedented reaction from the government, which committed a new massacre that was much more lethal than Carandiru, although now in the urban peripheries. As a result, the parties realised that it was not possible to proceed on the same basis: they need to re-establish minimal agreements that would make life more predictable. The truce that followed – reinforced by a new price list of financial incentives among individuals inscribed in both government and crime, for each tense interaction that needed to be made between them – led to the significant fall in homicides that unfolded until 2011.

This unlikely scenario of tense coexistence between two orders – whose actors, on both sides, are heavily armed, internally coordinated and capable of directly unsettling the urban order as a whole – constitutes the landscape of relations between government and crime to this day. In the decade since 2011 the balance between the force and the legitimacy among them tended to strengthen state policies. The military police has appeared daily in popular television shows about crime and against politicians; police officers are today well established in São Paulo's lower- to middle-class neighbourhoods, participating in WhatsApp groups, Consegs (Conselhos de Segurança) and being part of formal municipal and federal politics. Nevertheless, the coexistence between crime and state policies still establishes the urban order and frames developments in São Paulo's homicide rates. In a first reading, centred on the alterity between the social groups that legitimise one or other of these two orders, the tension that surrounds interactions between them highlights the magnitude of the social fracture that has emerged. These effectively constitute the production of social and political ontologies in dispute, whereby each group believes that its legal-political-administrative system, norms and values, aesthetic markers and even its markets form an autonomous totality in the face of what they identify as an implacable enemy. Analytically, however, the intrinsic relations between these supposedly autonomous regimes are plain to see. Second, we can see that through the conflict between the state policies and those of crime there is a kind of 'outsourcing' of public security, whereby the government continues to be the central actor in decision making and crime organises specific territories and groups in the peripheries of the city. If *bandidos* being killed in the 'settling of accounts' is unimportant to government, since within this regime these subjects lie beyond the frontiers of humanity (Arendt, 1989), high 'homicide rates' do matter. If crime can help to reduce them without the need for substantive political change, all the better.

Low homicide rates do not mean that there were no violent and periodic confrontations between police forces and the PCC in São Paulo. These clashes were very strong in 2012 and, with the governments elected in 2018 explicitly calling for the extermination of 'bandits' in the favelas, intensified in 2019. Preliminary data from different ethnographies indicate that, especially since 2006, there has been specialisation in policing the faction. Specific police groups specialise in extortion and homicide, targeting the PCC's 'brothers'. In some of these groups, therefore, the victims of police lethality do not have the same profile as always, not the young black of the peripheries, the low-down worker in the criminal markets. These police groups kill older, whiter criminal men who have passed through the prison system many times. This police lethality targets the well-established criminal entrepreneurs of São Paulo.

Another very important factor to consider about the urban order in Brazil, although less relevant in São Paulo because the PCC's hegemony in the 'world of crime' is stronger, is the ending of the harmony between the two main Brazilian criminal factions, Comando Vermelho (Red Command, a big criminal group, originally from Rio de Janeiro) and PCC, in 2016. This harmony, which aided in the production of peace in the prisons and peripheries of many Brazilian cities, also prevented local confrontation in several urban regions of the country. When it ended, very bloody massacres, especially in the North and Northeast of the country, increased local tensions and brought about local questioning of the legitimacy of the criminal order in suburban neighbourhoods. The more violent the presence of the 'world of crime', or of the police in everyday life, the less legitimacy its policies will enjoy. Political theory had already taught us about that. The emergence of the 'world of crime' in Brazilian cities is a major political issue for governments and public debate. It needs mediation.

Conclusion

[B]ut in São Paulo, God is a hundred bill. (Racionais MC's, 2002)

There has been intense debate in recent years, among those who study urban peripheries, regarding the Brazilian 'social question' – encompassing poverty and policies aimed at strengthening social protection as well as the repression of marginality, crime and violence. While there has never been consensus in the Brazilian literature on these themes, debates have been structured around arguments that are as consistent as they are divergent.[1] On the one hand, the literature has emphasised the expansion of citizenship, evidenced by greater coverage of policies and improvement of social indicators (including income inequality), and by the maintenance of progressive legal frameworks, the consolidation of community participation in councils, the stability of institutional democracy and a huge expansion of popular consumption and access to credit.[2] On the other hand, it has highlighted an increase in insecurity, the militarisation of the urban order, both the criminalisation of poverty and its instrumentalisation by the real estate and private security markets, along with increased incarceration and forced internment of drug users, and attacks on civil rights and social movements.[3] The same empirical phenomena – whether in debates about changes to the Statute of the Child and the Adolescent, the legalisation of drugs, affirmative action, funk music or even the reduction of homicides in São Paulo – could be taken as indicators supporting either the most optimistic or most pessimistic diagnoses about the consolidation of democracy or of economic development.

Without doubt, the distinct theoretical perspectives, sites of observation and research methods employed within each analytical current explain a part of these divergences, and are thus largely a healthy feature of the debate that will help it to develop and mature. However, I would like to suggest that one of the main causes of this confusion is the excessive analytical aggregation, presupposing empirical homogeneity (even if we claim otherwise), that categories like 'urban poverty', 'urban periphery' or 'popular classes' carry with them. Especially because today these words encompass everyone from a waste picker to a taxi driver; from a transgender sex worker to a builder with three cars in the garage; from small-town girls working at Hooters to pay for university in the metropolis, to a high school student caught up in the youth offender system; from a beneficiary of affirmative action at a good public university, to a homeless ex-convict and crack addict; from a patient at a rehabilitation centre trying to quit cocaine, to a Bolivian textile worker or a Nigerian street vendor; from an Evangelical Community Health Agent to a small car trader who is a member of the Rotary Club; from a sixty-year-old black private security guard from the Northeast of Brazil, to a 'brown' nineteen-year-old prisoner from a favela; a police officer, an unemployed mechanic or the owner of an illegal car scrapyard.

When we delimit the social field by broad population indicators, we know that all these subjects could live in the same street of the same 'peripheral' district in São Paulo. Using occupational or income categories, all could be considered 'members of the working classes'. Their life prospects, their geographic, family and religious backgrounds, their norms of conduct and the social programmes that come to them via NGOs, government or churches, as well as their insertion into different markets and the ways in which 'urban violence' touches their lives are fundamentally divergent. Heterogeneity intensified in urban peripheries (Caldeira, 2009; Cabanes, 2014), while dominant literature arguments become more aggregative (Wacquant, 2009a; 2009b).

Having participated in numerous debates about violence, social movements and urban transformations since 2008, I have come to realise that our arguments, although coming from different points of departure, are almost always based on totalising representations about the 'periphery' or of 'poverty'. More recently, I have perceived that we almost always take a particular image – that of the member of the PCC, the crack addict, the prisoner, the priest, or of indebted families who buy cars or social housing apartments through the real estate financed by public banks – as representing the peripheries as a whole.

This book has tried not to take this totalising and almost always dichotomous way of representing the poor – through the perspective either of 'urban violence' or of 'economic development' – as a presupposition, but rather as an object of reflection. Thus, I write here based on my experiences in recent years, both intellectual and political, in participating in countless debates about the 'peripheries'. The heterogeneity of the popular sectors and the way in which they are delimited by social programmes, by churches or by the 'world of crime', are themselves the point of departure. My research in the peripheries of São Paulo, therefore, is not its only source of data, although ethnography, the translation of a lived experience into text, remains the basis of the knowledge presented.

My argument here presupposes tense boundaries between different sectors of the population of the 'peripheries', whether classified as 'Classe C' (the upper fraction of peripherical families) or '*marginal*', but especially in relation to more affluent social groups (understood by all as '*playboys*', '*madames*' or '*bacanas*'). These are the two lines of social conflict that I am interested in studying, based on these delimitations. The modes of governing this conflict, which produces social and urban order, thus become privileged objects for analysis. As a hypothesis, in this book I proposed that today's social conflict is not only mediated by Christian values, a foundation for cohesion between unequals in Brazil, or by the rise of law as a privileged mediator (law, order, citizenship); nor is it *only* the product of a punitive logic, although this is clearly visible in trends towards mass incarceration and the criminalisation of poverty, which attempt to subjugate the discontented by force.

Contemporary governance strategies of urban conflict seem to be based precisely on the situational variation of a repertoire of actually existing and relatively autonomous normative regimes (Machado da Silva, 1993; Feltran 2010a, 2011; Grillo, 2013), which include these strategies and many others based on *slicing the population* as precisely as possible. Central to these delimitations, essentialised in bodies and in words, is the idea of separating out the spheres of morality or of the law. However, it is clear that all of them are subject to a market logic, formally integrated by money, which produces a common way of life, desired by all and centred on the expansion of consumption. Although they are represented as living in distinct moral universes, workers and *bandidos* exchange monetarised goods and services, to the extent that the markets in which they operate are deeply interlinked; police and traffickers also have 'accounts to settle', which can only be financial, so that drug trafficking generates benefits for both; *playboys* and *manos* love the same bikes and cars, submitting to the innumerable direct relationships, though in different positions, of the labour and consumption markets in which they participate. Everyone respects wealth as a sign of status. *Money* is objectively elevated to the status of mediator between conflicting population groups, far surpassing the legitimacy of law and of morality, which would keep them apart.

Scanning the population and essentialising and objectifying the slices taken is the first function of the machinery of *government*, which for a long time has not only been performed by the state, especially at the margins of the social world (Das and Poole,

2004; Lancione, 2016); it is based on this essentialisation that the evaluation – always selective and unequal – of these groups occurs. The value attributed to each part, duly objectified in these classifications, can then be quantified and monetised (Simmel, 1990 [1900]).[4] It is, therefore, a market logic: this is exactly the same way that urban land or 'market niches' are divided up; so too must the populations be sliced, made to become, simultaneously, the 'target audiences' of marketers and government programmes.[5] Hence the constitutive nexus between the selective management of poverty and market development, hence the ideal of expanding consumption to the poor and their integration into markets as a fundamental political project. Expanding the circulation of money, now also significant at the margins of the social world, is thus the fundamental objective of the variable repertoire of regimes of governing poverty that slice up the poor based on the potential intensity of conflict which they can inflict on the market order.

In order to develop this perspective, this conclusion argues that the representation of 'urban violence' has displaced the contemporary 'social question' away from 'workers' and onto '*marginais*'; also because of this, social policies have moved away from the universalism of social rights and today think in terms of *social protection*, especially grounded in the prevention of violence. In this way, the representation of a moral continuum among the poor, with the *bandido* to be imprisoned at one pole and the 'consumer' or 'entrepreneur' to be inserted into the market at the other, becomes plausible. In government practices, also often referred to in market practices, this essentialisation produces different slices of the population, in which different 'social vulnerabilities' are targeted and varying degrees of 'complexity' for intervention with different 'target groups' are developed. Alterity becomes radicalised in cases where subjects are coded as *bandidos*. This selective mode of government – which combines interventions as disparate as the conditional income transfer programmes and incarceration, not to mention extermination – ends up, as a side effect, promoting the emergence of a repertoire of normative regimes in the urban peripheries – of the state, 'crime' and religion – all regulating monetarised markets. It is monetarisation, therefore, that centrally mediates the relation between the differentiated groups, which under other mediating perspectives – law and order or morality – would be in radical alterity. 'Development' centred on consumption, therefore, is elevated as a common way of life. A worker does not morally confuse himself with a *bandido*, nor does a policeman have the same position before the law as a drug dealer; both, however, have proximate relative positions within consumer markets. As money circulates indiscriminately through legal, illegal and illicit markets, market expansion connects these subjects and therefore also mediates the 'settling of accounts' between them, which makes illicit and 'political commodity' (Misse, 2006a) markets grow. Thus, the same hand that encourages the expansion of consumption of the new '*Classe C*' foments the urban violence that it claims to control.

From the social question to the urban order as security

There is relative consensus in the literature that the contemporary *social question* is the product of a decisive shift, present since the French and American revolutions (Arendt, 1959, 1977), but especially visible since the 1950s, that lies at the heart of the normative modern narrative about the universal expansion of democracy and citizenship (Castel, 1999; Agamben, 1998). In a wage society, the social question was guided by the efforts – introduced by governments following great social conflict which many times ended in violence – of public and state mediation of the unequal effects of capitalist accumulation, codified in the extension of national civil, political and social rights (Marshall, 1950). Citizenship was therefore understood as the universal counterpart to wage labour (Donzelot, 1984; Machado da Silva, 1993; Rosanvallon, 1995; Feltran, 2011;

Cabanes, 2014). The 'worker' was, therefore, the central figure from which the social problem and attempts at addressing it were constructed. Although this counterpart was not in fact universalised, the normative (cognitive and political) horizon of solving the 'social question' was formulated in terms of social welfare, placing limits on the commodification of social life, the internalisation of class conflict in the conception and administration of the state, and through the creation of national communities that aim at internal homogeneity. The 'foreign' came to be figured as radical alterity, justifying war. The state protects its citizens from external threats.[6] Integration, insertion and social inclusion, therefore, oriented the social problem and modes of state intervention on poverty around the creation a *community*, while at the same time clearly redesigning the technologies of power (Foucault, 1997).

Telles (2011) and Robert Castel (1999) demonstrated how this equation was challenged both in European countries and in Brazil, from the 1980s onwards. In a new scenario, characterised by 'productive restructuring' and 'neoliberal reform of the state', state mediations that guaranteed rights at the base were dismantled, throwing the figure of the 'formal worker' onto the defensive. The rise of the 'precariat', and its informality, made 'structural unemployment' the new sign of 'vulnerability'. If the scenario described by Castel in the late 1990s has continued to metamorphose up to the present day, this is undoubtedly due to the radicalisation of the same trends of transformation of the social question that he described. Informal markets and precarious jobs expanded all over the world, even in contexts of economic development and very low unemployment, such as the Brazilian case in the 2000s. But they also expanded remarkably in the central economies (Ruggiero and South, 1997). In Brazil, the *regulation* of citizenship (Santos, 1979) embodied a similar model and, in practical terms, barely reached places and people marked by sociability, language and codes of conduct that were considered informal. Those classified as poor lay at the edges of an incomplete structural process of modernity, hence the attribution of 'backwardness' that permeates readings, from common sense to universities, about the popular sectors. The very notions of *exclusion* or *detachment* would attest to this kind of evolutionism inscribed even in critical formulations of the social question.

However, the social conflict immanent to recent transformations, not only frustrates the ideal of citizenship, but also, it seems to me, has become radicalised. This may be because we are experiencing a moment of broad social renegotiation, or because this conflict does not emanate fundamentally from the working sectors, who can be integrated into the *national community* through the narrative of expanding both markets and rights. Although work and rights – as well as religiosity – continue to play fundamental roles, lending cohesion to social practices, social conflict today is centrally *represented* in terms of the expansion and progressive thematisation of 'urban violence', 'drugs' and 'marginality',[7] which construct subjects using definitions that do not allow for integration. If the struggle for workers' rights in the 1980s and early 1990s raised the social issue to a political level (Paoli, 1995), the central opposition on which the contemporary social conflict seems to be built is the *moral* cleavage that opposes the figure of the worker, understood as a 'good guy', a participant in a community that yearns for progress, that of the *bandido* or the 'druggie', the '*nóia*', the 'convict' – in short, of the enemy who, by its very existence, threatens the same community. In the different figurations of the *other* to be combated, the conflict inscribed in the social question is now reflected around an *existential threat* to public order, subjectivated in bodies, territories and words that are clearly defined and internal to the territories where they live. No longer foreign enemies: the threat comes from within, is closer to home, the enemy is internal.

It is no longer just a matter of acknowledging the 'social vulnerability' of homeless people, prisoners or crack users, and then managing their necessary 'reintegration' (Melo, 2014). It is a question of equating this 'vulnerability' with the potential risk they represent. On the other hand, depending on the moral performance of each subject or group, different doses are offered of the mixture of social protection–control–repression, expanding rights and deprivations, treatment and discipline, healthcare and criminalisation, legitimate authority and violent repression, always at the same time.[8] This is why always targeted social services have proliferated alongside equally targeted strategies of public and private security, surveillance and the militarisation of urban areas.

In Brazil, the expansion of access to home ownership through the Minha Casa, Minha Vida programme is therefore in complete harmony with the return of the forced displacement of urban undesirables, either to distant peripheries or to prisons and rehabilitation clinics offering chemical control through psychiatrisation. Support is provided for the 'New C Class' which expands markets, while at the same time isolating the slices of the population that impede its advance: the *favelados*. The problem appears only when it is discovered that the homes in which the 'New C Class' will live are situated in territories in which not only the law of the market exists; when it becomes clear that this new class isn't 'segregated' from 'crime', from the PCC or its dynamics but, rather, lives in the same neighbourhoods; when it is realized that the *other* that needs to be combated materialises, not infrequently, in one's own father, brother, husband, relative.

The framework for making sense of social problems explicitly shifts from the *social question* to the problem of *violence*, understood as a problem associated with *crime*, *drugs* and *poverty*. But there is a mismatch between this framework and the set of practices that it presumes to describe, which forces reclassifications, owing to distrust of previously well-established constructions, such as the worker versus the *bandido*. There are many more shades of grey between them when one notes that the 'world of crime' in the peripheries also has legitimacy to safeguard values such as peace, justice, freedom and equality; which generates income and produces jobs and belonging, if not new kinship structures (Feltran,

2011; 2013a). Publicly, and especially among elites, the reclassification of the world is much slower than in popular everyday practice. Thus, in their public representations, workers and *bandidos* continue to be placed in opposition, and the fundamental normative basis of politics shifts from the integration of the workers into the community to debates about personal security and property, based on the control of spaces and of populations that threaten these (drug users, *marginais*, thieves, traffickers). It is no longer a question of the universal extension of citizenship rights (no rights are offered to such enemies), nor of the universality of democratic guarantees (the exception is tolerated, it may even become a rule when it comes to 'defending society').

Brazil's contemporary social conflict therefore requires slicing up the population and distributing it across the repertoire of different modes of government, ranging from substantive democracy to extermination. This mosaic of different ways of managing the poor is radically different from that anchored in the myth of racial democracy in the first half of the twentieth century, or subsequent attempts at the social insertion of migrant workers in cities, regional integration or the regulated extension of social rights to the *excluded*. In recent years, the social conflict has been expressed in a seemingly contradictory scenario: rising crime rates accompany increases in formal employment rates; mass incarceration policies coincide with the greater provision of social services; major urban regeneration programmes emerge alongside the compulsory hospitalisation of crack users; pacification means the military occupation of favela territories; incarceration produces the consolidation of criminal factions.

The constitutive contemporary paradox, therefore, is the association between economic development and the modernisation of markets, on the one hand, and the diffuse spread of the representation of 'urban violence', on the other. Analytically disaggregating the populations and, especially, the situations in which each of these regimes acts is therefore fundamental. In Brazil, traffickers, prisoners, rough-sleeping homeless people and crack users are at the centre of the public thematisation of contemporary social problems – on the covers of newspapers and magazines, across all media. We are not called upon to treat these figures as citizens, of course, except among those groups – in the face of growing public ridicule – who insist on the defence of human rights. Their incarceration, or even extermination, is legitimised by groups considered as *included* and, in the public debate, is directly linked with the dominant validation of instrumental notions of the democratic state and development. Diverse works have shown that *bandidos*, *favelados*, drug addicts and traffickers – points of gravitation for popular understandings of Brazil's social problems today – have long been publicly represented in terms of radical alterity (Misse, 2010; Biondi, 2010; Lyra, 2013; Grillo, 2013); the international bibliography demonstrates similar processes in other countries (Das and Poole, 2004; Jensen, 2008; Bourgois and Schonberg, 2009). With these enemies at its centre and with the demoralisation of narratives of universal social integration, or even of legitimate political struggle over common rights, the social is conceived as constrained by an irreducible conflict that restricts and reinforces its borders: there is always an inside and an outside of social life, which is no longer confused with national life. This figuration clashes with the central suppositions of political modernity inscribed in the democratic formula. It is in *political* terms, therefore, that the *social question* should be posed: it is a redefinition of what constitutes the life of the nation, of the political community. However, it has mainly been diffused through the moral terms in which 'urban violence' is represented.

Urban violence and welfare[9]

Luiz Antonio Machado da Silva warned us over two decades ago of the mistake of deploying the notion of 'urban violence' as an analytical category. On the contrary, we must treat this representation as part of the problem we are trying to understand, since it is a historical construction and constitutes, in the way it is routinely used, what it claims to describe (Machado da Silva, 1993). Michel Misse has verified the centrality of this statement across the whole field of studies on crime and violence, as well as the assumptions it reveals and the analytical developments that it proposes, which are also valid for those who study urban peripheries (Misse, 2006a). In addition, he has taught us that the first of the 'five misconceptions about urban crime in Brazil' is that 'poverty is the cause of crime, or of the increase of urban violence' (Misse, 2006b; 2010).

In order to engage with these arguments with a minimal level of rigour, it seems to be necessary to avoid *reifying* the concepts in question and representing them as a 'reality'. As such, there is no urban violence in itself. The representation of 'urban violence' is fundamentally a process of *arbitrary association* between distinct concepts and phenomena over time, that form a single phenomenon only as they are reified – via mechanisms of objectification, that are never disinterested – and thus come to be *apprehended* as constituting reality.[10] In our case, phenomena and concepts as diverse as *crime, illegal drugs, illicit markets, firearms, factions, gangs, brown and black bodies, urban territories* and *poverty* are interconnected in this representation. If analytical rigour demands that each of these concepts be treated separately, taking into account the obvious distinctions between them, in the representation of 'urban violence' they are undifferentiated, each of them potentially representing a facet of the broader phenomenon, if not simply synonymous with it. In São Paulo, during my field research, there were many situations in which to say 'violence', especially among individuals not inserted within the 'world of crime', was the same as saying 'trafficking' or 'PCC'. Along the same lines is the idea that any social programme dedicated to a young favela resident is necessarily a form of 'violence prevention'.

It does not matter that use of 'drugs' transcends class and that 'trafficking' is transnational; in the meanings of 'urban violence' both are embodied in hills and favelas, in a skin colour, in a particular age, in an aesthetic that must be contained. It doesn't matter if a country like India has immense poverty and homicide rates that are much lower than in a country like the United States. It doesn't matter that local dealers in São Paulo's favelas worked unarmed during the 2000s. The business of trafficking continues to be represented as something so violent that, in the escalating demands for punishment, it can be treated as legally equivalent to heinous crimes. It doesn't matter that crime depends on the law that classifies it, and is always much wider than the set of acts that involve violence; the construction of 'urban violence' reduces 'crime' to violent acts committed by only one race (that built upon the racialisation of the poor), now defined around the aesthetics of the young people in the peripheries. It doesn't matter, either, that legal and illegal economies are today interdependent; because it is implausible, thinking beyond the legal versus illegal dichotomy contained in this representation, to believe that formal economic growth should diminish the size of globalised informal and illegal markets. It is not what happens transnationally, and evidently has not occurred in Brazil in recent decades (Telles, 2011).

If such disparate concepts and phenomena appear in this dis-cursive regime as naturally connected, the subjects and spaces that materialise this connection, giving it unquestionable concreteness, are elevated as 'typical' in the representation of 'urban violence'. Their physical existence thus becomes the empirical demonstra-tion of how all the elements listed effectively combine in practice. Sabotage, a rapper with a lot of melanin in his skin and a long his-tory in the favela, sang what Michel Misse (2010) described about criminal subjectivation: 'I don't know what it is / If they see me, they retreat!' The figure of the '*nóia*' (crackhead), inhabitant of '*cracolândias*', is equally relevant for noting how the categories of 'drugs' (Fiore, 2012) and 'violence' become reified in their connec-tion. Even though empirically it is a very small portion of users of the substance (Rui, 2012) who use it to such an extent that they end up living on the streets, this is the immediate image conjured up by the word 'crack'. The part becomes the whole, but not by chance: this small part allows for the immediate naturalisation of all the elements on which the representation of violence is based – indignity, dirtiness, disorder, crime, violence, evil, abjection, immorality, risk, threat. If the vast majority of young people in the periphery are not 'in the crime', and if the immense majority of those in 'the crime' do not commit violent crimes, it is likewise this tiny criminal and violent portion that will represent *the entire periphery* when 'urban violence' is mobilised as the framework of intelligibility.

This representation thus produces a cognitive boundary that defines the limits to which the meanings of words can be distended. Within these parameters, the word 'crime' cannot, for example, be stretched to include people whose speech and actions are considered legitimate. In this representation, the law defines crime as its opposite and, as it presents itself as valid 'for all' in a given territory, it is not plausible to think otherwise. The valuation fund that accompanies the expression 'violence' is always negative (Misse, 2006b). The representation of 'urban violence' operates, therefore, within the limits of previously determined associations attached to subjects and territories that in their essence, and unambiguously demonstrated in their actions, express the violence that underpins this. It is not plausible, within this representation, to break with the central evaluation, which, as a result, is able to overflow and signify surrounding concepts, reifying them in each new situation in which they are mobilised. The word 'crime', however, even if it carries negative associations in the dominant state construction of law and order, can possess highly positive normative connotations for significant portions of the Brazilian population (Hirata, 2018; Malvasi, 2012). This implies that in our analysis we must also study use of these terms in completely distinct *situations* in which they also appear. Such dissensus refers not only to arguments, but to the arguable; that is, to the different parameters by which the world can be conceived and those who inhabit it.

The public thematisation of 'urban violence' in this way represents an active way of producing *reality* and investing it with content, which *at the same time* conceals what exists in the world, formulated in a way that is alien to its own terms. What is not plausible in terms of this representation can therefore be considered non-existent: that the 'world of crime' makes homicides diminish in the peripheries of São Paulo in the 2000s, for example (Telles and Hirata, 2007; Feltran, 2012). What is not publicly said, however, is discussed in private. Among the very poor, especially but not only in São Paulo, 'crime' has gained other meanings since the late 1970s. The accumulation of conflict around the meaning of these words made 'crime', in specific situations in the 'peripheries', a normative and figurative counterpoint to the representation of 'urban violence' itself. It seems to me that today the performance of these two representations is centred on the attempt to produce precise sub-groups of the population, in order to distribute a repertoire of different governmental regimes depending on 'who is speaking' across the social fabric.

The 'new generation of social policies' has already been conceived under the aegis of this representation of 'urban violence', in a framework opposed to the universalism of citizenship. It acts by cutting the social into different groups, requiring different intervention strategies. In field research, we can see the effects of the contemporary radicalisation of this logic: the same transgender individuals classified as 'sex workers' by health policies became 'rough sleepers' when assisted by CREAS Pop and 'drug users' when hospitalised in an evangelical rehabilitation clinic (Martinez et al., 2014). Their 'identities', in each case, demand very different doses of the assistance–repression equation, which were nevertheless always present. This also occurs in many other cases that we have studied: programmes aimed at the marginalised distribute repression–protection in distinct mixtures along an imaginary *continuum* that has, at one pole, the figure of the 'dangerous' to be controlled and, at the other, the new consumer eager for credit.

Conclusion

Between these poles are the notions of 'vulnerability' and 'complexity', extracted from registers and case discussions, in meetings of social workers, psychologists, teachers, occupational therapists, sometimes lawyers (Matsushita, 2012), which produce the state's selective governance regime.

In all cases, the aim is to 'refer' the adolescent in conflict with the law, the 'unstructured' family, the addict, the individual with special needs, the homeless person, someone with a 'mental disorder' and, with greater emphasis, those known to be *potential* criminals, to other treatment programmes (professional referral, family protection, health, education, psychological care, disciplinary control, chemical control, internment). When they escape the so-called social-assistance network, and it is not uncommon for them to do so, these same individuals pass through internment units, prisons or, more rarely but not a negligible possibility, are murdered. Recent studies with street dwellers and young people involved in criminal markets show that, even with so many resources for different forms of treatment, a lot of people are still killed (Vianna and Farias, 2011; Santos Silva, 2014).

Killing, however, is a last resort. The argument 'against the repressive hypothesis', prominent in the study of sexuality, also seems to be valid for many situations produced by what might be called, in Foucauldian language, the *dispositif* of 'urban violence'.[11] Like sex in modernity, never have *marginais* been so visible, so thematised, with so many policies aimed at them or organised around their existence. Firearms, *bandidos* with their faces covered, policemen, drugs seized and bodies stretched out on the ground crowd news reports; perhaps the great object of cinematography today. To incite, to classify; never has so much been invested in the imprisonment of those who are *classified* as being violent: young black men, *pardos* or *favelados*, who took seriously the orgiastic incitement to a *'vida loka'* (crazy life) – the *consumption* of drugs, cars, motorcycles and women, but above all the extreme experiences of the nightclub, of criminal acts, escapes and confrontations with the

217

police, all aiming for, or facilitated by, 'easy money'. The so-called 'prison population' continues to grow, with precise targets, having quintupled since 1992 in São Paulo, and its average age is only just over twenty. If in some situations the arrest occurs when social assistance does not work, in this system assistance seems to be the continuation of internment and imprisonment. According to this perspective, the pre-eminent 'other' of public order is no longer the unemployed worker, who asks for social integration because he wants to be a worker, because he has the nature and religion of a worker. The other is now the *bandido*, the public enemy.

War appears more and more in the lexicon and logic of state policies. Every war, however, encourages organisation by the different sides in conflict. Both inside and outside the prisons are administrative and political authorities such as the PCC, and the diffuse influence of the evangelical churches, other powers quite present in the territories in question. The policies of the state, those produced by 'crime' (Feltran, 2012; Santos Silva, 2014) and those of the churches coexist in practices within the territories, but they seek autonomy from one another on the plane of representations (Fromm, 2016; Machado, 2013; Vital da Cunha, 2018).

Normative regimes and their mediations

In this book I have worked on the hypothesis of the coexistence of normative regimes in the peripheries of São Paulo, provisionally called *state* and *criminal*. These regimes seek to regulate the urban order, progressively autonomising their discourses in relation to their coexistent, while at the same time energetically negotiating the active consent, impositions, hybridisations and exchanges between one another in their ordinary practices. The regimes validate discourses and guide practices from very specific locations, such as evangelical churches of different denominations; drug sale points, prisons and criminalised markets; health centres, schools, NGOs and social movements, all significant sites in the

Conclusion

peripheries. In their beliefs and values, pastors, 'brothers' of the PCC and public servants all ritualise the normativity and totality of the law of God, of the codes of the 'Party' and its process, or of the state's administrative and regulatory functions. But their daily practices are deeply hybridised, producing unexpected interfaces when looked at from the perspective of each regime.[12]

In developing this idea, however, I have focused on the internal modes with which moralities operate in each regime and have given very little thought to the fact, and consequences, of these regimes and their mediations operating in monetarised markets and seeking to regulate them, stimulate their growth and feed off them for their own expansion. Legal markets, criminal markets, religious markets; markets that, if they do not interact from a moral or legal perspective, are absolutely connected in monetary terms. Here I explore some of these dynamics, still open to dialogue and revision. I begin with the meanings of morality and justice that seem to operate both in state and criminal regimes. Then I examine the relationships that these senses of justice produce in relation to the modes of monetary circulation that connect them, without producing syntheses between these.

The state regime mobilises the republican legal lexicon, with categories like 'law' and 'order', and their correlates 'rights', 'citizenship' and 'democracy', as the great normative mediators of social conflict. Its discourse is promoted both by state agencies through 'public' institutions and policies and by NGOs and social movements. This regime is formally regulated by the legislature, produced as an ideal of justice by the judiciary and idealised as the basis for the regulation of markets. The quotation marks here refer mainly to the distance between what the abstract principles of these notions imply and how they operate practically, especially in urban peripheries. On the one hand, there are public security programmes such as the Unidades de Polícia Pacificadora (Pacifying Police Units; UPPs), the Choque de Ordem, the Operações de Saturação, civil and military police, and the increasingly militarised state order, as demonstrated by Daniel Hirata (2018) or Cibele Rizek (2006). On the other hand, this order is also key to interpreting the 'other' state policies for the management of social conflict in the peripheries: targeted health programmes, education, training, housing, culture, sports, urban policies and the myriad 'social projects' that abound in the urban territories considered to be poor and violent. Entities as diverse as schools and health centres, trade unions and NGOs, cultural, leisure and sports centres, when focused on serving the poor, justify their actions as 'violence prevention'.

The presumption that in the absence of these programmes youths from the peripheries would act violently against other social groups justifies, in a remarkable way, the importance and urgency of developing ever more innovative forms of 'social action' in the peripheries. Pronasci, Lula's National Programme for Security with Citizenship, had repressive and welfare arms, the UPP is accompanied by UPP Social, security has 'social rights' as its counterpart, rather than opposite. This approach, of course, tends to ignore and delegitimise other forms of community, social or political organisation in the daily lives of the poor themselves, many of which have long traditions and nevertheless continue to exist and shape practices and values.

The 'crime' regime and 'evangelical' churches that are in between the two are based on moralities of another kind, centred on agonistic debates, ideally face to face, which are prevalent in all social sectors but have special legitimacy among the popular classes. They are responding to a moral logic very different from that of the law, and not governed by formal rules or, *by definition*, by so-called legitimate institutions. The narrative dimension – recounting what happened – carries much more weight in these spaces than the conceptual dynamics of formal legislation. Collective judgements are reached about something that has happened based on narratives performed by the interlocutors. These debates are based on moral values almost always inspired by Old

Testament Christian religiosity (an eye for eye, a tooth for tooth, a moral logic that is valid among both evangelical 'believers' and 'thieves'). In these countless daily debates, defining *what is right* in the peripheries, the participants seek practical and always situational definitions, which do not ritualise pre-established codes but, rather, shared values. These values that are almost never defined abstractly a priori, but are signified individually and collectively during and after these everyday performances, allowing the *correctness of conduct* and the *reputation of the subjects* to be deliberated. The values that ground these communities, such as 'respect', 'humility', and 'equality', while immaculate in principle, are not abstractions or general principles but, rather, perceived as being (or not) demonstrated daily in acts that are commented upon, gossiped about, evaluated (Marques, A.J. 2010).

The set of attitudes recognised by peers as 'correct', in São Paulo, gives practical meaning to words like 'proceeding', 'procedure' or 'walking the right path' that induce the subjectivation of men and women as simultaneously 'well respected', 'cool' and 'humble' in different social spaces. Literature carefully studied this shared sense of justice, highly praised in the 'world of crime' of São Paulo, whose ultimate intention is not only to avoid violent outcomes but also to construct a social universe in which these values, while never absolutely reifiable, are guidelines for ordinary life. I would go as far as to say that in this it is non-republican and fully performative, 'against the State' (in the sense of Pierre Clastres), and that it operates on principles *put to the test on a situational basis* (Cefaï) as 'believers' and 'workers' in the peripheries, and also 'thieves' and *bandidos*, define in their lives what is 'right' in resolving their conflicts. This mode of resolution can be more or less institutionalised, sacralised or ritualised, and certainly has the Christian universe as its backdrop (Takahashi, 2014). One can thus see why evangelical and Pentecostal religiosity, and even the strict morality of 'crime' can be so pervasive, and expand much more than state 'law and order' in the peripheral universe. It is the dispute between locally legitimate moral grammars, opposed to state language conceived, mostly, as exogenous, elitist or even morally wrong. Wittgenstein, in *Philosophical Investigations*, thinks of *meaning* as produced only in the *situational use* of words, not as contained in their semantics. The senses of 'right', 'just' and 'beautiful' in the peripheries are, without doubt, subject to this interpretation.

But the normative regimes do not only act in the moral or administrative dimension of the territories studied, producing codes of conduct and meanings of justice. All of them, and the evangelical mediation, also operate *monetised markets* that also mediate potentially conflictual relationships such as those between police and 'traffickers' who, because they do not find ways to mediate their necessary interactions either in the law or in morality, use money as an objective means of settling their differences: payments to 'settle accounts' (or '*arregos*', as they say in Rio de Janeiro), which vary in amount and are negotiated in different ways between police and operators of illegal markets. Michel Misse (2006a) has already demonstrated how the circulation of *political commodities*, in this way, modulates the always-tense relations between the legal order and the day-to-day operation of informal, illegal and illicit markets. Carolina Grillo (2013) shows that this interpretation is also perfectly applicable to other contexts.

Samuel is one of Ivete's grandchildren. He was born and raised in Sapopemba.[13] On a Tuesday in April 2015, the fifteen-year-old black boy worked as a seller at a busy corner in the eastern part of town and earned R$300. His twelve-hour shift ended at midnight, and Samuel went straight home. He found his mother crying because he was 'becoming a drug dealer'. The next day, Samuel woke up and went straight to the nearest shopping mall, which had opened in the 2000s, during the Lula da Silva and Dilma Rousseff administrations (2003–16), when the economic policy of expanding the low-income consumer market was in place. This policy, designed to boost economic growth and which economists refer to as bottom-up economics, continued the state reforms and privatisations begun by Fernando Henrique Cardoso in the 1990s, and preceded the even more radical liberalism of the Michel Temer and Jair Bolsonaro administrations.

At the mall, Samuel spent the day's income – which corresponded to one third of the monthly minimum wage of his grandmother, who also lives with them – on a pair of Oakley sunglasses, for which he paid in cash. They were on sale for only R$275 reais (US$72), down from the usual R$450 (US$117) or more. With the change, he was also able to eat a sandwich at Subway and an ice cream at McDonald's. What had been *dirty* money, obtained by selling drugs illegally, became just money the following day. Samuel paid taxes and honoured the global brands he admires: Oakley, Subway and McDonald's, like so many others. Companies and governments are thankful.

Dirty money, especially from drug dealing, is laundered mainly through *consumption*. Drug dealers' commissions in São Paulo range from 25% to 50% of the amount sold. Marijuana, cocaine and crack are sold retail, almost always by teenagers prone to compulsive shopping. They do not save the money they receive, which therefore goes straight into official economies. Insurance and auctions also serve as legal connections between those economies, which thereby are mutually strengthened, as is seen below. There are countless other ways to launder money, and new ones are devised every day.

From perspectives of economic sociology and anthropology, Samuel's money underwent a qualitative change at that very moment (Guyer 1995, 2004; Neiburg 2007; Zelizer 2011). That qualitative change of Samuel's money, from dirty to clean in seconds, involved no legal problem for the boy or for those who sold him the items. It was not money laundering, but merely shopping. That is what is expected in the global economy, in much of the state's justice system and even in small local businesses, precisely because, on that impersonal level, there is absolutely no concern for the *quality* of Samuel's money, only for the *amount* he has in his pocket (Simmel, 1990 [1900]).

It is therefore clear that Samuel is not the only one making money from illegal markets. Oakley, McDonald's, their franchisees, the mall and the governments levying consumption taxes also profit from them. On the other hand, some still reject that money. Samuel's mother, my research interlocutor and friend since 2005, has never accepted his money in her household despite a serious lack of means. In fact, she made her son pack up and leave home in 2016, when she was sure he had already become a drug dealer.

On another April Tuesday, this time in 2017, the teenager was shot in the back by a police officer while trying to escape a routine blockade on an avenue near his home. By then, the police considered Samuel not only a drug dealer, but also a motorcycle thief, and he was on the run. His girlfriend was pregnant, and he recovered from his bullet wound after many days in the hospital. His baby daughter is now eighteen months old. Still wanted by the police, sometime soon Samuel will be arrested. In contrast, his dirty money circulates freely. Illicit economies create criminals, and the war between the police and criminals breeds great urban violence. How can we grasp this boundary between dirty and clean money, licit and illicit economies, so relevant for Samuel's mother, but so irrelevant for a fast food restaurant from a global chain in a shopping mall? What is Samuel's position in an illicit market such as that of drug dealing or vehicle theft in São Paulo?

The key issue seems to be the scale, the depersonalisation of money. *'Money is one thing; a lot of money is something else,'* as the wise *Brazilian singer Tim Maia would say.* On a local level, illegal money creates people like Samuel – thieves – and 'urban violence' by perpetuating from generation to generation a vicious cycle of durable inequality and violence (Tilly, 1999). Samuel embodies Tilly's finding. His mother is keenly aware of the fate of favela dwellers involved in illicit activities. It is the same as that of Samuel's father and uncles: jail or death, even if they achieve economic success. Outlaws like Samuel spark a public outcry for *repression*, and there are many young black Samuels living in favelas and occupying low positions in illegal markets. They repeatedly go to prison and appear in murder statistics in São Paulo. The day after one of them is arrested or killed, there is another in his place.

However, the same illegal money that takes Samuels to prison boosts certain industries and becomes brands, profit, a global financial market and economic development, calling for *growth*. Whenever money circulation increases in illegal economies, more jobs are created in their drug, arms, car theft, bribery, fraud and smuggling businesses. As a result, more opportunities arise to employ other Samuels, who have no access to the formal labour market. Samuel obviously went no further than elementary school and had difficulty completing it. He went to no libraries, speaks no foreign languages and cannot write easily even in Portuguese.

Even today he supports his daughter with money he makes from illegal economies, mainly by dealing cocaine and by selling motorcycle parts, also obtained from thefts in São Paulo, in a small business run by a friend. With the money they obtain by dealing drugs, Samuel and his friend either buy motorcycles legally and illegally to resell them or buy stolen or legally acquired ones to strip for parts. Likewise, major global brands fund national economies, international markets and even social initiatives, as well as pay lawyers' fees, with proceeds from illegal economies, among other sources. Illegal businesses are almost always associated with legal enterprises, not least because of the need to launder money. As a result, the boundary between legal and illegal creates, on the one hand, big business people and, on the other hand, petty criminals and major criminal factions.

Driven by criminal populism, in today's Brazil governors, presidents and senators receive big business people from their states directly in their offices and undertake to devise policies to boost economic growth and create jobs, with the country's prosperity

in mind. The same governors, presidents and senators are keen
to buy military drones in Israel, to have police cars armoured and
to toughen laws against criminals, who cause so much damage to
society. Little do they know – if they know at all – that the money
that produces business people produces criminals in Brazil.

Brazil's peripheries have been, directly or indirectly, fundamental to national capitalist accumulation and 'free markets', from the
extraction of surplus value in the very process of urbanisation as
noted by Lucio Kowarick (1987) or Francisco de Oliveira (1982),
to the more recent development of profitable forms of flexible
capitalist accumulation: the illicit markets such as drug trafficking, smuggling and car theft, which are highly profitable, given
the much lower level of institutional mediation. The works of
Galdeano (2013) and Côrtes (2007, 2018) indicate how an entre-
preneurial logic crosses between 'evangelicals', *bandidos* and state
actors, turning them all into diverse market operators. The Conde
de Sarzedas Street in São Paulo (devoted to evangelical commerce) and also the media-savvy evangelical churches described
by Patricia Birman and Carly Machado (2012) are based on market
logics. Contemporary social housing is the tip of the operation of
transnational financial markets (Shimbo, 2012). The armed youths
studied by Lyra (2013) work for transnational trafficking. Thus,
street-level police and prison wardens, when negotiating with their
'antagonists' in the '*biqueiras*' and prisons, make money circulate
at different scales and in different situations, from the most to the
least legitimate (Hirata, 2014; Hirata and Grillo 2019).

The expansion of popular consumption, stimulated from the
centre, radicalises the objectification of numerous social conflicts.
To reduce these phenomena to analytic economism would be to
miss the basis of the critique which I, alongside those authors cited
above, propose to rethink the margins of the city. Not recognising
the obvious forms of monetisation present here, including how
to regulate conflicts between different normative regimes, would
perhaps be even more serious. Miagusko (2014) demonstrates the

Conclusion

escalation of lethal violence in a Rio de Janeiro favela when a trafficker unilaterally decides to stop paying '*arregos*' to police officers. Without money in the mediation of this conflict, it becomes much more lethal. Without the payment of wages, labour conflicts escalate. Many drug workers, smugglers, stolen car vendors, pastors and 'brothers' of the PCC are also entrepreneurs; all those who relate to them, on a daily basis, fuel the circulation of money, steadily expanding in Brazil's peripheries, with their labour and consumption. The expansion of popular income, the minimum wage and credit and income transfer programmes also fuel the growth and development of illegal, informal and illicit markets.

These three equations of mediation of potential conflicts – the law, the locally embedded senses of divine 'justice' and the money – that ultimately regulate violence and produce order do not always succeed. The urban order in São Paulo has been marked by the ever more radical construction of alterity as public expression of social plurality continues to retreat. Distributed across increasingly autonomous urban regimes, the conflict that is of interest today is not that of opinions elaborated from a shared epistemic background, a same political community. The notion of a *war* between sliced-up sub-sections of the population, which no longer make up a single moral or legal community but only a commercial community, seems to make more and more sense for understanding contemporary conflicts. When neither the law nor what is considered 'right' can mediate the relationship between population slices and their progressively autonomous ways of conceiving themselves and others, money appears as the only objective way of mediating their relations. Instead of politicising the social question or the pillars of community life, therefore, it seems to me that the hybrid of these equations of mediation – money – has instead greatly heightened the intensity of the latent conflict between different forms of life that are engendered in the biopolitical governance practices to which Brazilian cities are subject today. Values, customs and common beliefs no longer present themselves as a foundation for the cohesion between social groups; money seems to be the primary mechanism fulfilling this function. Sufficient money for mediation between these groups can inhibit the violent manifestations of the conflict that divides, segregates, separates them. An economic crisis would make us see the violence in its unmediated expression, as we have seen since 2014 in Rio de Janeiro or Fortaleza.

The framework for *public* intelligibility of the 'social question' in contemporary Brazil has shifted from the integration of the poor into a *national* development project to be achieved through the expansion of labour markets and citizenship, to another framework based on social and urban conflict that today is understood as *caused* by the poor. Monetisation of social relations between groups that are increasingly different was the government's bet from 2003 to 2016. Among the poor, those that are functional to the monetised market fit into the design of the nation. The diagnosis of our social problems has thus changed so radically that the policies designed to heal it have had their meaning inverted. If two or three decades ago it was possible to think of social conflict as fundamentally caused by inequality and dictatorship, to be overcome structurally, today it is a question of stimulating the market that can develop the country and control the violence that emerges from the poor, thus creating obstacles to 'our' material progress. Social policies, public discourses about poverty and its territories, state strategies, civil society and religious management of social conflict are now guided by the instrumental logic of market efficiency, of cost-benefit, in an aggressive tendency towards the objectification of social relations. Putting thousands of prisoners to work almost for free within the prisons is considered a cutting-edge 'social programme' by governments and entrepreneurs. Everyone profits. Managing the social is therefore, and fundamentally, about expanding markets.

It is noted, however, that if the drug market stimulates the economy, parts of the city benefit from it but are not 'integrated'.

Conclusion

Expanding markets and incriminating subjects who create problems – without ever suppressing the circulation of value by the markets in which they operate – are thus different sides of the same coin. The *markets* of drug trafficking, smuggling or car theft, for example, are not being repressed. The repression is applied to low-level traffickers or thieves who, when selectively incriminated and placed in detention units or prisons, give up their jobs so that others like them enter the economy, and so the same old logic of social control, of producing urban order by money, morality and violence, continues to operate.

Notes

NOTES TO INTRODUCTION

1 Grilagem is the illegal, private appropriation of land, typically using falsified documents. It remains a common practice in Brazil and played an important role in the urbanisation of São Paulo's periphery.

2 This heading invokes James Ferguson's (1999) eponymous book, which has been an inspiration to me.

3 www.seade.gov.br/produtos/midia/boletim-ped/rmsp/rmsp_anual_19 97.pdf

4 www.seade.gov.br/produtos/midia/boletim-ped/rmsp/rmsp_set2010. pdf

5 The 's' in 'state' is written in lowercase in order to reinforce the differentiation sought here, in contrast to the more common use of 'State' merely representing a set of public institutions or ideological apparatuses. The notion is Weberian, as we refer to an objectified state: a human community that successfully imposes a legitimate monopoly of forces on a particular territory (Weber, 1967). However, state is also an agent and, like all agents, it is produced during and as a result of its actions. The theory that substantiates this objective and ordered definition of state in Weber is a theory of action. Abrams (2006) warned of the difficulty imposed by the study of the state, precisely because it implies studying under the perspective of the Simmelian theory of objectification (state as idea, state as system). Vianna (2014) and Souza Lima (2002) have demonstrated how it is more productive to understand what are known as state processes in motion, observing its will to be progressive and its instances of reification. Das and Poole (2004) have demonstrated that there is no state centre and that operations of legitimisation and constructing legibility are fundamental to its validation in legal terms.

6 'Or depuis cinquante ans, les travaux convergent pour montrer qu'il ne suffit pas d'une loi ou d'une annonce pour modifier les comportements.

Notes

Les exemples abondent de décisions répétitives qui restent de peu d'effet et manifestent plutôt l'impuissance de l'État. [end note] L'exemple le plus ancien est la cascade d'édits royaux sur la répression du vagabondage qui ne purent empêcher l'émigration rurale et une forte circulation des populations du XIVe au XIXe siècle. Au XXe la question des personnes sans domicile fixe n'a cessé d'augmenter' (Lascoumes and Le Galès, 2012, p. 18).

7   Brazilian middle classes and elites are very heterogeneous but could not be described by the 'globalised mind' found in Europe by Andreotti, Le Galès and Moreno-Fuentes (2015).

8   I have chosen to continue using the term 'peripheries', despite recognising their problems (especially the implication of a watertight division between 'centre' and 'periphery' and, depending on the context, a range of associated social stigmas). I made this choice, above all, because it strikes me as the most intelligible category for highlighting the set of social dynamics to which I refer throughout this book. 'Urban poor', 'working' or 'popular classes', 'low income sectors' or related concepts seemed less effective, in relative terms, when switching between ethnographic description and analysis of the structure of public debates. When I speak of the 'peripheries' of São Paulo, therefore, I refer to environments situated in time and space, in which real people relate to one another and to other spheres of the social world in ways that are plural and heterogeneous. On the other hand, and at the same time, the term 'peripheries' helps us to recognise the regularities that are reproduced in these regions of the city and which demand significant analytical investment.

Notes to Chapter 1

1   In Brazil's racial identity's puzzle most Italians, as well as Arabs or Jews, are considered to be white, despite the fact that this is different in many other national and regional ethnic-racial puzzles.

2   It would be from lived experience rather than abstract explanation that categorical meanings would emerge. Inspiration for this debate stems from Rancière (2002) and Wittgenstein (2009) (particularly paragraphs 98–106).

3   'On the one hand, it is clear that every sentence in our language is "in order as it is". That is to say, we are not striving after an ideal, as if our ordinary vague sentences had not yet got a quite unexceptional sense, and a perfect language awaited construction by us. On the other hand, it seems clear that where there is sense there must be perfect order. So there must be perfect order even in the vaguest sentence' (Wittgenstein, 2009, paragraph 98, p. 44). The debate would be a lengthy one, sparked by that between Durkheim and William James, before being taken up by

Notes

pragmatists and interactionists. For a new approach to the debate, see Werneck (2012).

4 For a debate on routine as structure, see Machado da Silva (2008). Das (1995, 2006a and 2012), performs in-depth studies on the relevance of everyday life in the construction of meaning, as do Bayat (2013) and Blokland, Giustozzi and Schilling (2016).

5 I sought to address the problem of difference, particularly in terms of the public and emic notions of 'periphery' in Feltran (2013, 2014).

6 Author Laura Moutinho (2006) analyses the life stories of three poor black men in Rio de Janeiro, stating in an introductory summary that 'homophobia overlaps with racism' (Moutinho, 2006, p. 112) in her characters' broader negotiation of difference. Moutinho also gives authorial clues as to how one category of difference is objectified in a more central fashion than others in the defining of situations, without implying that the other categories are not simultaneously and mutually objectified. For an excellent review of the debate on intersectionalities, see Piscitelli (2008) or Cho, Crenshaw and McCall (2013).

7 Aesthetic and politics are also considered here in terms of a concept proposed by Jacques Rancière (2005, p. 18): 'Such forms are revealed to be tied to a certain political regime related to indeterminate identities, the delegitimation of words' positions, of the deregulating of the sharing of space and time. Such an aesthetic political regime befits democracy, the regime of assemblies of craftspeople, intangible written laws and the theatrical institution.'

8 Categorical judgements of value may therefore be constructed even if they are not immediately objectified into words and action. The life of categories is processed at every moment in the flux of experience, albeit silently (Das, 1999). In theoretically suggesting a reflection very similar to that of the present text, even reflecting on aesthetics and intersectional politics, Lowenkron (2015) notes how federal police treated a 'male' transvestite with respect while working, rendering her a target for jokes and insults outside of their professional interaction.

9 Notes on a scene from everyday life observed in January 2017 in São Carlos, São Paulo state, Brazil.

10 Available at www.youtube.com/watch?v=AgJdeavBa8g (accessed 1 March 2017). The scene lasts a little over seven minutes, and is fully transcribed here.

11 Laura Moutinho resumes the debate on the 'Mediterranean model' of 'honour and shame' in which, 'while men enjoy wide sexual permissiveness, women are controlled by a rigid sexual set of morals, whose righteousness serves as the custodian of male honour: shame falls on women and it is the male control that maintains family honour' (Moutinho, 2006, p. 100).

Notes

12 Simmel discusses this division among women in Europe at the beginning of the twentieth century by means of a study on prostitution, proclaiming: 'as long as marriage exists, so will prostitution' (Simmel, 2006, p. 10).

13 http://g1.globo.com/sao-paulo/noticia/2016/03/policia-matou-duas-pessoas-por-dia-nos-2-primeiros-meses-de-2016-em-sp.html (accessed 31 March 2016).

14 For an excellent debate on the human status as community-based and political, see Arendt, (1951) or Cavell, (2006).

15 'The adjective 'authoritarian' and the noun 'authoritarianism' are specifically employed in three contexts: the structure of political systems, the psychological devices related to power and political ideologies. In the typology of political systems, regimes privileging governmental authority are known as authoritarian, diminishing the consensus in a relatively radical fashion, concentrating political power in the hands of a single person or in a single body and placing representative institutions in second place. (…) In a psychological sense, an authoritarian personality is used to refer to a personality type formed by various characteristic traits centred on the coupling of two strictly linked attitudes: on the one hand, a concerned obedience towards superiors, sometimes including favours and adulation for all those retaining strength and power; and on the other hand, an arrogant and condescending treatment of hierarchical inferiors and anyone who does not have power and authority. (…) Authoritarian ideologies are therefore ideologies that negate equality among men in a relatively decisive manner, focusing on the hierarchical principle as well as arguing in favour of authoritarian regimes and often exalting some of the components of the authoritarian personality as virtues' (Bobbio, Matteucci and Pasquino, 1998, p. 94).

Notes to Chapter 2

1 This first interview with Pedro was carried out by myself and Ana Paula Galdeano Cruz, whom I thank. Thanks also to Alexandre Werneck for the comments on the first draft of the chapter.

2 Pedro says his cousin was executed after a 'debate'. The following chapter discusses the reinforcement of these debates during the expansion of the PCC in São Paulo.

3 'Sign the LA' means to attend Casa Foundation (the former FEBEM) on a monthly basis, where their Community Service is monitored in accordance with judicial decision.

4 Pedro's brother wasn't involved with the 'crime' at this time, but did become so again when he was older. He was in prison at the time of this first interview, having been caught during a robbery he carried out in the centre of São Paulo.

Notes

5 Semi-release is an intermediate socio-educational measure between Assisted Freedom and Internment, which is similar to the semi-open regime for adults.

6 The fatal results of these trajectories are often highlighted in this literature. In São Paulo the homicide rate among adolescents and young people remains high, even if it has fallen significantly in recent years. The average number of homicides in the capital, which had been around 30 per 100,000 by the end of the 1990s, dropped steadily from 2000 onwards. Average rates in the Sapopemba district also declined steadily, from 209 in 2000 to 51 in 2007 (PRO-AIM, 2008), remaining stable from then onwards (Santos Silva, 2014; Ruotti et al., 2017).

Notes to Chapter 3

1 In 2019 the ages of Ivete and her children were: Ivete (61); Ivonete (43); Marcela (42); Anísio (30†); Raúl (39); Neto (36); Alex and Lázaro (twins, 35); and Fernando (21†).

2 In the programme *Roda Viva*, screened in October 2007 on the channel TV Cultura.

3 Durham (1973, chapter 8) discusses precisely this attempt to reproduce the patronage model in São Paulo, especially among families that, like Ivete's, were qualified to engage in only marginal jobs, without the protection of a contract or formal salary.

4 I study Marcela's trajectory in Feltran (2007). Rui (2014) offers an in-depth ethnography of this circuit.

5 'But I continue to be respected by them [the traffickers]. When I pass, they say hello, they know that I'm a person who won't give them any trouble, or mess with the police. On the contrary, if one comes running and says they need to hide, I'll hide them, because I can't do anything, I won't hand them in. Because they have their own lives, each one makes their choices, don't they?' (Ivete)

6 The new structure of the group implied that each one took responsibility for his or her own life. As the dynamics of cycles into and out of prison stabilised, Ivete stopped visiting the prisoners, and they stopped expecting visits.

Notes to Chapter 4

1 In short, politics refers not only to disputes between already existing subjects on a pre-constituted terrain (the state, councils, civil society etc.) but, above all, to the dispute underlying the very institution of these terrains and subjects (Rancière, 1996a, 1996b), that is, the very definition of what is socially legitimate.

Notes

2 That amounted to fifteen weeks without being able to work, since the usual work schedule for adolescents on the retail side of the traffic in Sapopemba is a rotation, in which each individual works one morning and one night per week.

3 This is a report shown on the channel Rede Record's 'Domingo Espetacular' ('Sunday Special') programme, available at: http://you tube.com/watch?v=XVs9yı1XfZQ.

4 The expressions and names used in the report are maintained here. All the detained PCC members who participated in the conversations recorded by the police are identified as 'prisoner'.

5 'Checkmate' must end not only the life of the individual(s) sentenced, but the whole potential cycle of private revenge.

6 The average number of homicides in the capital, which reached around 30 per 100,000 by the end of the 1990s, declined steadily from 2000 onwards. The average rate in the Sapopemba district, where I have conducted most of my fieldwork, declined by a factor of six between 2001 and 2008 in a steady way, falling from 60.9 per 100,000 in 2001 to only 8.8 per 100,000 in 2008. Source: author's calcuations based on data from PRO-AIM, City Council of São Paulo, January 2010.

7 Official data from the Secretaria de Administração Penitenciária (Ministry of Prison Administration) for the State of São Paulo show that the prison population rose from 55,000 in 1994 to almost 190,000 in 2011. See www.sap.sp.gob.br. It is estimated that, on average, 5,800 people are released from São Paulo's prisons every month, compared to 6,600 entering. Meanwhile, there are 30,000 people who have been sentenced, but whom the prison system cannot accommodate. For a critique of the policy of mass incarceration, its motivations and consequences in the USA, the work of Wacquant (2009a, 2009b) is a key reference. Caldeira (2009) goes beyond criticising the author's argument.

8 Mano Brown (2009), available at www.youtube.com/watch?v=PQ4dP 2evx9w.

Notes to Chapter 5

1 Among other activities, CEDECA monitors adolescents from the neighbourhood in their compliance with 'socio-educational measures' in open areas (Assisted Liberty and Community Service, according to the Child and Adolescent Statute). These measures apply to individuals sent there by the judiciary upon being charged with committing an offence.

2 Translator's note: A cavaquinho is a very small stringed instrument used to play samba, similar to a ukulele.

3 In Feltran (2010b) I study the regulating of the 'world of crime', from the

Notes

assassins typical of 1980s São Paulo, to the present scenario of arbitration via 'debates'.

4   Machado da Silva (1999) identified the legitimate coexistence of two orderings with other contents in Rio de Janeiro's favelas, with his argument retrieved and debated in Misse (2006a).

5   The police officer informed Ricardo of the name of his division; however, I have omitted any references in this chapter that would identify police officers, divisions and police stations, also using fictional names and changing street and favela names, in order to preserve the interlocutors' anonymity.

6   On the Portuguese expression '*dar um psicológico*' ('to use psychology') and its meanings in context, see the analysis by Marques A.J. (2007, 2010).

7   'Idea' is practically synonymous with conversation, making 'exchanging ideas' conversing and 'giving ideas' giving advice or speaking with someone, opening up the possibility of dialogue. According to Ricardo, the police officer enquired as to the possibility of 'conversing' about the boys' situation, opening up the possibility of a financial agreement. See Zaluar (1985).

8   I have been studying Ivete's family for years (Feltran, 2007, 2008, 2009).

9   The news wasn't easy for me to digest; perhaps of all the stories I had followed in Sapopemba that of Marcela is the one to have created the greatest personal impression on me. I discuss her trajectory in Feltran (2007).

10   I have briefly reflected on the transference of 'crime' to the body of the criminal, and then to those who are similar to him/her, in Feltran (2008). Misse deals with this phenomenon – conceived of as criminal subjectification – in Misse (2010).

11   Zaluar and Ribeiro (2009) reflect and theorise more specifically on the paradox of close neighbourly relations in areas with high rates of violence in Rio de Janeiro.

12   This is the term given to assaults on individuals who make substantial withdrawals in bank agencies or from ATMs. One person stays inside the bank observing and passing information to another person outside, who follows the customer and approaches them when the opportunity strikes.

13   Fernando used the following three categories: *Comando* (Command), which would have been the expression used by the police, then PCC and then *Partido* (Party). The police wouldn't have used the common expression 'brothers'.

14   A military police officer once told me in an informal conversation that in the fifteen minutes between arresting a dealer and escorting him to the nearest police station, he received no less than three calls from lawyers and police officers, asking about what had happened and informing him of 'who he was dealing with'.

Notes

15 The family has four cars, with three stolen and Neto's being paid for in instalments.

16 A month later, a newspaper in wide circulation reported on a corruption scandal involving stolen cars, bribes and money laundering using the patio of this same police station as a privileged territory.

17 Although divine justice is the most abstract among these, its absolute superiority in relation to the others is enunciated very frequently, such as in these lyrics by São Paulo's leading hip-hop group, Racionais MC: 'the Prosecutor is only a man / God is the Judge'.

18 In the rainy season, landslides that destroy homes are common on the favela hillsides. In such cases, residents' first port of call is a television network that has been there before. They do the same when attempting to prove paternity or for intervention in police cases etc.

19 Das (2006a), especially chapter 9.

20 See Foucault (2001, p. 227); an appropriation of his argument in contemporary Brazil is found in Telles (2009).

Notes to Chapter 6

1 Expressions commonly used by both government and criminal actors are presented in italics. This acknowledges the argument made by Machado da Silva (1999) regarding the notion of urban violence, and discussed by Misse (2006a) with reference to the idea of public security, that these categories are not neutral tools of analysis but representations that are a significant part of the objects of analysis themselves.

2 As proposed by Boltanski and Thevenot (1991) and Thevenot (2006). To offer one example, the governor updates the government matrix of justification when he declares that he 'does not bargain with a bandido', or that he 'dismantled the PCC'. But the PCC-affiliated kidnappers of a *Rede Globo* reporter did not mobilise a different but, rather, the same discourse of the government when they advocated the use of the Law of Penal Executions on a broadcast network. However, a different matrix – that of 'crime' – is mobilised to justify the death of someone in a PCC 'debate' (Marques, 2007; Hirata, 2018; Feltran, 2010a, 2010b; Kessler and Telles, 2010).

3 This analogy was at least evident in my fieldwork: Marcela told me in 2005 that 'the PCC is like the GOE [Special Operations Group] in prison'. Lázaro, her brother, told me also in 2005 that having the PCC in prison 'was the same as having the prison staff. It's also a form of discipline, the same form of discipline: they don't let fights or riots happen, they run things. [Can everyone be part of the chain of command?] Anyone, someone from another faction can't join. But aside from that everyone can join, because it's not a faction, anyone can join, everyone

is respected. A guy will have the same respect for us as he has for his brother, who is in the Command.' About this symmetry between the PCC and government in the 'dominated prisons', see Mallart (2012).

4 As an ex-prison officer, recruited in 1998 at the peak of this intense restructuring process, recounted: 'there were five directors [per prison, who delivered the preparatory course for the officers]. (…) I stayed in this "school" for about forty days. It was where I had classes in Criminal Law, Criminology, we had an Ethics class, we had a Personal Defence class, we had a class in Penitentiary Security, with professors who later became the directors of the prison, and with professors from the Prison Administration Secretariat for the State of São Paulo. (…) The classes were interesting. One of the most interesting things was that the slogan of all teachers, including those who became directors, was rehabilitation. According to the new Penal Code (…) humanitarian treatment of prisoners was fundamental. (…) Violence was only to be used as a last resort.' (Paulo).

5 The same Paulo, who during the training course had been convinced by the rhetoric of rehabilitation, saw his hopes dashed after only three months in the new prison. 'Until then I had not seen any attitudes of violence among the directors. I had only seen them among older employees. Then I started to see it among the directors themselves. Those that talked about rehabilitation, and this happened on my shift, which was the night shift. Some prisoners arrived from the City Penitentiary [fictitious name]. There was trouble at that prison and they brought the leaders. They gave them a truck and took it to Municipality [fictitious name]. (…) The director called the head on duty, my friend, and said he wanted the biggest guys to receive the "*bonde*" [vehicle used to transport prisoners]. They called me, called several people, the highest ranking. They called Paulo, who later got the nickname Superman, who was an extremely violent guy. They called Pedro, who was a good guy, but later became violent. And then we went to an inclusion sector (…), we got there and the directors came. (…) The guys who worked up there brought a lot of clubs, we called it "lowering the pipe". They were water pipes, made of iron, and at the base there was a slightly larger pipe, made of PVC, and it was pierced, with a piece of string [tied in a loop, shows how they wrapped the handle], so it wouldn't fall. (…) He brought the pipes, each director took one. One of the directors brought a wooden club that looked like a baseball bat. (…) All of it was to welcome the arrivals. The director said, "Look, is there anyone who does want to participate?" I said, "I don't want to." (…) It's funny that the employees were anxious, isn't it? It's a mix, but I think there was a desire to give some beatings. That was the conclusion I came to later. The prisoners arrived and started to come down one by one, with heads down in their underwear. (…) I only heard

Notes

the prisoners' screams: "Stop sir, it hurts! It hurts, sir! Stop, stop!" There
were ten guards beating them, one by one, with the directors there. One
by one.'

Notes to conclusion

1   The position occupied by the poor in Brazilian democracy and in
    Brazilian cities, as well as the relation between poverty, development and
    citizenship, has always been a central theme of the literature. It has been
    approached from a Marxist perspective (Kowarick, 1987; Oliveira, 1982),
    including within both Gramscian (Machado da Silva, 1993; Dagnino,
    1994, 2002) and Thompsonian (Sader, 1988; Telles and Paoli, 1994) tradi-
    tions, as well as more culturalist approaches (Caldeira, 2000; Durham,
    1977) or with Arendtian (Telles, 2001) or Habermasian (Zaluar, 2004)
    influences.

2   An example of this is the prolific work of the Centro de Estudos de
    Metrópole, dedicated to gathering evidence, using methods ranging
    from demography to ethnography, to develop hypotheses and contribute
    to debates around a range of current arguments in the literature on
    themes such as inequality (Marques and Bichir, 2011), labour relations
    (Guimarães, N.A., 2009, 2012), urban territory and poverty (Marques
    and Bichir, 2011), social policies (Arretche, 2010), state strategies for gov-
    erning the 'social' (Feltran, 2011, 2012; Marques, 2014) and race relations
    (Guimarães, A.S.A., 2012), among others.

3   In different ways, Telles and Cabanes (2006), Rizek and Oliveira (2006),
    Cabanes, Georges, Rizek and Telles (2011) and Vieira and Feltran (2013),
    as well as the work of NECVU-UFRJ (Núcleo de Estudos da Cidadania,
    Conflito e Violência Urbana-Universidade Federal do Rio de Janeiro
    [Centre for Studies of Citizenship, Conflict and Urban Violence-Federal
    University of Rio de Janeiro]), CEVIS-IESP/UERJ (Coletivo de Estudos
    sobre Violência e Sociabilidade–Instituto de Estudos Sociais e Políticos/
    Universidade do Estado do Rio de Janeiro [Collective Studies about
    Violence and Sociability–Institute for Social and Political Studies/
    State University of Rio de Janeiro]) and the Urban Ethnography Group
    (Núcleo de Etnografias Urbanas) at CEBRAP (Centro Brasileiro de
    Análise e Planejamento [Brazilian Center for Analysis and Planning]),
    especially Rui (2012), Fiore (2013) and Malvasi (2012), are example of this
    strand within the bibliography.

4   This reflection is inspired by analyses by Simmel (2014) and Arendt (2001)
    of how cultural objects are monetised. Monetisation must be preceded
    by work that makes the question 'how much does it cost?' plausible for
    objects for which it was previously unthinkable, as it would be today to
    ask 'how much does your child cost?'

5 It is in this way symptomatic that the Municipal Secretary of Security, in personal conversations, has three times referred to the Public Security programme 'Crack, it is possible to win' (Crack, é possível vencer) as a 'fantasy name'. Public programmes have long had slogans formulated by marketers, obeying the logic of fragmentation between market niches.

6 If the notion of 'social question' had become pronounced in French debates about the welfare state (Ewald, 1986), the contradictions between political and economic modernity (Telles and Paoli, 1994) have led us to a critical, although paradoxical, horizon, in the sense that it is presumed that the problems arising from modernity must be overcome within the framework of modern teleology itself, through the creation and progressive extension of citizenship rights. Citizenship would thus be a measure of social relations (Telles, 1994).

7 It is not, for example, the aesthetics of the worker that, at present, dictate the criteria of belonging to the social world among the younger generation in the peripheries; forms of aesthetic expression that have become widespread there in recent decades, such as rap or funk, show a division of sensibility (Rancière, 1995) centred on a more radical alterity than in the past (Bertelli, 2014; Feltran, 2013b; Takahashi, 2014).

8 The prevailing logic of coalition governments at the national level since Brazil's 'democratic transition', the synthesis of the coexistence of Sarney and the MST, financial capital and the solidarity economy, environmentalists and agribusiness, the third sector and evangelicals, for example, favours the type of schizophrenia – in a theoretical sense – characteristic of these social (but also environmental, political and economic) actions. It seems that it is within this framework that contemporary government can be best understood.

9 This section synthesises and develops arguments previously made in Feltran (2013b; 2014).

10 'Thus, our relations develop on the basis of mutual knowledge, and this knowledge on the basis of the real relation, as two indissociably intertwined elements which, through their alternation within interaction, makes it seem like one of the points in which being and representation make their mysterious unity empirically perceptible' (Simmel, 2010a, pp. 30–31).

11 Michel Foucault (1997) argues that the dispositif of modern sexuality is not primarily concerned with suppressing sex in a non-specific way; hence the profusion of modern discourses that, on the contrary, even today instigate it, from Sunday afternoons to Saturday nights. It was of more interest to legitimise an authority – sovereign, disciplinary, governmental – from which one could legitimately classify sexuality: to describe it, categorise it, hierarchise it. The modern administration of sex would benefit from this operation of capture and reification inscribed

in the act of naming, also the act of moralising. The meaning of names would become routine as part of nature; would normalise the kind of sex that could plausibly be integrated into family and productive life, distinguishing it from the one to be banished from the dominant moral code, within the limits of legality. From the dark rooms of family patriarchs to the most abject slaves, the dispositif of sexuality would act by classifying, in order to rule.

12 Not only 'evangelical thieves' or the 'settling of accounts between police and criminals', but hybrids between religious and criminal norms, for example (Marques, 2012). Hybridisms between different regimes are, in practice, constant in the peripheries – religious syncretism, the fusion of political ideologies etc. Liberation theology, associating historical materialism and Christianity, for example, was extremely successful for at least two decades in Brazil.

13 Samuel's real name, as well as parts of his trajectory, have been withheld so as to protect his identity. I had contact with him during my field research between 2005 and 2018.

References

Abrams, P. 2006. Notes on the Difficulty of Studying the State. In: Sharma, A.; Gupta, A. (eds), *The Anthropology of the State: A Reader*. Oxford: Blackwell, pp. 58–89.

Adorno, S.; Salla, F. 2007. *Criminalidade organizada nas prisões e os ataques do PCC*. Estudos Avançados: Dossiê Crime Organizado, n. 61.

Agamben, G. 1998. *Homo Sacer: Sovereign Power and Bare Life*. Stanford: Stanford University Press.

Almeida, R. 2019a. *A onda quebrada: evangélicos e conservadorismo na crise brasileira (2013–2018)*. Tese de Livre-Docência, Campinas, Unicamp.

Almeida, R. 2019b. Bolsonaro presidente: conservadorismo, evangélicos e a crise brasileira. *Novos Estudos CEBRAP*, v. 38, n.1, pp. 185–213.

Almeida, R. 2018. Religious Transition in Brazil. In: Arretche, M. (ed.), *Paths of Inequality in Brazil: A Half-century of Changes*. 1. ed. Cham: Springer, v. 1, pp. 257–284.

Almeida, R. 2017. A onda quebrada: evangélicos e conservadorismo. *Cadernos Pagu*, v. 50, pp. 5–30.

Almeida, R. 2009. *A igreja universal e seus demônios*. São Paulo: Terceiro Nome, v. 1500.

Almeida, R. 2004. Religião na Metrópole Paulista. *Revista Brasileira de Ciências Sociais (Impresso)*, São Paulo, v. 19, n. 56, pp. 15–27.

Almeida, R; D'Andrea, T.; De Lucca, D. 2008. Situações periféricas: etnografia comparada de pobrezas urbanas. *Novos Estudos CEBRAP*, v. 83, pp. 109–130.

Anderson, B. 1991. *Imagined Communities: Reflections on the Origin and Spread of Nationalism*. London: Verso.

Anderson, N. 1923. *The Hobo: Sociology of Homeless Man*. Chicago: University of Chicago Press.

Andreotti, A.; Le Galès, P.; Moreno-Fuentes, J. M. 2015. *Globalised Minds, Roots in the City: Urban Upper-middle Classes in Europe*. Oxford: Wiley.

References

Arendt, H. 2001. A crise na cultura: sua significação social e política. In: *Entre o Passado e o Futuro*. São Paulo: Perspectiva, pp. 248–281.

Arendt, H. 1997 [1958]. *Rahel Varnhagen: The Life of a Jewess*. Baltimore: Johns Hopkins University Press.

Arendt, H. 1989. O Declínio do Estado-nação e o fim dos direitos do homem. In: *Origens do totalitarismo*. São Paulo: Companhia das Letras, pp. 300–337.

Arendt, H. 1977. *On Revolution*. New York: Penguin.

Arendt, H. 1959. *The Human Condition: A Study of Central Dillemas Facing Modern Man*. New York: Doubleday Anchor Book.

Arendt, H. 1951. The Decline of the Nation-state and the End of the Rights of Man. In: *The Origins of Totalitarianism*. New York: Schocken Books, pp. 267–302.

Arias, E. D. 2017. *Criminal Enterprises and Governance in Latin American and the Caribbean*. New York: Cambridge University Press.

Arias, E. D.; Barnes, N. 2017. Crime and Plural Orders in Rio de Janeiro, Brazil. *Current Sociology*, v. 65, n. 3, pp. 448–465.

Arias, E. D.; Goldstein, D. (eds). 2010. *Violent Democracy in Latin America: Toward an Interdisciplinary Reconceptualization*. Durham, NC: Duke University Press.

Arretche, M. (ed.). 2015. *Trajetórias das desigualdades: como o Brasil mudou nos últimos cinquenta anos*. São Paulo: Editora da UNESP, v. 1.

Arretche, M. 2010. Federalismo e igualdade territorial: uma contradição em termos? *Dados* (Rio de Janeiro: Impresso), v. 53, pp. 587–620.

Auyero, J. 2003. *Contentious Lives: Two Argentine Women, Two Protests, and the Quest for Recognition*. Durham, NC: Duke University Press.

Auyero, J. 2000. *Poor People's Politics*. Durham, NC: Duke University Press.

Batista, L. G. 2012. O mundo do crime e a produção do espaço nas periferias: um estudo etnográfico da sociabilidade em torno dos pontos de venda de droga. Relatório de Iniciação Científica.

Bayat, A. 2013. *Life as Politics: How Ordinary People Change the Middle East*. Stanford: Stanford University Press.

Bertelli, G. B. 2014. 'O riso do antropófago: cumplicidade e dissidência na estética de Oswald de Andrade'. Doctoral thesis. São Carlos: Universidade Federal de São Carlos.

Biondi, K. 2016. *Sharing this Walk: An Ethnography of Prison Life and the PCC in Brazil*. John F. Collins (ed., trans.). Chapel Hill, NC: University of North Carolina Press.

Biondi, K. 2010. *Junto e misturado: uma etnografia do PCC*. São Paulo: Terceiro Nome/Fapesp.

Birman, P. 2012. O poder da fé, o milagre do poder: mediadores evangélicos e deslocamento de fronteiras sociais. *Horizontes Antropológicos* (UFRGS. Impresso), v. 18, pp. 133–153.

Birman, P.; Machado, C. 2012. A violência dos justos: evangélicos, mídia e

References

periferias da metrópole. *Revista Brasileira de Ciências Sociais* (Impresso), v. 27, pp. 55–69.

Blokland, T. V. 2017. *Community as Urban Practice*. Oxford: Polity Press.

Blokland, T. V. 2008. Facing Violence: Everyday Risks in an American Housing Project. *Sociology*, v. 42 n. 4, pp. 601–617.

Blokland, T. V. 2003. *Urban Bonds*. Cambridge, Oxford, Malden: Polity Press.

Blokland, T. V.; Giustozzi, D.; Schilling, H. 2016. *Creating the Unequal City: The Exclusionary Consequences of Everyday Routines in Berlin*. Berlin: Ashgate.

Bobbio, N.; Matteucci, N. E.; Pasquino, G. 1998. *Dicionário de Política*, 3. ed. Brasília: Editora UNB.

Boltanski, L.; Thevenot, L. 1991. *De La justification: les économies de la grandeur*. Paris: Gallimard.

Bourdieu, P. et al. 1999. *The Weight of the World: Social Suffering in Contemporary Society*. Stanford, CA: Stanford University Press.

Bourgois, P. 1995. *In Search of Respect: Selling Crack in El Barrio*. San Francisco: San Francisco State University.

Bourgois, P.; Schonberg, J. 2009. *Righteous Dopefiend*. Berkeley: University of California Press.

Brah, A. 2006. Diferença, diversidade, diferenciação. *Cadernos Pagu*. v. 26, pp. 329–365.

Breviglieri, M.; Lafaye, C.; Tromm, D. 2009. *Competences critiques et sens de la justice*. Paris: Econômica.

Brown, M.; Prado, J. 2002. *Diário de um detento. Sobrevivendo no Inferno*.

Cabanes, R. 2014. *Économie morale des quartiers populaires de São Paulo*. Paris: L'Harmattan.

Cabanes, R. 2003. Travail, famille, mondialisation, Récits de la vie ouvrière. São Paulo, Brésil, Karthala: IRD.

Cabanes, R.; Georges, I.; Rizek, C. S.; Telles, V. S. (eds). 2011. *Saídas de Emergência – ganhar/perder a vida na periferia de São Paulo*. 1. ed. São Paulo: Boitempo Editorial, v. 1.

Caldeira, T. P. R. 2009. Marginality, Again?! *International Journal of Urban and Regional Research*. v. 33, n. 3, pp. 848–853.

Caldeira, T. P. R. 2006. 'I came to sabotage your reasoning': Violence and Ressignifications of Justice in Brazil. In: Comaroff, J.; Comaroff, J. (eds). *Law and Disorder in the Postcolony*. Chicago: University of Chicago Press, pp. 102–149.

Caldeira, T. P. R. 2000. *Cidade de Muros: crime, segregação e cidadania em São Paulo*. São Paulo: Edusp.

Castel, R. 1999. *Les métamorphoses de la question sociale: une chronique du salariat*. Paris: Folio, Gallimard.

Cavell, S. 2006. Foreword. In: Das, V., *Life and Words: Violence and the Descent into the Ordinary*. Berkeley, CA: California University Press, pp. ix–xiv.

References

Cefaï, D. 2010. Provações corporais: uma etnografia fenomenológica entre moradores de rua de Paris. *Lua Nova,* n. 79, pp. 71–110.

Cefaï, D.; Gardella, E. 2012.Comment analyser une situation selon le dernier Goffman? In: *Erving Goffman et l'ordre de l'interaction.* Paris: Presses universitaires de France, pp. 234–266.

Cefaï, D.; Terzi, C. 2012. *L'expérience des problèmes publics.* Paris: Éditions de l'EHESS.

Cho, S.; Crenshaw, K. W.; McCall, L. 2013.Toward a Field of Intersectionalities Studies: Theory, Application, Praxis. *Journal of Women in Culture and Society.* v. 38, n. 4, pp. 725–810.

Clastres, P. 2004. *Arqueologia da violência – pesquisas de antropologia política.* São Paulo: Cosac & Naify.

Clastres, P. 2003. *Sociedade contra o estado.* São Paulo: Cosac & Naify.

Cohen, C. 2015. Boko Haram, une impossible sociologie politique? *Afrique contemporaine.* n. 255, v. 3, pp. 75–92.

Côrtes, M. 2018. O dispositivo pentecostal e a agência dos governados. *Em Debate.* v. 1, pp. 31–38.

Côrtes, M. 2007. O bandido que virou pregador: A conversão de criminosos ao pentecostalismo e suas carreiras de pregadores. 1st edn. São Paulo: Aderaldo & Rothschild Editores Ltda, v. 1.

Dagnino, E. 2002. Sociedade civil, espaços públicos e a construção democrática no Brasil: limites e possibilidades In: Dagnino, E. (ed.), *Sociedade Civil e Espaços Públicos no Brasil.* São Paulo: Paz e Terra, pp. 279–302.

Dagnino, E. 1994. Os Movimentos Sociais e a emergência de uma nova noção de cidadania. In: Dagnino, E. (ed.), *Os Anos 90: Política e Sociedade no Brasil.* São Paulo: Brasiliense, pp. 103–118.

Darke, S. 2018. *Conviviality and Survival: Co-producing Brazilian Prison Order.* Houndmills: Palgrave Macmillan.

Das, V. 2012. Entre palavras e vidas: entrevista a Michel Misse, Alexandre Werneck, Patrícia Birman, Pedro Paulo Pereira, Gabriel Feltran e Paulo Malvasi. *Revista Dilemas.* n. 5. v.2.

Das, V. 2006a. *Life and Words: Violence and the Descent into the Ordinary.* Berkeley, CA: California University Press.

Das, V. 2006b. The Signature of the State: The Paradox of Illegibility. In: Das, V. *Life and Words: Violence and the Descent into the Ordinary.* Berkeley: California University Press, pp. 162–183.

Das, V. 1999. Fronteiras, violência e o trabalho do tempo. *Revista Brasileira de Ciências Sociais.* v. 14, n. 40, pp. 31–42.

Das, V. 1995. *Critical Events: An Anthropological Perspective on Contemporary India.* New Delhi: Oxford University Press.

Das, V; Poole, D. (eds). 2004. *Anthropology in the Margins of the State.* New Delhi: Oxford University Press.

Dewey, J. 1938. *Logic: The Theory of Inquiry.* New York: Holt & Co.

References

Dewey, J. 1927. *The Public and its Problems*. New York: Holt & Co.

Dias, C. N. 2011. Da pulverização ao monopólio da violência: expansão e consolidação da dominação do PCC no sistema carcerário paulista. Tese (Doutorado em Sociologia). Programa de Pós-Graduação em Sociologia. Universidade de São Paulo.

Dias, C. N. 2008. Práticas punitivas na prisão: institucionalização do legal e legalização do arbitrário. In: 32ª Reunião Anual da Anpocs. Caxambu.

Dias, C. N.; Darke, S. 2015. From Dispersed to Monopolized Violence: Expansion and Consolidation of the Primeiro Comando da Capital's Hegemony in São Paulo's Prisons. *Crime, Law and Social Change* (print), v. 1, pp. 1–20.

Doimo, A. M. 1995. *A Vez e a Voz do popular: movimentos sociais e participação política no Brasil pós-70*. Rio de Janeiro: Relume Dumará/ANPOCS.

Donzelot, J. 1984. L'invention du social. Essai sur le déclin des passions politiques. Paris: Fayard.

Douglas, M. 1976. *Pureza e Perigo*. São Paulo: Perspectiva.

Duneier, M.; Kasinitz, P.; Murphy, A. (eds). 2014. *Urban Ethnography Reader*. Oxford, University of Oxford Press.

Durham, E. R. 1977. *A dinâmica cultural na sociedade moderna*. São Paulo: Ensaios de Opinião , pp. 32–35.

Durham, E. R. 1973. *A caminho da cidade*. São Paulo: Perspectiva.

Elias, N. 1978. *The Civilizing Process*. New York: Urizen Books.

Ewald, F. 1986. *L'État providence*. Paris, Grasset.

Feltran, G. S. 2019. (I)llicit Economies in Brazil: An Ethnographic Perspective. *Journal for Illicit Economies and Development*. v. 2, n. 1. pp. 1–10.

Feltran, G. S. 2018. *Irmãos: uma história do PCC*. São Paulo: Companhia das Letras.

Feltran, G. S. 2014. Crime e periferia. In: Lima, R. S.; Ratton, J. L.; Azevedo, R. G. (eds), *Crime, Polícia e Justiça no Brasil*. 1. ed. São Paulo: Contexto Editora, v. 1, pp. 299–307.

Feltran, G. S. 2013a. Questão social e lumpen. In: Ivo, A. B. L.; Kraychete, E. S.; Borges, A.; Mercuri, C.; Vitale, D.; Sennes, S. (eds), *Dicionário Temático Desenvolvimento e Questão Social*. São Paulo: Annablume, v. 1, pp. 400–404.

Feltran, G. S. 2013b. Sobre anjos e irmãos: cinquenta anos de expressão política do 'crime' numa tradição musical das periferias. *Revista do Instituto de Estudos Brasileiros*, v. 1, pp. 43–72.

Feltran, G. S. 2012. Governo que produz crime, crime que produz governo: o dispositivo de gestão do homicídio em São Paulo (1992–2012). *Revista Brasileira de Segurança Pública*. São Paulo. v. 6, n. 2, pp. 232–255.

Feltran, G. S. 2011. Fronteiras de tensão: política e violência nas periferias de São Paulo. São Paulo: Editora da Unesp/CEM.

Feltran, G. S. 2010a. Crime e castigo na cidade: os repertórios da justiça e a questão do homicídio nas periferias de São Paulo. *Caderno CRH*, v. 23, n. 58, pp. 59–73.

References

Feltran, G. S. 2010b. The Management of Violence on the Periphery of São Paulo: A Normative Apparatus Repertoire in the PCC era. *Vibrant*. Florianópolis, v. 7, n. 2, pp. 109–134.

Feltran, G. S. 2010c. Periferias, direito e diferença: notas de uma etnografia urbana. *Revista de Antropologia*. v. 53, n. 2, pp. 565–610.

Feltran, G. S. 2009. Travailleurs et bandits dans la même famille. In: R. Cabanes; I. Georges (eds), *São Paulo: la ville d'en bas*. Paris: L'Harmattan. pp. 359–378.

Feltran, G. S. 2008. O legítimo em disputa: as fronteiras do 'mundo do crime' nas periferias de São Paulo. *Dilemas Revista de Estudos de Conflito e Controle Social*, v. 1, n. 1, pp. 93–126.

Feltran, G. S. 2007. A fronteira do direito: política e violência nas periferias de São Paulo. In: Dagnino, E.; Tatagiba, L. *Democracia, sociedade civil e participação*. Chapecó: Unochapecó, pp. 537–566.

Feltran, G. S. 2005. *Desvelar a política na periferia: histórias de movimentos sociais em São Paulo*. 1st edn. São Paulo: Associação Editorial Humanitas (FFLCH/ USP) / FAPESP, v. 1.

Feltran, G. S. 2004. Isolamento, solidão e superfluidade: sobre abismos cotidianos. *CADERNOS IFCH*, Instituto de Filosofia e Ciências Humanas, UNICAMP, CAMPINAS, BRASIL, v. 1, n. 31, pp. 173–196.

Ferguson, J. 1999. *Expectations of Modernity: Myths and Meanings of Urban Life on the Zambian Copperbelt*. Berkeley, CA: University of California Press.

Fiore, M. 2013. Uso de drogas: substâncias, sujeitos e eventos. Doctorl thesis. Campinas: Universidade Estadual de Campinas.

Fiore, M. 2012. O lugar do estado na questão das drogas: o paradigma proibicionista e as alternativas. *Novos Estudos CEBRAP* (Impresso), v. 92, p. 9–21.

Foucault, M. 2001. *Vigiar e Punir*. 24. ed. Petrópolis: Vozes.

Foucault, M. 1997. *Il faut défendre la societé. Cours au Collège de France* [1976]. Paris: Hautes Études, EHESS, Gallimard, Seuil.

Foucault, M. 1987. *Maquiavel, a política e o Estado moderno*. 8. ed. Rio de Janeiro: Civilização Brasileira.

Fraser, N. 1992. Rethinking the Public Sphere: A Contribution to the Critique of the Actually Existing Democracy. In: Calhoun, C. *Habermas and the Public Sphere*. Massachusetts: MIT Press, pp. 109–142.

Fromm, D. R. 2016. Deus e o Diabo na Terra do Crack: a Missão Cristolândia. In: Rui, T.; Martinez, M.; Feltran, G. (eds), *Novas Faces da Vida nas Ruas*. 1. ed. São Carlos: EdUFSCar, v. 1, pp. 245–266.

Galdeano, A. P. 2013. Gestion sociale de la violence dans une banlieue de São Paulo: trois logiques d'engagement citoyen. *Bresil(s)*, v. 4, pp. 169–192.

Goffman, A. 2014. *On the Run: Fugitive Life in an American City*. Chicago; London: University of Chicago Press.

Goffman, E. 2005. *Interaction Ritual*. New Brunswick, NJ: Aldine Transaction.

References

Goffman, E. 2003. On Face-Work: An Analysis of Ritual Elements in Social Interaction. *Reflections: The SoL Journal.* v. 4, n. 3, pp. 7–13.

Gomide Freitas, L. 2014. O Sal da Guerra. Padre Antônio Vieira e as tópicas teológico-jurídicas na apreciação da guerra justa contra os Índios. Uberlândia, Universidade federal de Uberlândia, tese de doutorado.

Gramsci, A. 1987. *A questão meridional.* Rio de Janeiro: Paz e Terra.

Gregori, M. F. 2000. *Viração: Experiências de meninos nas ruas.* São Paulo: Companhia das Letras, v. 1.

Grillo, C. 2013. Coisas da Vida no Crime: Tráfico e roubo em favelas cariocas. Tese de doutorado (Antropologia e Sociologia). Universidade Federal do Rio de Janeiro.

Guimarães, A. S. A. 2012. The Brazilian System of Racial Classification. *Ethnic and Racial Studies* (print), v. 35, pp. 1157–1162.

Guimarães, N. A. 2012. A procura de trabalho: uma boa janela para mirarmos as transformações recentes no mercado de trabalho?. *Novos Estudos* CEBRAP (Impresso), v. 93, pp. 123–144.

Guimarães, N. A. 2009. À Procura de Trabalho. Instituições do Mercado e Redes. Belo Horizonte: Argvmentvn.

Guyer, J. 2004. *Marginal Gains: Monetary Transactions in Atlantic Africa.* Chicago: University of Chicago Press.

Guyer, J. 1995. Introduction. In: Guyer J. (ed.), *Money Matters: Instability, Values and Social Payments in the Modern History of West African Communities,* London: James Currey, pp.1–33.

Habermas, J. 1992. 'L'espace public', 30 ans après In: Quaderni, N. *18. Les espaces publics,* pp. 161–191.

Hall, S.; Schwarz, B. 2017. *Familiar Stranger: A Life Between Two Islands.* Durham NC: Duke University Press.

Hirata, D. V. 2018. Sobreviver na adversidade: entre o mercado e a vida. São Carlos: EdUFSCar.

Hirata, D. V. 2014. Street Commerce as a 'Problem' in the cities of Rio de Janeiro and São Paulo. *Vibrant* (Florianópolis), v. 11, p. 97.

Hirata, D. V.; Grillo, C. C. 2019. Movement and Death: Illicit Drug Markets in the Cities of São Paulo and Rio De Janeiro. *Journal of Illicit Economies and Development,* v. 2, pp. 5–16.

Hirschman, A. O. 1970. *Exit, Voice, and Loyalty: Responses to Decline in Firms, Organizations, and States.* Cambridge, MA: Harvard University Press.

Hobbs, D. 2013. *Lush Life: Constructing Organised Crime in the UK.* Oxford: Oxford University Press.

Hobbs, D. (ed.). 2011. *Ethnography in Context.* Sage Benchmarks in Social Research Methods, 4 vols. London: Sage.

Holston, J. 2007. *Insurgent Citizenship: Disjunctions of Democracy and Modernity in Brazil.* Princeton: Princeton University Press.

IPEA/FBSP. 2018. Atlas da violência 2018. Available at: www.ipea.gov.br/

References

portal/index.php?option=com_content&view=article&id=33410&Itemid =432. (Accessed 12 March 2019).

Jensen, S. 2008. *Gangs, Politics and Dignity in Cape Town*. Oxford, Johannesburg and Chicago: James Currey, University of Witwatersrand Press, and University of Chicago Press.

Kessler, G. 2007. Transformaciones en la frontera: trabajo y delito en jóvenes del Gran Buenos Aires. *Revista Medio Ambiente y Urbanización*, v. 1, n. 52, pp. 23–37.

Kessler, G. 2004. *Sociología del delito amateur*. Buenos Aires: Paidós.

Kessler, G.; Telles, V. 2010. Apresentação ao dossiê 'Ilegalismos na América Latina'. *Tempo Social*, USP, v. 22, p. 9–16.

Kowarick, L. 1987. The Logic of Disorder. In: Archetti, E.; Cammack, .P; Roberts, B. (eds), *Sociology of 'Developing Societies': Latin America*. London: Macmillan Education, pp. 221–229.

Kowarick, L. 1979. *A espoliação urbana*. Rio de Janeiro: Paz e Terra.

Lancione, M. (ed.). 2016. *Rethinking Life at the Margins. The Assemblage of Contexts, Subjects and Politics*. London: Routledge.

Lascoumes, P.; Le Galès, P. 2012. *Sociologie de l'action publique. (2e édition)*. Paris: Armand Colin.

Lessing, B. 2017. Counterproductive Punishment: How Prison Gangs Undermine State Authority, *Rationality and Society*. v. 29, n. 3, pp. 257–297.

Lima, J. C. 2016. The digital workers in Brazil: between creativity and precariousness. *Sociologies in Dialogue*, v. 2, pp. 157–179.

Lowenkron, L. 2015. Corpos em trânsito e o trânsito dos corpos: a descons-trução do tráfico de pessoas em investigações da Polícia Federal. Paper apresentado na XI Reunión de Antropologia del Mercosur.

Lyra, D. 2013. A república dos meninos: juventude, tráfico e virtude. Rio de Janeiro: Mauad X.

Machado, C. 2018. Evangélicos, mídias e periferias urbanas: questões para um diálogo sobre religião, cidade, nação e sociedade civil no brasil contemporâneo. Debates do NER (UFRGS), v. 19, pp. 58–80.

Machado, C. 2017. The Church Helps the UPP, the UPP Helps the Church: Pacification Apparatus, Religion and Boundary Formation in Rio de Janeiro's Urban Peripheries. *Vibrant* (Florianopolis). v. 14, pp. 75–90.

Machado, C. 2016. Peace Challenges and the Moral Weapons of Pacification in Rio de Janeiro. *L'Homme* (Paris. 1961). v. 3–4, pp. 115–148.

Machado, C. 2013. 'É muita mistura': projetos religiosos, políticos, sociais, midiáticos, de saúde e segurança pública nas periferias do Rio de Janeiro. *Religião e Sociedade*. v. 33, pp. 13–36.

Machado da Silva, L. A. 2016. Fazendo a cidade: trabalho, moradia e vida local entre as camadas polulares urbanas. Rio de Janeiro: Mórula Editorial.

Machado da Silva, L. A. 2011. A política na favela (reedição). *Dilemas: Revista de Estudos de Conflito e Controle Social*, v. 4, n. 4, pp. 699–716.

References

Machado da Silva, L. A. (ed.). 2008. *Vida sob cerco: violência e rotina nas favelas do Rio de Janeiro*. Rio de Janeiro: Nova Fronteira/Faperj.

Machado da Silva, L. A. 2004. Sociabilidade violenta: por uma interpretação da criminalidade contemporânea no Brasil urbano. *Sociedade e Estado*, Brasília. v. 19, n. 1.

Machado da Silva, L. A. 1999. Criminalidade violenta: por uma nova perspectiva de análise. *Revista de Sociologia e Política*, Curitiba. n. 13, pp. 115–124.

Machado da Silva, L. A. 1993. Violência Urbana: representação de uma ordem social. In: Nascimento, E. P.; Barreira, I. (eds), *Brasil Urbano: cenários da ordem e da desordem*. Rio de Janeiro: Notrya, pp. 144–155.

Mallart, F. M. 2012. Cadeias dominadas: dinâmicas de uma instituição em trajetórias de jovens internos. Master's dissertation. São Paulo: Faculdade de Filosofia, Letras e Ciências Humanas, Universidade de São Paulo.

Malvasi, P. 2012. Interfaces da vida loka: um estudo sobre jovens, tráfico de drogas e violência em São Paulo. Doctoral thesis. São Paulo: Faculdade de Saúde Pública, Universidade de São Paulo.

Mandani, M. 2001. *When Victims Become Killers: Colonialism, Nativism, and the Genocide in Rwanda*. Princeton, NJ: Princeton University Press.

Manso, B. P. 2012. Crescimento e queda dos homicídios em sp entre 1960 e 2010. Uma análise dos mecanismos da escolha homicida e das carreiras no crime. Doctoral thesis. São Paulo: Universidade de São Paulo.

Manso, B.; Dias Nunes, C. C. 2018. *A guerra: ascensão do PCC e o mundo do crime no Brasil*. São Paulo: Todavia.

Marques, A. J. 2010. Liderança, proceder e igualdade: uma etnografia das relações políticas no Primeiro Comando da Capital. *Etnográfica*, Lisboa. v. 14, pp. 311–335.

Marques, A. J. 2008. 'Faxina' e 'pilotagem': dispositivos (de guerra) políticos no seio da administração prisional. *Lugar Comum* (UFRJ) v. 25–26, pp. 283–290.

Marques, A. J. 2007. 'Dar um psicológico': estratégias de produção de verdade no tribunal do crime. In: *VII Reunião de Antropologia do Mercosul*. Anais. Porto Alegre, CD-ROM.

Marques, E. C. 2014. *Governo e governança em grandes cidades: Paris, Londres, Cidade do México e São Paulo*. Projeto de Pesquisa (mimeo). Financiamentos: CNPq, CAPES, FAPESP.

Marques, E. C. 2012. *Opportunities and Deprivation in the Urban South: Poverty, Segregation and Social Networks in São Paulo*. 1st edn. Farnham: Ashgate Publishers.

Marques, E. C. 2010. *Redes sociais, segregação e pobreza*. São Paulo: UNESP.

Marques, E. C.; Bichir, R. 2011. Redes de apoio social no Rio de Janeiro e em São Paulo. *Novos Estudos CEBRAP* (Impresso), v. 1, pp. 10–32.

Marques, E.; Torres, H. (eds). 2005. *São Paulo: Segregação, pobreza e desigualdades sociais*. São Paulo: Senac.

References

Marques, V. 2015. Fé&Crime: evangélicos e PCC nas periferias de São Paulo. São Paulo: Fonte Editorial.

Marshall, T. H. 1950. *Citizenship and Social Class*. Cambridge: Cambridge University Press.

Martinez, M. M.; Pereira, L. F. P.; Barbosa, A. R.; Oliveira, L. M. F.; Pazzini, D. P. 2014. A produção e a gestão da população de rua: a trajetória de Luciene. *Dilemas: Revista de Estudos de Conflito e Controle Social*, v. 7, pp. 741–767.

Martins Junior, A. 2014. Lives in Motion: Notebooks of an Immigrant in London. Helsinge: Whyte Tracks.

Matsushita, L. L. 2012. Perspectivas do Caso Beth. Monografia de Conclusão de Curso (Ciências Sociais), Universidade Federal de São Carlos.

Mattos, C. 2016. Uma etnografia da expansão do mundo do crime no Rio de Janeiro. *RBCS*. v. 31, n. 91, pp. 1–15.

Mbembe, A. 2003. Necropolitics. *Public Culture*, v. 15, n. 1, pp. 11–40.

Melo, F. A. L. 2014. *As prisões de São Paulo: estado e mundo do crime na gestão da*. 1st edn. São Paulo: Alameda Casa Editorial, v. 1.

Menezes, P. 2015. Entre o 'fogo cruzado' e o 'campo minado': uma etnografia do processo de 'pacificação' de favelas cariocas. Doutorado em Sociologia, IESP/UERJ.

Miagusko, E. 2014. A produção das margens do Estado no centro de São Paulo: sem-teto nas ruínas de um presídio abandonado. The production of the state margins in São Paulo's central area: homeless in the ruins of an abandoned prison. *Etnográfica*, v. 18, n. 1, pp. 33–52.

Misse, M. 2018. Violence, Criminal Subjection and Political Merchandise in Brazil: An Overview from Rio. *International Journal of Criminology and Sociology*, v. 7, pp. 135–148.

Misse, M. 2010. Crime, sujeito e sujeição criminal: aspectos de uma contribuição analítica sobre a categoria 'bandido'. *Lua Nova – revista de cultura e política*, n. 79, pp. 15–38.

Misse, M. 2007. *O Estigma do passivo sexual: um símbolo de estigma no discurso cotidiano*. Rio de Janeiro: Booklink: NECVU/IFCS/ UFRJ; LeMetro/ IFCS/UFRJ, v. 3.

Misse, M. 2006a. Crime e violência no Brasil contemporâneo: estudos de sociologia do crime e da violência urbana. Rio de Janeiro: Lumen Juris.

Misse, M. 2006b. Sobre uma sociabilidade violenta. In: Misse, M. *Crime e violência no Brasil contemporâneo: estudos de sociologia do crime e da violência urbana*. Rio de Janeiro: Lumen Juris, pp. 167–182.

Moutinho, L. 2006. Negociando com a adversidade: reflexões sobre 'raça' (homos)sexualidade e desigualdade social no Rio de desigualdade social no Rio de Janeiro. *Estudos Feministas*, Florianópolis. v. 14, n. 1, p. 336.

Moutinho, L. 2004. Condenados pelo desejo? Razões de Estado na África do Sul. *Revista Brasileira de Ciências Sociais*. v. 19, n. 56, pp. 95–112.

References

Neiburg, F. 2007. As moedas doentes, os números públicos, e a antropologia do dinheiro. *Mana* (UFRJ Impresso), v. 13, pp. 45–77.

Oliveira, F. 1982. O Espaço e o Urbano no Brasil. *Espaço e Debates*, São Paulo. n. 6, pp. 36–54.

Oliveira, F.; Rizek, C. S. (eds). 2006. *A Era da Indeterminação*. 1st edn. São Paulo: Boitempo Editorial, v.

Oliveira, J. P. de 2014. Pacificação e tutela militar na gestão de populações e territórios. *Mana*, v. 20, n.1, pp. 125–161.

Oliveira, M. C.; Vieira, J. C.; Marcondes, G. S. 2015. Cinquenta anos de relações de gênero e geração no Brasil: mudanças e permanências. In: Arretche, M. (ed.) *Trajetórias das desigualdades: como o Brasil mudou nos últimos 50 anos*. São Paulo: Edunesp/CEM, pp. 309–333.

Paoli, M. C. 1995. Movimentos sociais no Brasil: em busca de um estatuto político. In: Helman, M. (ed.), *Movimentos sociais e democracia no Brasil: 'sem a gente não tem jeito'*. São Paulo: Marco Zero; Princeton, NJ: Princeton University Press.

Perlongher, N. 2008. *O negócio do michê*: a prostituição viril em São Paulo. São Paulo: Perseu Abramo.

Piscitelli, A. 2008. Interseccionalidades, categorias de articulação e experiências de migrantes brasileiras. *Sociedade e Cultura*, v. 11, n. 2 , pp. 263–274.

PRO-AIM. 2012. Mortalidade no Município de São Paulo. Prefeitura Municipal de São Paulo/Sempla. Disponível em: www.nossasaopaulo. org.br/observatorio/analises_distritos.php (Accessed 20 July 2012).

PRO-AIM. 2008. Mortalidade no Município de São Paulo. Prefeitura Municipal de São Paulo. Disponível em: www2.prefeitura.sp.gov.br/.../ saude/TABNET.2008. (Accessed 21 May 2008).

Rancière, J. 2005. *A partilha do sensível: estética e política*. São Paulo: EXO Experimental.

Rancière, J. 2002. O mestre ignorante: cinco lições sobre a emancipação intelectual. Belo Horizonte: Autêntica.

Rancière, J. 1998. *Aux bords du politique*. Paris: La Fabrique Éditions.

Rancière, J. 1996a. *O desentendimento*. São Paulo: Editora 34.

Rancière, J. 1996b. O dissenso. In: Novaes, A. (ed.), *A crise da razão*. São Paulo: Companhia das Letras, pp. 367–383.

Rancière, J. 1995. *La mésentente: politique et philosophie*. Paris: Galilée.

Richmond, M. A. 2019a. Review of Angotti, T. (ed.), Urban Latin America: Inequalities and Neoliberal Reforms. *Journal of Latin American Studies*, v. 51, n. 1, pp. 198–200.

Richmond, M. A. 2019b. 'Hostages to both sides': Favela Pacification as Dual Security Assemblage. *Geoforum*, v. 104, pp. 71–80.

Rizek, C. S. 2006. Comunidade e Violência nas Fronteiras da Cidade. 25ª Reunião Brasileira de Sociologia, Goiânia. Anais da 25ª Reunião da Associação Brasileira de Antropologia. Mimeo.

References

Rizek, C. S.; Oliveira, F. (eds). 2006. *Francisco de Oliveira – A tarefa da crítica*. 1st edn. Belo Horizonte: Editora da Universidade de Minas Gerais.

Robinson, J. 2006. *Ordinary Cities: Between Modernity and Development*. London: Routledge.

Rodgers, D.; Baird, A. 2015. Understanding Gangs in Contemporary Latin America. In: Decker, S.; Pyrooz, D. (eds), *Handbook of Gangs and Gang Responses*. New York: Wiley, pp. 478–502.

Rosanvallon, P. 1995. *La nouvelle question sociale*. Repenser l'Etat-providence, Paris: Seuil.

Ruggiero, V.; South, N. 1997. The Late City as a Bazaar: Drug Markets, Illegal Enterprise and the Barricades. *The British Journal of Sociology*, v. 48, n.1, pp. 54–70.

Rui, T. 2014. *Nas tramas do crack: etnografia da abjeção*. 1nst ed. São Paulo: Editora Terceiro Nome (Coleção Antropologia Hoje).

Rui, T. 2012. Corpos abjetos: etnografia em cenários de uso e comércio de crack. Tese (Doutorado em Antropologia), Instituto de Filosofia e Ciências Humanas, Universidade Estadual de Campinas.

Rui, T.; Feltran, G. S. 2015. Guerra e Pacificação: palavras-chave do conflito urbano contemporâneo (Nota do Comitê Migrações e Deslocamentos). *Boletim Informativo*. n. 18/2015-ABA.

Ruotti, C.; Regina, F. L.; Almeida, J. F.; Nasser, M. M. S.; Peres, M. F. T. 2017. A ocorrência de homicídios no município de São Paulo: mutações e tensões a partir das narrativas de moradores e profissionais. *Saúde e Sociedade* (online), v. 26, pp. 999–1014.

Sader, E. 1988. Quando novos personagens entraram em cena: Experiências, falas e lutas dos trabalhadores da Grande São Paulo, 1970–80. Rio de Janeiro: Paz e Terra.

Salla, F. A. 2007. De Montoro a Lembo: as políticas penitenciárias de São Paulo. *Revista Brasileira de Segurança Pública*, v. 1, pp. 72–90.

Salla, F. A. 2006. As rebeliões nas prisões: novos significados a partir da experiência brasileira. *Sociologias*, UFRGS. v. 16, pp. 274–307.

Santos, W. G. 1979. Cidadania e justiça; a política social na ordem brasileira. Rio de Janeiro: Ed. Campus.

Santos Silva, D. 2014. Se o irmão falou, meu irmão, é melhor não duvidar: políticas estatais e políticas do 'crime' em relação a homicídios em São Paulo. Master's dissertation. São Carlos: Universidade Federal de São Carlos.

Shimbo, L. Z. 2012. *Habitação social de mercado: a confluência entre Estado, empresas construtoras e capital financeiro*. 1st edn. Belo Horizonte: C/Arte.

Simmel, G. 2014. O conceito e a tragédia da cultura. *Crítica Cultural*, Palhoça, SC. v. 9, n. 1, pp. 145–162.

Simmel, G. 2010a [1918]. Life as Transcendence. In: *The View of Life: Four Metaphysical Essays with Journal Aphorisms*. Chicago: University of Chicago Press, pp. 1–19.

References

Simmel, G. 2010b. *El secreto y las sociedades secretas*. Madrid: Sequitur.

Simmel, G. 2009. Sociology: Inquiries into the Construction of Social Forms. Leiden: IDC Publishers.

Simmel, G. 2006 [1892]. Algumas reflexões sobre a prostituição no presente e no futuro. In: Simmel, G. *Filosofia do Amor*. São Paulo: Martins Fontes, pp. 25–29.

Simmel, G. 1990 [1900]. *Philosophy of Money*. London: Routledge.

Simone, A. M. 2018. *Improvised Lives: Rhythms of Endurance in an Urban South*. Cambridge: Polity.

Souza Lima, A. C. (ed.). 2002. *Gestar e Gerir: estudos para uma antropologia da administração pública no Brasil*. Rio de Janeiro: Relume Dumará. (Coleção Antropologia da Política).

Stepputat, F. 2018. Pragmatic Peace in Emerging Governscapes. *International Affairs*. v. 94, n. 2, pp. 399–416.

Stepputat, F. 2015. Formations of Sovereignty at the Frontier of the Modern State. *Conflict and Society: Advances in Research*. New York: Berghahn Books, v. 1, pp. 129–143.

Stepputat, F. 2013. Contemporary Governscapes: Sovereign Practice and Hybrid Orders Beyond the Center. In: Bouziane, M., Harders, C.; Hoffmann, A. (eds), *Local Politics and Contemporary Transformation in the Arab World – Governance Beyond the Center*. Basingstoke: Palgrave Macmillan, pp. 25–42.

Takahashi, H. Y. 2014. 'Evangelho segundo Racionais MC'S: ressignificações religiosas, políticas e estético-musicais nas narrativas do rap'. Master's dissertation. São Carlos: Universidade Federal de São Carlos, São Carlos.

Teixeira, A. 2009. Prisões da exceção: política penal e penitenciária no Brasil contemporâneo. São Paulo: Juruá.

Teixeira, C. P. 2011. A construção social do ex-bandido: um estudo sobre sujeição criminal e pentecostalismo. Rio de Janeiro: 7letras.

Telles, V. S. 2011. *A cidade nas fronteiras do legal e ilegal*. São Paulo: Argvmentvm/USP.

Telles, V. S. 2009. Ilegalismos urbanos e a cidade. *Novos Estudos CEBRAP*, v. 84, pp. 142–173.

Telles, V. S. 2001. *Pobreza e Cidadania*. São Paulo: Editora 34.

Telles, V. S. 1994. Sociedade civil e a construção de espaços públicos. In: Dagnino, E. (ed.), *Anos 90: Política e Sociedade no Brasil*. São Paulo: Brasiliense, pp. 30–45.

Telles, V. S.; Cabanes, R. (eds). 2006. *Nas tramas da cidade: Trajetórias urbanas e seus territórios*. São Paulo: Associação Editorial Humanitas/IRD, pp. 69–116.

Telles, V. S.; Hirata, D. V. 2007. Cidades e práticas urbanas: nas fronteiras incertas entre o ilegal, o informal e o ilícito. *Estudos Avançados, Dossiê Crime Organizado*, São Paulo. n. 61, pp. 173–191.

References

Telles, V. S.; Paoli, M. C. 1994. Social Rights: Conflicts and Negotiations in Contemporary Brazil. In: Dagnino, E.; Escobar, A.; Alvarez, A. (eds), *Cultures of Politics/Politics of Cultures*. Boulder, CO: Westview Press, v. 1, pp. 64–92.

Thevenot, L. 2006. L'action au pluriel: sociologie des régimes d'engagement. Paris: La Découverte.

Thevenot, L. 1990. L'action qui convient. In: Pharo, P.; Quéré, L. (eds), *Les forms de l'action*, Paris, Ed. de l'EHESS (Raisons Pratiques 1), pp. 39–69.

Tilly, C. 1999. *Durable Inequalities*. Berkeley, CA: University of California Press.

Tilly, C. 1985. *War Making and State Making as Organized Crime*. In: Evans, P., Rueschemeyer, D.; Skocpol, T. (eds), *Bringing the State Back*. Cambridge: Cambridge University Press, pp. 169–187.

Vianna, A. R. B. 2014. Violência, Estado e Gênero: Entre corpos e corpus entrecruzados. In: de Souza Lima, A. C.; Garcia-Acosta, V. (eds), *Margens da Violência: Subsídios ao estudo do problema da violência nos contextos mexicano e brasileiro*. 1 ed. Brasília: ABA, v. 1, pp. 209–237.

Vianna, A. R. B. 2005. Direitos, moralidades e desigualdades: considerações a partir de procesos de guarda de crianças. In: Lima, R. K. (ed.), *Antropologia e Direitos Humanos*. Prêmio ABA Ford Direitos Humanos. Niterói: EdUFF, v. 1, pp. 13–68.

Vianna, A. R. B.; Farias, J. 2011. A guerra das mães: dor e política em situações de violência institucional. *Cadernos Pagu* (UNICAMP. Impresso), v. 37, pp. 79–116.

Vieira, N. C.; Feltran, G. S. 2013. *Sobre periferias: novos conflitos no Brasil contemporâneo*. 1st edn. Rio de Janeiro: Lamparina Editora/FAPERJ.

Vital da Cunha, C. 2018. Pentecostal Cultures in Urban Peripheries: A Socio-Anthropological Analysis of Pentecostalism in Arts, Grammars, Crime and Morality. *Vibrant*, v. 15, pp. 93–115.

Wacquant, L. 2009a. *Punishing the Poor: The Neoliberal Government of Social Insecurity*. Durham, NC and London: Duke University Press,.

Wacquant, L. 2009b. *Prisons of Poverty*. Minneapolis: University of Minnesota Press.

Waiselfisz, J. J. 2015. Mapa da Violência. Disponível em: www.mapadaviolencia.org.br/pdf2015/MapaViolencia_2015_mulheres.pdf (Accessed 12 May 2016).

Weber, M. 1967. A política como vocação. In: Gerth, H. H.; Wright Mills, C. (eds), *Max Weber: Ensaios de Sociologia*. Rio de Janeiro: Livros Técnicos e Científicos, pp. 97–154.

Werneck, A. V. 2012. *A Desculpa: As circunstâncias e a moral das relações sociais*. Rio de Janeiro: Civilização Brasileira.

Werneck, A. V. 2009. O invento de Adão: o papel do ato de dar uma desculpa na manutenção das relações sociais. Doctoral thesis. Rio de Janeiro: Universidade Federal do Rio de Janeiro.

References

Whyte, W. F. 2005 [1943]. A estrutura social do gansterismo. In: *Sociedade de Esquina: a estrutura social de uma área urbana pobre e degradada*. Rio de Janeiro: Zahar, pp. 129–162.

Willis, G. D. 2015. *The Killing Consensus: Police, Organized Crime, and the Regulation of Life and Death in Urban Brazil*. Oakland, CA: University of California Press.

Wittgenstein, L. 2009. *Philosophical Investigations*. London: Basil Blackwell.

Zaluar, A. M. 2004. *Integração perversa: pobreza e tráfico de drogas*. 1. ed. Rio de Janeiro: Fundação Getúlio Vargas.

Zaluar, A. 1985. *A Máquina e a Revolta*. São Paulo: Brasiliense.

Zaluar, A.; Ribeiro, A. P. A. 2009. Teoria da eficácia coletiva e violência: o paradoxo do subúrbio carioca. *Revista Novos Estudos*, CEBRAP. v. 84, pp. 175–196.

Zelizer, V. 2011. *Economic Lives: How Culture Shapes the Economy*. Princeton, NJ: Princeton University Press.

Index

Index

Index

Index

Index